More Praise for *Fortress America*

"Challenging and provocative, *Fortress America* will stir stimulating debate in the classroom and in the living room about the state of America in the post–World War II world."

—**William Chafe, Alice Mary Baldwin Professor, emeritus, Duke University; former president, Organization of American Historians**

FORTRESS AMERICA

★ ★ ★

How We Embraced Fear and Abandoned Democracy

ELAINE TYLER MAY

BASIC BOOKS
New York

Basic Books
Hachette Book Group
1290 Avenue of the Americas, New York, NY 10104
www.basicbooks.com

Printed in the United States of America

First Edition: December 2017

Published by Basic Books, an imprint of Perseus Books, LLC, a subsidiary of Hachette Book Group, Inc.

Library of Congress Cataloging-in-Publication Data
Names: May, Elaine Tyler, author.
Title: Fortress America : how we embraced fear and abandoned democracy / Elaine Tyler May.
Description: First edition. | New York : Basic Books, [2017] | Includes bibliographical references and index.
Identifiers: LCCN 2017023376| ISBN 9780465055920 (hardcover) | ISBN 9780465093007 (e-book)
Subjects: LCSH: Crime—United States—History—21st century. | Violence—United States—History—21st century. | Public safety—Social aspects—United States—History—21st century. | United States—Social conditions—21st century. | United States--Civilization—21st century.
Classification: LCC HV6789 .M359 2017 | DDC 364.10973—dc23
LC record available at https://lccn.loc.gov/2017023376

ISBNs: 978-0-465-05592-0 (hardcover), 978-0-465-09300-7 (ebook)
LSC-C

10 9 8 7 6 5 4 3 2 1

In Memory of Jonathan Kaminsky, 1978–2016,
Whose light left this world too soon
And for
Ezrah Josephine May and Isaiah Nelson May
With hopes that they will grow up in a post-fortress world

CONTENTS

Introduction

THE BUNKER MENTALITY

Fear is a potent force in America, and it has taken many forms throughout this nation's history. Perhaps at no point was fear more widespread than in the years after World War II, which witnessed major political, social, and cultural upheavals. In particular, fears of atomic attack, communist subversives, crime, and physical harm at the hands of strangers have affected social norms, election results, public policies, and daily life. This fear has generated the security state defining the place of the United States in the world ever since the early years of the Cold War. At the same time it has fostered a security culture, a bunker mentality, within the country. This book is an effort to understand how that state of mind developed, how it evolved throughout the twentieth century, and what it has meant for the nation and its citizens up to the present day. Why have Americans become so fearful? How has that fear been expressed and addressed in the nation's culture, institutions, and laws? What have citizens done to achieve personal safety and security?

Americans learned to fear dangers from both inside and outside the country in the early years of the Cold War and the Atomic Age. Citizens came to believe that the government would not protect them, so they had to protect themselves. Over time, they turned their attention to other presumed dangers, especially crime and social unrest. Fear increased far out of proportion to any real threat, leading millions of Americans to undertake security measures that did not make them any safer.

Misplaced fear drove Americans away from true security. To be secure is to be safe, out of harm's way, and to have the essentials for a comfortable life: adequate food, shelter, and clothing. In the United States, security is embedded in the nation's founding documents, particularly the Declaration of Independence, which promises the right to "life, liberty and the pursuit of happiness." Traditions of individualism and free enterprise embody the belief that security originates from self-sufficiency. American democratic practices foster an expectation that virtuous citizens who work hard will be rewarded with security, the good life, and the fulfillment of the American dream. Although throughout the nation's history large numbers of Americans never had the opportunity to achieve this level of security, it has remained an aspirational goal and a national ideal.

There was never a "golden age" of security. But there were moments in the twentieth century when citizens and policymakers believed that the government had a responsibility to create the conditions in which Americans could achieve safety and a decent standard of living. Those moments resulted from two beliefs in particular: that the government was a force for social betterment, and that all citizens shared responsibility for the common good. That vision was never perfect—in fact, it never fully became reality—but it had political, cultural, and social traction, especially in times of hardship.

One such time was the Great Depression of the 1930s. The economic crisis moved large numbers of Americans to abandon the belief in self-sufficiency and turn to the government for assistance. At that time, for most people, insecurity was understood in economic terms. President Franklin D. Roosevelt's New Deal offered programs, such as Social Security, to provide a safety net for the many Americans who had lost jobs, income, and opportunities. The New Deal rested on a widely shared belief that the government had a responsibility to assist citizens in need.

The safety net did not reach everyone, however. African Americans who worked as household workers or sharecroppers were not included, for example; nor were many others who labored at the edges of the economy. Indeed, the vision of security that prevailed prior to World War II belonged largely to the white middle class. It rested on hierarchies of race and gender that many white Americans believed to be rooted in biology. The belief that people of color were inferior, and that women were innately destined to be wives and mothers, maintained social arrangements that upheld the power and authority of white men. Those boundaries of race and gender were enforced by both violence and law. Lynching and Jim Crow segregation were among the strategies that kept the racial hierarchy in place; exclusionary practices and gender-based laws restricted opportunities for women and maintained their subordination. The social order that resulted from these discriminatory practices enforced oppression for some while offering predictability and stability for others.

Another pre–World War II source of security for mainstream Americans came from the belief that the nation was safe from attack from abroad. Although the United States had participated in wars, no international wars had been fought on American soil for more than a century, and Europe had taken the brunt of World War I. The oceans on either side of the country seemed to offer protection; civilians did not imagine that war would threaten their safety. But that sense of security was shattered in December 1941 with the Japanese attack on Pearl Harbor, which brought the United States into World War II.

War revived the economy, putting millions of Americans to work in the defense and other industries, and thereby ending the Depression. At the same time, the war unleashed a new definition of and new urgency about security. After the attack on Pearl Harbor, national security took on a different meaning rooted in danger emanating from abroad. Security concerns became focused on protecting the nation from foreign enemies as well as protecting individuals from threats to their physical safety.

The war marked significant changes in the quest for security in other ways, too. An uneasy peace arrived in 1945, when the United States dropped atomic bombs on two Japanese cities, ushering in the Atomic Age. The war was over, but new anxieties emerged. Postwar prosperity eased economic insecurities for many, but the Cold War raised new fears about personal safety, and especially about the threat of nuclear attack from abroad and communist subversion at home.

In this new era of danger, in which the physical safety of civilians was suddenly at risk, national security became the responsibility of the government, while citizens became responsible for their own protection. In the face of possible atomic attack, officials warned Americans that the government could not protect them—they had to protect themselves. By acknowledging that the government was powerless to provide safety in such a dangerous world, political leaders and civil defense authorities unwittingly sowed the seeds of dwindling faith in government, the police, and other public institutions.

Cold War ideology promoted a fierce commitment to self-sufficiency and privatized protection. It wove together several strands of American political culture into a tough fabric constructed to withstand the harsh postwar climate and protect the American way of life. These strands included beliefs in individual freedom, unfettered capitalism, and the sanctity of the home. Many Americans came to see the world as a dangerous place, inside as well as outside the nation's borders, and became accustomed to the threat of nuclear annihilation, which fueled the development of a militarized society. They also became accustomed to the idea that communists were among them, which prompted suspicions of "outsiders" of every kind.[1]

During the Cold War, the news media, political leaders, and large numbers of Americans became preoccupied with both national and personal security. The two were profoundly connected. At the dawn of the Atomic Age, protection against external dangers took the form of a nuclear arsenal, while protection against internal enemies took the form of a nuclear family. The United States vigorously opposed international control of nuclear arms, instead choosing to accumulate weapons, helping to cause a spiraling nuclear arms race. Rather than defusing international tensions to achieve a safer world through democratic practices in the global arena, the nation's leaders chose preparedness in the face of danger.

Americans responded with similar strategies at home. Although some citizens called upon the nation's leaders to stop the arms race, others acquiesced to the dangers of the Atomic Age by fortifying themselves with privatized protection, constant vigilance, and a bunker mentality—and for some, actual bunkers. They turned to the nuclear family, with a homemaker mother and a breadwinning father, to maintain social stability, nurture self-sufficient citizens, and provide protection in a dangerous world.[2]

Like World War II, when the nation came together to face its enemies, the Cold War called for national unity. Many scholars have argued that the "Cold War consensus" that prevailed in the postwar era—in which the two mainline parties, Democrats and Republicans, opposed communism, supported a nuclear arms race, and maintained remnants of New Deal liberalism—disintegrated in the 1960s. According to this view, American politics became increasingly polarized over the final decades of the twentieth century and continued along this path well into the twenty-first, leading to a situation in which the two parties are in agreement on practically nothing today. I argue in this book that in fact a new consensus developed over the last half of the twentieth century, rooted in a new definition of "security" that was grounded in fear and that both major parties adopted and most Americans across the political spectrum accepted. While the two major political parties became locked in fierce battles in the twenty-first century, large numbers of citizens retreated from the political process altogether and into their own private lives. As a result, active citizenship declined and the common good withered. The path to our current situation began more than half a century ago.

The Cold War defined the framework of security through the 1950s. The sources of danger began to pivot in the 1960s and 1970s in the wake of rising crime, urban unrest, protests against the war in Vietnam, and the civil rights and feminist movements. Public opinion polls and survey data demonstrate that Cold War anxieties morphed into fears of crime and social disruption. Those fears far exceeded actual threats. Even as the Cold War waned and crime rates fell, fear continued to rise. The fear that developed was neither neutral nor abstract.

Then as now, African Americans were more likely than whites to be victims of crime and violence. They had good reason to fear for their safety and well-being. But many whites in the 1960s watched inner-city black neighborhoods being consumed by flames and worried that the violence would spread to white neighborhoods. Domestic disruption and a growing sense of personal vulnerability led to a new definition of security that was grounded in fear of violence and physical assault. According to this notion, nobody was really safe, regardless of their wealth, race, or gender.

At the same time, the postwar economic boom that had lifted many Americans into the middle class began to falter. The nuclear family, with a father whose income could support a wife and children, and a mother who would provide daily care of the home and family, had been the bulwark of security in the early postwar years. With so much turmoil in the world, many believed that a home in which parents conformed to clearly defined roles and responsibilities would provide stability and a solid safeguard against the dangers emanating from outside. That ideal became increasingly difficult to achieve, both because of changing economic realities and because of the discontent among women and men who felt trapped by their assigned roles. Men found it difficult to support a family on a single income, and women joined the paid labor force to help pay the bills. The nuclear family began to unravel, with declining rates of marriage, soaring rates of divorce, and a declining birthrate. Social, cultural, and political upheavals disrupted the sense of security that the nuclear family had offered, and Americans of all backgrounds and classes felt the ground shifting beneath their feet.

As the family faced new challenges, the home itself became a site of vulnerability. Houses that once *provided* protection became places that *needed* protection. Homeowners transformed their houses into barricaded fortresses, with alarm systems, metal grates, fences, and locks. City planners designed streets that reflected "bunker architecture."

Domestic security appeared to be threatened not only by Cold War dangers, economic woes, and urban upheavals but also by the social and political challenges to the racial and gender status quo that took shape in the 1960s. The economy weakened just as the civil rights and feminist movements began to force the government and employers to grant greater opportunities and a more equitable legal status for racial minorities and women. While the successes of the civil rights and feminist movements changed millions of lives for the better, they also caused considerable anxiety for many whose lives had been ordered by time-honored racial and gender inequalities. Coming at a time of increasing economic instability, these developments gave rise to new fears.

With rising crime and urban unrest making headlines, and feminism, civil rights, the counterculture, and the sexual revolution turning the traditional domestic order upside down, political leaders and the mainstream media fanned fears with calls for "law and order." They revived fictitious tropes of racial danger that had prevailed for centuries, especially in the South, promoting unfounded assertions that black men were dangerous and white women were vulnerable. Media messages warned women to stay home and avoid city streets, when statistically they were safer outside than in their own homes, where most violence against women occurred. Many women absorbed these messages and changed their behavior in order to avoid attack, or learned how to defend themselves if assaulted.[3]

Precautions to avoid harm are, of course, a normal part of life. But when fears become exaggerated or misdirected, they can be harmful to individuals and to society. In the United States, "security" in the last decades of the twentieth century came to mean a particular kind of safety, safety from the threat of physical violence from strangers. For the vast majority of citizens, "stranger danger" has never been a serious threat. Most physical harm to Americans comes at the hands of people they know.

Still, most Americans took for granted the daily rituals of security culture: the avoidance of certain streets, the reluctance to walk alone at night, the many locks on doors and the installation of security systems, the private security guards, the importance of personal firearms. Few stopped to think whether any of these measures actually provided personal safety, and whether there might be different strategies for improving the well-being of all.

How did this happen? There is no single "cause" of the security obsession that emerged in the second half of the twentieth century. There were many factors involved, and many dimensions to the fears that led millions of Americans to seek safety from perceived dangers. Uncovering this history requires delving into a wide range of sources. Fear is not only a response to reality, such as the development of nuclear weapons, economic insecurity, urban unrest, or the presence of crime. It is also fostered by messages carried in the news media, Hollywood films, and political speeches, and spread by businesses seeking to profit from fear. Hence this book relies not only on public opinion data, but also on the view of American life reflected in blockbuster movies, such as the *Dirty Harry* films, and not only on crime statistics, but also on the rhetoric of politicians who exaggerated danger to create fear.

Insightful observers have examined various aspects of our nation's culture of security. Many scholars have studied the impact of US foreign policy, and some have argued persuasively that our military adventures around the world in the name of national security have actually made the United States less safe, while causing untold death, destruction, and misery. Others have written extensively about the many misguided efforts to limit or cut off immigration and seal the nation's borders, and the disastrous consequences of an unnecessarily punitive criminal justice system.[4]

Fortress America looks primarily at the personal side of the security quest: the ways in which Americans have endeavored to protect themselves on a daily basis in a world they perceive as dangerous. It builds on the rich body of scholarship that has yielded insights into the domestic ramifications of the Cold War and the militarization of American life that followed in its wake. The central aim of the book is to point out the distance between our fears and reality, to show how unwarranted fears have damaged our country, and to suggest more sensible, humane, and democratic routes to safety and well-being.

The quest for security—and its resounding failure to achieve a safer society—propels the story that unfolds in the following chapters. The book's narrative is both thematic and chronological. It starts with how Americans learned to be fearful for their personal safety in the early years of the Cold War and came to understand that they were responsible for their own protection against both external and internal enemies. Over time, these warnings, and the fears they generated, took on a life of their own. As a result, large numbers of Americans—especially, but not only, white Americans—began to behave in new security-minded ways. They bought guns and promoted gun rights over gun control.[5] They bunkered themselves in their homes and hired private security companies for protection. They retreated from public streets. They promoted draconian laws that resulted in mass incarceration. They turned away from the government, seeing it as part of the problem rather than part of the solution.

By the early twenty-first century, because of ill-founded and unjustified fears, millions of Americans were locked up in prisons for no good reason. Millions more locked themselves up behind gates, walls, and security systems—also for no good reason. Americans came to fear strangers who might attack them, retreating to fortified homes. Fear of crime rose, even when rates of crime fell. Parents debated whether to hover over their children like surveillance helicopters or to give them "free range," allowing them to play freely within their own neighborhoods, or even walk to and from school without supervision, like the parents themselves had been able to do when they were children.

With the dubious distinction of leading the world in both gun possession and gun violence, Americans ignored all the data demonstrating that more guns led to more gun violence, consistently opposing gun control legislation. Citizens remained hostile to government and distrustful of the police. The government and the police did quite a bit to deserve that distrust and very little to earn back public confidence.

Millions of Americans hunkered down in gated communities and fortified homes. Although climate change began to gain public and political attention, affluent, security-seeking Americans drove around in gas-guzzling, military-style vehicles that endangered not only the environment but also those who rode inside them and those who encountered them on the streets.[6]

Americans believed they were protecting themselves. But they were not. Decades of "law-and-order" policies made the United States a lawless and disordered society. Legislation on gun rights and "stand-your-ground" laws advanced to such an extent that vigilante violence—once the very definition of lawlessness—became legal. In many states, the kind of vigilante outlaws that had been valorized in frontier myths and Hollywood films were legally defined as law-abiding citizens.

Meanwhile, the security obsession caused unintended consequences that harmed our democracy and led to the neglect of real threats to the security of Americans, such as severe and increasing economic inequality; poorly maintained and dangerous infrastructure, such as bridges, levees, and drinking water; environmental degradation and climate change; and threats to the safety of food and other consumer products. In the rush toward self-protection, true security has eluded ordinary citizens.

There has been some pushback. Some citizens and leaders have objected, resisted, dissented, organized, or simply refused to allow misplaced fear and security concerns to affect the way they live. They have participated in a wide variety of social and political movements to dismantle the apparatus of security and strengthen the democracy. But the security obsession endures.

As large numbers of Americans came to believe that their personal safety was more important than the common good, and that safety could be achieved by living life at a distance from public spaces, a thriving democracy and a vibrant, healthy society became increasingly unattainable. As in the realm of foreign policy, where the effort to achieve national security led to questionable results, in the realm of personal security there is no evidence that the relentless quest has made Americans any safer or better off. In fact, the obsession with security over the past half-century has only made Americans less safe and less secure, and the country less democratic.

Our security obsession is unnecessary and counterproductive. The vast majority of Americans have no desire to cause physical harm to others. We do not need to be so frightened of each other. But we have become a paranoid, armed, militarized, racially divided, and vastly unequal vigilante nation. The pursuit of security has damaged our public as well as our private lives and hindered our ability to trust each other and our government. In other words, we face a serious risk that our democracy could be totally destroyed. In order to understand how we arrived at our current situation and where our nation might be headed, we need to look back to the moment when fear began to shape how we live.

Chapter 1

GIMME SHELTER: SECURITY IN THE ATOMIC AGE

Every Home a Fortress!

—*Leo Hoegh, head of the Office of Civil and Defense Mobilization, 1958*[1]

In January 1945, the cover of *House Beautiful* magazine featured a photograph of a World War II veteran returning to his family at their modest but cheerful home in Beverly Hills, California. As he opens the gate of his white picket fence, his smiling wife waves to him from the front door, and his young daughter bounds gleefully down the path through the garden toward him. The cover asks, "Will you be ready when Johnny comes marching home?" While the photo is idyllic, the question reveals uncertainty about the domestic world to which the veteran is returning. "Will you be ready" to properly welcome him back to a well-appointed private home, in an uncertain postwar world, where he can find comfort and security as the master of his house, with a devoted wife and well-behaved children? This vision of domestic bliss, appropriately set in the postwar paradise of Southern California, offers "the American ideal of good living—one of the ideals these veterans have fought for, and which they can now look forward to attaining."[2]

The photo of the returning veteran, carefully posed and staged by photographer Maynard Parker, captures the postwar American dream in all of its aesthetic and ideological dimensions. But it was not a real family. Parker had constructed the scene, and the "family members" were models. Parker's photographs, mostly taken in Southern California, often reflected the ideal, though not the reality, of suburban domesticity. The photo is benign and optimistic, depicting a private vision of security, self-sufficiency, affluence, and family solidarity behind the picket fence.

The real-life homecomings of American war veterans were rarely picture-perfect. Hidden from this view were the countless men suffering from posttraumatic stress disorder (then known as "shell shock"), along with their fears of unemployment, their disconnection with family members after the long separation, the grief endured by those who lost loved ones, shrinking opportunities for women—who had enjoyed lucrative home-front jobs during the war—and the violence inflicted on the men of color who had risked their lives for their country. The joy of victory was dampened by the realization of the horrors coming to light in the wake of the war: the ghastly images of the Holocaust, in which the Nazis murdered 6 million Jews, and the horrifying aftermath of the United States' decision to drop atomic bombs on two once-thriving Japanese cities and their inhabitants. What would the postwar world look like, and how would Americans adapt to it?

A major motion picture captured the anxiety of the immediate postwar years. *The Best Years of Our Lives*, winner of seven Academy Awards, including one for Best Picture, in 1946, garnered an audience of 55 million in the United States alone.[3] In the film, three veterans return to their small town after the war. They are not the same as when they had left, and neither are their town and their families.

One of the three men is a wealthy banker. In his absence, his daughter has become a mature young woman; his son rejects his war souvenirs and questions him about the horrible effects of the atomic bombs. His wife tends to him as if he were a child and attempts to control his

Photographer Maynard Parker stages a homecoming scene for the cover of the January 1945 issue of *House Beautiful* magazine. The scene represented the dream of GIs returning after World War II, complete with the smiling wife, welcoming child, and white picket fence.

Source: Maynard L. Parker collection. Courtesy of the Huntington Library, San Marino, California.

drinking, but without much success. A second man, a soda jerk before the war, returns a hero, but he is shell-shocked. The corner drugstore where he used to work has been bought out by a corporate chain, and he is without a job. His wife, whom he wed just before going overseas, loses interest in him absent the glamour of his uniform, turns to other men, and leaves him. When he spends a fitful night at the banker's home, it is the banker's daughter who comforts him and eases his nightmares. The third man, a sailor, has lost his arms along with his sense of self; his devoted and loving girl-next-door sweetheart finally restores his sense of manhood.

All three come home broken in mind and body, and all three are nurtured back to mental health and manly competence by strong women. In the end, the women's efforts are successful: they heal their men to the point that they can reassert their proper roles as husbands. The war hero relives the nightmares of combat at an airfield full of abandoned aircraft like the ones he flew during the war, and he is offered a job taking the planes apart and turning the scrap metal into materials to be used to build suburban houses, like the one he hopes to live in with his new wife (the banker's daughter). But in spite of the happy ending, the world had changed. The couples face new challenges and insecurities, just as the film's large and appreciative audiences did in real life.[4]

As reflected in *The Best Years of Our Lives*, the postwar moment was a complicated mix of optimism, anxiety, and uncertainty. The war was over, and the United States was powerful and prosperous. Yet an uneasy peacetime unfolded in these years. Two strands of postwar America became intertwined, one celebrating the family-centered American dream, the other darkened by fear. Victory propelled the United States to global superpower status; the nation was armed with the most powerful weapon ever developed, a weapon that no other country could match, at least for a while. The atomic bomb gave the United States military superiority, but it also gave the world a new and horrifying threat.[5]

From the start, it was clear that peacetime would not necessarily be peaceful.[6] Soon enough, in 1949, the Soviets, too, had the bomb. Already fearful of communist subversion, now Americans faced the thought of

In this still from the Academy Award–winning 1946 film *The Best Years of Our Lives*, the calm and confident young woman eases the nightmares of the returning soldier suffering from shell shock (now known as posttraumatic stress disorder).

Source: Margaret Herrick Library, Academy of Motion Picture Arts and Sciences.

an atomic attack on the homeland. How would Americans protect themselves against these looming threats? How would the nation respond to a foreign enemy that could destroy its cities in an instant, or internal enemies who might infiltrate the citizenry with communist doctrine? Would suburban homes, like the one pictured on the magazine's cover, help Americans adapt to the new realities of the Cold War and the Atomic Age?

AT THE DAWN of the Atomic Age, "national security" became an urgent concern. US State Department officials spoke of "national security" rather than "national defense" to describe the "close relationship between domestic politics, foreign policy, and military affairs." The term encapsulated the need to fortify the nation against the myriad dangers of the age, internal as well as external.[7]

The biggest perceived threat to national security after World War II was the Soviet Union, along with its American sympathizers. The two nations had a long history of hostility, beginning with the Russian Revolution in 1917, when the communists defeated the czar's army and founded the Soviet Union. Many left-leaning Americans supported the Russian Revolution against the brutality and excesses of the czar. The Communist Party of the United States of America (CPUSA) was founded in 1919, ultimately claiming 50,000 to 60,000 members at its first peak in the 1920s.

The party seemed to have little staying power. Within a decade, membership fell to 24,000, and by 1932 it was down to 6,000. Yet membership swelled again during the years of the Great Depression, owing to widespread disenchantment with the failed capitalist system. In the face of economic hardship, many Americans were drawn to the communist alternative. Membership in the CPUSA rose to about 65,000, and many other Americans, who did not join, were sympathetic to the cause.

But the CPUSA was never a major force in American politics. Anticommunist sentiment far outweighed communist sympathy. In the late 1930s, as Adolf Hitler marched across Europe conquering one nation after another, the majority of Americans polled—61 percent in 1937, and 58 percent in 1938—said they would choose fascism over communism. At the same time, Americans claimed to uphold the principles of the US Constitution: 97 percent said they believed in freedom of speech. But when it came to communists, they were prepared to violate their democratic principles. Only 38 percent said that if it was up to them, they would allow communists to hold meetings and express their views. In 1938, Congress established the House Un-American Activities Committee (HUAC) to investigate any individuals or organizations suspected of having communist ties.

On the eve of the United States' entry into World War II to fight alongside the Soviet Union, most Americans still had deep antipathy to communism. According to surveys taken at the time, 67 percent of them preferred denying Communist Party candidates the same amount of free radio time that Democratic and Republican candidates received. Vast majorities believed that communists could not be "good Christians" and should not be allowed to hold government jobs. Eighty percent wanted to do away with the Communist Party altogether; 64 percent favored policies that would "take repressive measures" against communists; and 5 percent supported the arrest and imprisonment of anyone identified as a communist. Only 8 percent thought it best to leave communists alone.

When the United States and the Soviet Union formed an alliance against the Axis powers, that hostility did not disappear. Although membership in the CPUSA rose slightly during the war years, it never reached above 80,000. Suspicion persisted throughout the war. In 1947, even after the Russians had made extreme sacrifices to defeat the Nazis, hostility to communism remained fierce in the United States, with 67 percent of Americans opposing the idea of allowing communists to hold civil service jobs. By 1949, 87 percent of survey respondents said that all communists should be immediately removed from vital defense industries.[8]

The World War II alliance between the United States and the Soviet Union quickly fell apart. When the Soviet Union emerged as the world's only other superpower, Americans began to see communism as a global as well as a domestic threat. Many feared that communist subversion would undermine American democracy, threaten capitalism, and erode the values of individualism and self-reliance. The conflict between the two nations framed postwar American foreign policy and suffused domestic politics. In what became known as his Truman Doctrine speech of 1947, President Harry Truman pledged that the United States would oppose communist aggression wherever it threatened democratic nations.[9]

National security was on the agendas of both major political parties during the presidential campaign of 1948. Republican candidate Thomas Dewey, calling upon the nation to "move out of this desperate darkness of today," claimed that the Republican Party was best equipped to confront "a fearful world." Dewey lost to Truman, the Democratic incumbent, whose view of the world was equally dire. Truman heeded the advice of Republican senator Arthur Vandenberg of Michigan, who argued that to wake up the citizens to the dangers of the age, the president needed to "scare the hell out of the country."[10]

Amid fears of a war with the Soviet Union, anticommunist fever swept the nation. Political leaders fueled a panic over the possibility that communists or communist sympathizers had infiltrated the government, universities, schools, and other institutions. Truman established a federal employee loyalty program. Attorney General Tom Clark gave a list of supposedly subversive organizations to the FBI with instructions to investigate them. Senator Joe McCarthy, a Republican from Wisconsin, built his political career on blaming allegedly disloyal Americans for weakening the country and making it vulnerable to communism. The anticommunist hysteria he promoted came to be known as McCarthyism.

HUAC, the congressional arm of the anticommunist crusade, launched investigations of government agencies, universities, and the entertainment industry in an effort to root out "internal enemies" from institutions with cultural and political power. As a result of this "red scare," thousands of people lost their jobs, their lives and careers ruined. In addition to government agencies, such as the State Department, Hollywood was the site of a major purge of suspected communist sympathizers. Many actors, screenwriters, directors, and other artists were blacklisted and unable to find work, from that point forward, in the film industry.[11]

Anticommunists also targeted anyone whose identity or lifestyle deviated from the nuclear-family norm. Breadwinning fathers and stay-at-home mothers who raised well-adjusted children were the model citizens of the era. Those who did not fit the norm were suspect, especially homosexuals, who were targeted in what historians later termed the "lavender scare." Thousands of gay men and lesbians, who were believed to be vulnerable to blackmail, were caught in the anticommunist purges and lost their jobs in government, the educational system, and other institutions.[12]

Truman saw the threat of subversion at home and the danger of attack from abroad as two sides of the same coin, and he and many others worried that communist sympathizers within the United States might undermine national security. As early as 1948, a year before the world learned that the Soviet Union had developed an atomic bomb, 71 percent of those polled agreed that the United States should "take certain steps in order to make an agreement with Russia more likely" and announce to the world "that we will not use the atom bomb except in self-defense."[13]

When the Soviet Union exploded its first atomic bomb in a controlled test in 1949, the United States developed a strategy of "deterrence." The idea was to build and stockpile so many nuclear weapons that no nation would dare to attack the United States, for fear that retaliation would result in the aggressor's utter annihilation. But there were no guarantees that deterrence would work. People knew that nuclear war could happen, because it had already happened, and there was only one country that had waged it: the United States. If the good guys were willing to drop the bombs, there was every reason to believe that the bad guys would do the same. The Russians could ignite World War III, noted the young war hero and congressman John F. Kennedy, with an "atomic Pearl Harbor." According to NSC-68, a top-secret State Department report of 1950 that outlined the policy of deterrence and called for an arms buildup, "the cold war is in fact a real war in which the survival of the free world is at stake."[14]

The vast majority of Americans at the time believed that communists should be treated like war criminals. When a Gallup poll in 1950 asked what should be done with American communists if the United States got into a war with Russia, 40 percent of respondents said that they should be put into internment camps or imprisoned, and 28 percent said they should be exiled or sent to Russia. Fully 13 percent said that law-abiding American citizens who had committed no crime, but were communists, should be shot or hanged.[15]

By the time Dwight D. Eisenhower became president, the policy of nuclear deterrence had strong bipartisan support and defined the terms of an epic battle.[16] In his First Inaugural Address in 1953, Eisenhower warned the nation "that forces of good and evil are massed and armed and opposed as rarely before in history. . . . Freedom is pitted against slavery; lightness against the dark."[17]

In 1954, Eisenhower signed the Communist Control Act, which outlawed the CPUSA and criminalized membership in, or support for, the party or "Communist-action" organizations. Few Americans protested this affront to the Bill of Rights, even though there was no wartime emergency at the time that might have spurred support for such a draconian measure. Anticommunist fear had reached new heights. According to a Gallup poll conducted that year, two-thirds of Americans believed the government should have the right to listen in on citizens' telephone conversations if they were suspected of communist sympathies, that an admitted communist should not be allowed to make a speech in their community, that books by communists should be banned from the public library, and that any communist radio singer should be fired. A majority favored putting admitted communists in jail, and 77 percent said they should have their American citizenship revoked.[18]

This fear was far out of proportion to any threat American communists may have posed. By 1957, membership in the CPUSA had dwindled to fewer than 10,000, with an active base of approximately 5,000. A small number spied for the Soviet Union. But those who joined or sympathized with the CPUSA were not necessarily interested in overthrowing the government of the United States. In fact, many supported the ideals on which the nation was founded: equal opportunity for all, the value of hard work, and a belief in American progress. Some of the authors and teachers who lost their jobs, or were blacklisted by publishers, for example, used pseudonyms to write books for children that encouraged racial tolerance, equality between boys and girls, and individual creativity.[19]

Nevertheless, many Americans believed that the country was crawling with dangerous communists who threatened the nation and its citizens.[20] High-profile cases of suspected communist spies contributed to this misperception. The media gave extensive coverage to suspected spies, including Alger Hiss, as well as Julius and Ethel Rosenberg. The 1953 execution of the Rosenbergs created a media frenzy around the supposed traitors, even though the question of their guilt was and remains a matter of much controversy and debate.

Newspapers, magazines, and television in the 1950s exaggerated the dangers of communism much as the media would exaggerate the prevalence of violent crime in later decades. Political leaders warned that communist ideas were as dangerous to American security as Soviet weapons. Faced with these alarming messages, it appeared as though the idealized American way of life was vulnerable. Citizens needed to fortify themselves and their families, not only physically—with appropriate preparedness—but also psychologically and ideologically.

As AMERICANS SOUGHT ways to protect themselves and their families from Cold War dangers, they turned to the home as a place that would offer both physical and psychological security. The home provided a private space isolated from the public world where dangerous people and ideas might be lurking. In the early postwar years, those dangers seemed to emanate from the perceived communist threat. In later years, the suburban home promised a refuge from new dangers that seemed to emerge from urban centers: crime, violence, and upheaval. Over time these fears merged as Americans retreated into increasingly fortified private spaces.

In the immediate aftermath of World War II, numerous factors converged to point Americans toward the single-family suburban home as the epitome of the domestic ideal. The communist threat encouraged citizens to reject ideas associated with the Soviet Union, such as collectivism and socialism, and to embrace values of individualism and self-reliance. Those values found expression in private homes, where men provided financial support and women stayed home and tended to the family. For large numbers of Americans weary of war and eager to take advantage of postwar prosperity, this domestic ideal was a personal dream as well as a national symbol of the virtues of American political freedoms and free-market capitalism.

The government actively encouraged and supported the proliferation of these homes along with the values and lifestyle they represented.

Thanks to government programs, millions of middle- and working-class families were able to afford homes like the one pictured in Maynard Parker's *House Beautiful* cover photo of 1945. The Servicemen's Readjustment Act of 1944, known informally as the GI Bill, provided many benefits to returning veterans, including access to low-interest home mortgages. In addition, public policies fostered suburban expansion through zoning laws, transportation development, and tax benefits.

In other words, government officials made decisions to subsidize suburban expansion and home ownership, rather than putting resources into overcrowded urban centers. Ideally, nuclear families would move to the suburbs and stay home for fun and leisure, with minimal need to venture into risky public life, where they might encounter dangerous people and ideas. In the midst of both prosperity and anxiety, houses provided the first line of defense—both physically, as structures, and psychologically, as environments that fostered self-reliant citizens. The proper house, inhabited by the proper family, would protect Americans against the new threats of the postwar world. Safe within their domestic sanctuaries, Americans might nurture independent citizens and, with proper preparation, protect themselves against atomic attack.[21]

Postwar suburban growth accelerated a trend that had begun decades earlier. In 1910, the majority of Americans lived in rural areas; only 21 percent of the US population lived in central cities, and a mere 7 percent lived in suburbs. Beginning in 1940, suburbs accounted for more population growth than central cities. By 1960, 31 percent of the US population lived in the suburbs, almost equal to the 32 percent living in urban centers. Suburban residents were much more likely than residents of central cities to own their own homes.[22]

Along with postwar prosperity, demographic changes spurred the expansion of single-family homes in the suburbs. The marriage rate rose as the age of marriage declined, producing the "baby boom" and a dramatic increase in the number of nuclear families. By 1950, 78 percent of American households included a married couple—a number that would decline to 52 percent by the end of the century. These postwar nuclear families poured into the new suburban developments.

Although suburban home ownership represented the postwar American dream, it is unlikely that ideological reasons provided the prime motivation for the migration from city to suburb. For many of the young families who moved to the suburbs in the early postwar years, space and privacy were new luxuries. Those who had come from crowded urban neighborhoods, or had lived with relatives in crowded spaces, eagerly embraced the lifestyle that came with single-family homes.

But for planners and designers, privacy was intended to be a sign and source of security in an uncertain world. Elizabeth Gordon, the influential editor-in-chief of *House Beautiful* from 1941 to 1964, was one of the most outspoken advocates of suburban single-family dwellings as a bulwark against communist infiltration. In her widely read magazine, she articulated the interrelated Cold War themes of individualism, free enterprise, the sanctity of the home, and suspicion of outsiders. She railed against the International Style—an architectural design drawn from European modernism that characterized tall office buildings as well as large apartment buildings—which she considered collectivist and un-American:

> We don't believe the International Style is simply a matter of taste; any more than we believe that Nazism or Communism are matters of taste, matters of opinion. . . . Either we choose the architecture that will encourage the development of individualism or we choose the architecture and design of collectivism and totalitarian control. . . . The International Style . . . masses families together in one giant building so that relatively few, strategically placed, block leaders could check on all movements and conduct classes of ideological indoctrination. . . . [It is] a design for living that we associate with totalitarianism.[23]

Whether or not they purchased homes with these political considerations in mind, readers might have agreed with her, especially regarding privacy. In secluded residential spaces, families could protect themselves from dangers, noises, and intrusions from suspicious or potentially subversive unknown people. According to Gordon, families flourished in privacy, fenced in and walled off from public gaze. Joseph Howland, the magazine's garden editor, concurred: "Good living is NOT public living. . . . Do the neighbors know your business? We consider [privacy] one of the cherished American rights, one of the privileges we fought a war to preserve. . . . The very *raison d'être* of the separate house is to get away from the living habits and cooking smells and inquisitive eyes of other people."[24]

Privacy had not always been a desired feature of suburban housing design. Earlier advocates and designers of suburban homes did not call for houses to be separated from their neighbors and communities. As early as 1870, one suburban proponent, with little use for foreign traditions and cultural styles, complained, "The practice of hedging one's ground so the passerby cannot enjoy its beauty is one of the barbarisms of old gardening." As late as 1940, one architect suggested that homes should be inviting rather than secluding: "Looking out I see my garden, see the trees, the sun, the rain, see the birds and human neighbors pictured through my window pane. But my window has two pictures, one for them and one for me. My side too must be made lovely for those looking in to see." By the late 1950s, privacy, as a design feature, had won out over the open plan that had previously prevailed in the suburbs. The idea of opening one's home to the world outside vanished in favor of the benefits and protections afforded by privacy.[25]

For suburban residents, privacy offered the possibility of internal fortification. According to planners and advocates like Elizabeth Gordon, without intrusion from the outside, families could cultivate the virtues of independent citizenship that bolstered both individual autonomy and national strength. The home came to represent the place where Americans could find security and safety—and protect themselves from the dangers of the age. Safe inside the private home, Americans could enjoy the fruits of postwar prosperity.

A striking example of postwar private leisure was the rapid spread of backyard swimming pools. New and cheaper construction materials, generous payment plans, and low-interest bank loans made pools affordable for middle-class suburbanites. The number of private pools nationwide

In this typical postwar suburban house, the family's privacy is protected against intrusive eyes by solid walls and fences.

Source: Maynard L. Parker collection. Courtesy of the Huntington Library, San Marino, California.

grew from 10,000 in 1950 to 175,000 by 1959. Meanwhile, the number of public pools declined dramatically. Before World War II, tens of millions of Americans swam at huge public pools. Municipal pools were centers of civic life and community gathering. They were also segregated. The new ease of building private pools was not the only cause of the decline of public pools. They declined in part because of the successful efforts of black citizens to gain admission, largely by filing and winning discrimination lawsuits. It was partly in response to this new integration that between 1950 and 1970 millions of white Americans stopped swimming in public pools. Many public pools closed, and private pools proliferated.[26] As white middle-class Americans retreated from the racial and class diversity of the cities, they retreated from public amusements that would bring them into contact with potentially dangerous "others." At a time when anticommunists labeled civil rights activists as subversives, pervasive racism fused with fears of communism, hampering efforts to desegregate public accommodations in the North as well as the South.

Swimming pools may seem a benign accoutrement of the "good life" in the postwar years. But they represent a significant turn away from engagement in public activities and toward a more private life. Americans with pools, swing sets, and barbeques in their backyards were less likely to venture out to public parks, beaches, and amusement areas. Private leisure and entertainment reflected postwar prosperity and the fruits of American capitalism. They also kept families isolated from a public world where dangerous and subversive elements might be lurking.

Another important consumer item, besides swimming pools, to occupy a central place in the postwar home was the television. In the first decade after World War II, the number of American households with a television grew from 8,000 to 35 million. By 1962, that number reached 49 million—approximately 90 percent of all households.[27] In the privacy of their living rooms, Americans watched programs such as *The Adventures of Ozzie and Harriet* and *Leave It to Beaver*, in which fictional white middle-class families enacted proper suburban values. The tidy, consumer-laden home, managed by a competent wife and mother and supported by a responsible breadwinner, offered the formula and the setting for the cultivation of independent citizens with an appreciation for American capitalism.

To MORE AND more Americans in the postwar period, the suburban single-family dwelling came to represent the normative domestic abode. But it was not available to all. Those who were excluded not only lacked access to the comforts of suburban living, but also lost the claim to good citizenship that suburban home ownership conferred. According to widely shared assumptions at the time, markers of good citizenship included not only home ownership, which indicated a stake in society, but also conformity to the prevailing domestic ideal: a male breadwinner who earned enough to provide for his family, and a wife whose primary occupation was homemaker and mother, who together raised well-

The postwar suburban ideal celebrated family leisure within the walls of the home. In this photo, the family gathers for entertainment and fun in the privacy of their fenced-in backyard.

Source: Maynard L. Parker collection. Courtesy of the Huntington Library, San Marino, California.

adjusted children. A heterosexual married couple with children living in the suburbs gave evidence of these qualities of good citizenship. These were also the families who were presumably worthy of the safety and security that suburban living offered. Those who were left out—because they were single, or homosexual, or could not afford a suburban home, or were excluded because of racial restrictions—had neither the presumed attributes of good citizenship nor access to the security that suburban residences allegedly provided. That left them suspect. If they were not living the life that conferred good citizenship, perhaps they harbored subversive or criminal tendencies.

Yet it was public policies, along with widespread racism, that determined who had access to suburban home ownership. Although the

Federal Housing Authority (FHA) offered veterans government-subsidized mortgages and low down payments for new homes, families of color were blocked from most suburban developments, even if they were able to afford homes within them. Policies known as "red-lining" prevented nonwhite families from purchasing homes in certain neighborhoods. At the same time, African Americans who wanted to purchase suburban homes faced restrictions on housing loans. Even if law and public policy would allow them to move to a particular suburb, they might then face threats, and at times violence, from white neighborhood residents.[28]

Other groups were also excluded or discouraged from suburban home ownership. Single-family houses were constructed with one family type in mind: a heterosexual married couple and their children. White middle-class nuclear families inhabited neighborhoods filled with people like themselves, and these residents were not necessarily friendly to nonconformists. Housing designs fostered the nuclear-family structure, with back-facing windows for supervision of children, and interior spaces that included child-sized bedrooms and playrooms. Suburban neighborhoods were often zoned against apartment buildings and commercial establishments that would be more appropriate for single adults or gay couples.

And many families simply could not afford to purchase these homes. In 1950, the median value of a house was $7,354, while the median family income for a white family was $3,445. Black families earned, on average, about half of what white families earned. By 1960, the value of a house had increased to $11,900, on average, while the income of white families had increased to $5,835. Black families still earned only slightly more than half of what white families earned, with a median income of $3,230.[29] With this income gap, large numbers of black families were priced out of the housing market, along with other racial minorities and low-income whites. Some black families had the means to purchase homes in predominantly black suburbs, or in the very few suburban neighborhoods that accepted blacks as well as whites. But those who could not, or would not, buy a suburban house resided outside the parameters of normative postwar life.

The suburban dream was far from the celebrated embodiment of self-sufficiency that it allegedly represented. Suburban houses were privately owned, but their owners relied on public funding and government subsidies, such as tax breaks and mortgage subsidies. Nobody referred to suburban homes as "public housing," even though in many respects they were. "Public housing projects," or "subsidized housing," were terms associated exclusively with poor people in the inner cities who lived in multi-unit structures.

As the government poured subsidies into suburban developments, it ignored substandard housing in the cities, in part for ideological reasons. Many officials were intensely hostile to "public housing" in urban centers. City policymakers, who considered it akin to socialism, and real estate agents, who saw it as eroding their profits, campaigned vigorously against it. In Los Angeles, a 1952 ordinance directed against "socialist projects" virtually outlawed public housing.[30]

Some politicians and bureaucrats pushed back, often at the cost of their careers. Frank Wilkinson, a Los Angeles housing official, was one such casualty. Wilkinson had, in fact, joined the Communist Party, but he had no interest in any kind of action communists were usually suspected of, such as attempting to overthrow the US government. Raised in a devout Methodist family of solid Republicans, he visited poor neighborhoods in the nation's large cities. Seeing the suffering, he decided to dedicate his life to the eradication of poverty. In 1952, Wilkinson was head of the Los Angeles Housing Authority. Urban renewal—a new term for clearing out impoverished neighborhoods—was being implemented across the country. Although the disastrous consequences of uprooting communities and destroying neighborhoods only became apparent later, at the time urban renewal offered a vision of a future without slums.[31] In that reformist mode, Wilkinson proposed clearing out Chavez Ravine, a neighborhood of about three hundred Mexican American families, in order to build a project with thousands of public housing units.

The City of Los Angeles bought the land with funds from the federal government and cleared out the residents, promising them first choice of homes in the new development. But soon, opponents of the plan, including anticommunist politicians and corporate business owners who wanted the land for their own use, accused Wilkinson and other city leaders of promoting a socialist plot. Eventually, the city turned Chavez Ravine into a stadium for the Dodgers baseball team. The former residents lost their homes and received nothing in return. Wilkinson called it "the tragedy of my life." For his efforts, he was accused of being a communist and hauled before the House Un-American Activities Committee. He ended up in prison for refusing to answer the committee's questions.[32]

ANTICOMMUNIST GOVERNMENT OFFICIALS and business leaders saw government projects such as public housing as evidence of creeping socialism, and of the threat of subversion by internal enemies. Los Angeles mayor Fletcher Bowron articulated this view: "Our real threat here is sabotage. Our danger is from within. We must guard against this sabotage." The editors of the *Los Angeles Times* agreed with the mayor, noting the connection between internal and external threats: "He regards sabotage as a danger more likely to materialize than attack from *without* the continental limits. We know we have a local Communist fifth column of respectable numbers and unlimited fanaticism. They might, provided their Russian masters trust them, collaborate on an A-bomb smuggling venture into the city's heart. They need watching."[33]

Anticommunism was "in the air," according to the writer Patricia Hampl, and it was driven mainly by fear. Hampl, who grew up in St. Paul, Minnesota, describes in her memoir her terror as a child in the 1950s, when she was unable to sleep for fear of the "*Communists* who lurked in the dark." She did not know "whether to watch for man or beast, goblin or reptile, malicious intent or natural disaster, something large and looming or a thing so insidiously small that no degree of vigilance could assure safety: I didn't know, I didn't know." Noting the power of the new medium of television, she recalled watching TV shows, including the nightly news, filled with dire warnings about the communists. Still, she wrote, "I could not concoct my Communists. . . . They remained, simply, dread."[34]

Such anxieties were not merely figments of a child's overly active imagination. In addition to the television news that frightened Hampl, widely read publications warned not only that communists were dangerous, but that they were everywhere. A 1952 article in *Reader's Digest* warned, "The Russians do not grab merely real estate. They also grab people. . . . No-one is too small or insignificant, too young or too old, to be shackled and regimented or pauperized and destroyed."[35] Ominous warnings such as this one, from politicians, officials, and the media, not only promoted anticommunist policies, but also fueled primal fears.

Innocent children appeared to be particularly vulnerable. Stoking parental fears, in 1953 Norfolk and Western Railway placed a public service advertisement in *Newsweek* picturing a frightened boy at home at night in a dark hallway, with the caption: "You needn't be ashamed of being afraid in the dark, son. . . . The darkness is a hiding place for confusion, greed, conspiracy, treachery, socialism . . . and its uglier brother, communism." Urging vigilance against this subversion, the ad warned, "if you ignore this responsibility . . . what you lose in the dark may be your freedom." In the Los Angeles suburb of South Gate, local businesses sponsored a public service ad that asked, "Are you shutting your child behind an IRON CURTAIN?" The Freedoms Foundation warned, "It Could Happen Here," with an image of a father apologizing to his son for his lack of vigilance. In the caption, the father tells his son, "I am so sorry you are going to have to live under Communism. . . . Not enough of us spoke up for freedom when we had the chance."[36]

In these public service ads, businesses and political groups warned that communists were not the only threat. They asserted that the government itself was also dangerous. Antigovernment thought was nothing new in the United States, but to many, the Cold War attached a sinister meaning to government action and involvement in citizens' lives. A 1950 public service ad in *U.S. News and World Report* from the Electric Light and Power Companies warned of increasing government control, and assured readers that the company was "battling this move toward a socialistic government." The ad pictured a small boy in front of a table holding four symbols of freedom: a key, a Bible, a pencil, and a ballot.[37]

These public service ads, sponsored by private institutions, portrayed big government as akin to socialism and communism. Companies called upon men to protect their families through personal defense, and to trust private enterprise, not the government, to keep them secure. This message was nowhere more explicit than in ads for the insurance industry, which often promised "self-made security" for the "do-it-yourself American," who was responsible for "creating his own security." These messages assured men that if they purchased insurance from private companies, rather than relying on the government, they would be fulfilling their roles as self-sufficient breadwinners. As the head of the family, it was up to them to provide security for their families.[38]

These antigovernment messages stressed the responsibility of citizens to protect themselves, their families, and American capitalism from the threat of subversion. Private companies and trade associations poured resources into advertisements and educational films that promoted these themes. In 1950, the American Economic Foundation, an organization dedicated to free enterprise and limited government, along with the Inland Steel Company and Borg-Warner Corporation, produced an educational film, *In Our Hands*, depicting a fictional election. One candidate promises socialism, saying it will create full employment and economic equality. The other promotes capitalism, emphasizing strong unions and strong management engaging in negotiation and free choice. A family watches the candidates debate on television. The son likes the communist candidate, because he promises "full security," asking, "Why shouldn't the government take care of us?" After some discussion, they all decide to vote for the communist, and he wins.

The film then depicts the aftermath of the election, which produces an assault on the home, the family, private ownership, and religion. The "Master State" moves the family from place to place, seizing the family car. The mother cries and the father yells as they are taken away in the back of a truck, with the mother holding a baby. The mother asks the driver what will happen to the baby, who hasn't yet been baptized. The driver says he doesn't know what the party will do about the churches. The pointed message of the film is that the dictator was elected. The family, and others who voted for him, are responsible for their own ruin. They were duped in part because they failed to recognize the threats, in this case largely internal ones, right in front of them.[39]

Amid warnings by private enterprise against both communism and big government, public officials had to figure out the best way to respond to Americans' fears of an atomic attack. Hovering above all debates over domestic security was the image of the mushroom cloud, and the reality that the American dream could be snuffed out in an instant. Government officials faced a dilemma. They needed to reassure the public that the nation's leaders would protect them in the event of an attack, but at the same time, many wanted to avoid big government projects that might smack of socialism.

The question of how much the government should do to actively protect American citizens was a source of political contention, similar to the debate over public housing. Should the government build public shelters, or should individual citizens provide their own protection?

To address the most immediate and tangible threat of the Atomic Age, Truman, in 1951, established the Federal Civil Defense Administration (FCDA). The FCDA, framing civil defense as a "way of life," called for a national fallout shelter program. But acquiring the necessary funding proved an insurmountable hurdle. Opponents objected to the cost, the supposedly socialistic nature of such a program (they were aware, for instance, that the Soviets had built a large underground complex in Moscow capable of housing 30,000 state officials for several months), and what they saw as the impracticality of trying to protect citizens in vast underground shelters for any length of time. Congress rejected proposals for shelter funding in 1951, 1952, and 1953.[40]

President Eisenhower, for his part, vehemently opposed a national shelter system. The highly esteemed World War II general did not want the nation to become a "garrison state." At his first White House Conference of Mayors in 1953, he warned, "We can't be an armed camp. We are not going to transfer ourselves into militarists. We are not going to be in uniform, going around yelling 'Heil' anything."[41]

Eisenhower favored evacuation as the more efficient and economical, not to mention palatable, option. In an evacuation of a city, at the sound of the siren people would get into their cars and drive to a rural or suburban "reception area" fifteen or twenty miles away, where families would reunite. Eisenhower proposed—and Congress passed legislation for—a national highway system in part out of a belief that highways would facilitate swift evacuation in the event of an atomic attack. One official noted that commuters in cities like New York and Chicago were already well practiced in evacuation because of their daily retreat from city to suburb.[42] Still, these plans, like plans for shelters, depended on calm, orderly behavior on the part of citizens facing the prospect of imminent death.

Civil defense officials offered several different proposals for protecting citizens from nuclear attack, including publicly funded underground fortifications, plans to evacuate cities to suburbs, and private family shelters. Politicians debated various strategies. An alternative to new shelter construction was a public and private partnership to identify and fortify public spaces that could be used as shelters with no investment of government funds. The Los Angeles Civil Defense Ordinance of 1951, for example, required engineers in the city's Department of Building and Safety to locate and designate potential shelters. Government officials recruited city planners and architects to provide shelter space in public buildings. Many architects objected and refused to take part in civil defense efforts. They believed that shelters were useless and that, anyway, it was not the job of architects to design them. Others warned that the plans were unrealistic. The superintendent of buildings believed that people would panic in the event of an attack, "a state of affairs which might turn 'shelters' into 'tombs.'"[43]

The American Institute of Architects (AIA) fully cooperated, promoting civil defense planning as a means of boosting the status of the profession. Although it was useless to try to protect against atomic blast, providing shelter from the resulting fallout seemed feasible. In the 1950s and 1960s, thousands of architects identified more than 100 million shelter spaces as part of the National Fallout Shelter Survey. These spaces, marked with bold black and yellow signs, were stocked with food and supplies. Initially, shelter space was designated in existing buildings. Later, buildings were designed and built for both business and shelter, with heavy concrete blocks and small windows, giving rise to urban landscapes marked by "bunker architecture."[44]

The various strategies for shelters in public buildings all had drawbacks. Civil defense planners realized that public shelters would not provide adequate protection in the event of an attack. Individual citizens would need to do their part. Officials agreed that "primarily civil defense starts in the home." Eventually, civil defense officials reached a consensus that the government would educate the public, organize plans for a response in the event of an attack, and encourage individual citizens to provide protection for themselves and their families. This solution released the government from having to build large shelter projects and recruited American families—especially suburban families living in single-family homes—into the defense effort. In this way the government supported individual responsibility within the suburban family home.

Thus, as the 1950s unfolded, the private home became the primary location for civil defense planning. In 1958, Leo Hoegh, head of the Office of Civil and Defense Mobilization, announced that there would be "no massive federally financed shelter construction program"; he instead proposed a plan that focused on private shelters with the advice and guidance of the government. As Hoegh declared, "Every home a fortress!"[45]

Creating that fortress was a challenge for civilians, who took the threat of an atomic attack very seriously. In a 1946 poll, when the United States was still the only country with atomic weapons, 74 percent of Americans believed that regardless of how many atomic bombs and rockets the country produced, another country might attack them. By

1950, when the Soviet Union also had atomic weapons, over half of those polled worried about the possibility of another war. When asked in 1951 what disturbed them the most, they cited financial concerns as first; the threat of world war was next, above even the health of their families.[46]

Citizens were skeptical of unrealistic pronouncements by civil defense officials who tried to assure them that they could achieve safety from atomic attack with simple home preparedness. One expert declared, "No one ever needs to be scared of an A-bomb. Have respect for it but never fear it. Be prepared with first-aid training and stop, look and think." Few were convinced by such assurances. Americans had seen photos of Hiroshima and Nagasaki, and they knew the likelihood of surviving an atomic bomb attack was slim. Civil defense officials tried to offer useful advice, but they, too, were often at a loss.[47]

Nevertheless, officials continued to talk publicly about the importance of preparedness. In 1951, California governor Earl Warren was one among many who whipped up nuclear fears in order to spur citizens to personally take action on behalf of their safety and that of their families: "For our own protection, all Californians must realize, and realize quickly, that the danger is here, the task of preparation is great, and the time may be shorter than we think." Civil defense authorities tried to estimate the extent of potential death and destruction based on population numbers and patterns. State officials believed that California would be a prime target. They expected the Soviet Union to launch at least five strikes on California, resulting in 260,000 deaths. In case they needed reminding, on the tenth anniversary of the surprise attack on Pearl Harbor, the *Los Angeles Mirror* exhorted residents to ready themselves. A front-page headline announced, "EXTRA—Operation Wake Up," along with a full front-page photo of a mushroom cloud.[48]

What could responsible citizens do to protect themselves and their families? One California proposal made clear that, to many citizens, the external and internal threats were indeed inseparable. It called for a neighborhood-based block warden system involving volunteers who would keep an eye on their neighbors and report any suspicious activity that might suggest that Soviet spies were in their midst, ready to help the communists attack the United States. Civil defense officials called for 1.5 million volunteer wardens throughout the state. Many citizens responded to the call. In Pasadena, 14,000 volunteers signed up in one day.[49]

On the national level, a new federally funded program, called the Ground Observer Corps, was given the mission of preventing an attack by approaching aircraft through volunteer efforts. Beginning in 1950, a large number of volunteers—800,000, by one estimate—watched the sky looking for hostile aircraft from some 16,000 observation posts. The Ground Observer Corps ended in 1958, by which time both the United States and the Soviet Union had intercontinental ballistic missiles (ICBMs), which flew too fast and too high to be spotted by the human eye.[50]

As various plans for public protection against the threat of nuclear attack came and went, civil defense officials continued to call upon citizens to build shelters in their homes. Enterprising businesses supported this idea, hoping to cash in on shelter construction. The structure of suburban houses allowed for shelters to be built in basements or backyards. Home-centered civil defense also offered the possibility of bolstering traditional gender arrangements and patriarchal authority. Advocates claimed that, in addition to providing protection, private shelters would foster "privacy and decency," and give "the head of the family his natural place in making decisions in fateful circumstances." But the instructions for building shelters revealed officials' naïveté as they tried to persuade citizens that they could protect themselves in the event of a nuclear attack.

Guidelines for citizens were contradictory, puzzling, and unrealistic. For example, in 1951, California civil defense director Walter M. Robertson made shelter construction sound unconvincingly simple: "All one needs is a hole in the ground with a little overhead cover." Frustrated by such suggestions, citizens demanded more precise instructions, flooding officials with queries.[51] Many observers expressed skepticism that home shelters would provide protection, especially those built by homeowners themselves. The *Los Angeles Examiner*

The Portland Cement Association promoted its product for its beneficial use in the event of an atomic attack. The advertisement promised safety in the Atomic Age with the "all-concrete blast-resistant house."

Source: Courtesy of the Portland Cement Association.

warned against "bomb shelter fever" breaking out in "a rash of amateur construction activity." Others said any backyard shelter was folly, asserting that even professionally constructed shelters were wasteful "death traps." Explaining how home shelters could actually increase the possibility of death, John H. Alderson, the Los Angeles fire chief, told a reporter that "such dug-outs, if near a building, would have their oxygen exhausted as the nearby buildings burned and occupants would suffocate." One company offered the "all-concrete blast-resistant house" as an alternative to the underground shelter.[52]

In spite of the many critics of home shelters, FCDA officials and politicians of both parties made clear time and time again that families would need to provide for their own safety in the nuclear age. The government would supply guidelines and educational programs, but homeowners would be responsible for purchasing, installing, and equipping private shelters for their own families. Atomic Age safety came in only one form: a nuclear family inhabiting a fortified suburban home. Civil defense planners made no mention of the one in four Americans who were poor in the mid-1950s, or the half who were not homeowners, or the one in four who were not married or not living in single-family dwellings. Most nonwhite Americans, as well as the disabled, were left out of civil defense guidelines entirely.[53]

If the single-family home was the most promising site for protection, the suburb was the place to be in the event of a nuclear attack. Government publications, along with the news media, asserted that densely populated urban centers would be the primary targets for nuclear attacks. Accordingly, civil defense officials joined the chorus of government planners who were encouraging migration to the suburbs. By promoting suburban homes as essential for civil defense, the government underscored that the white middle-class nuclear family represented not only the "normal" American family, but also the family most deserving of protection from external and internal threats.

The entire civil defense program was premised on the notion that civilians could survive a nuclear war. That premise was unrealistic, but it allowed government officials to provide some rationale for the buildup of nuclear weapons. In the event of an attack, the country would be equipped to retaliate. If civilians were alert and prepared, they could minimize their risk of harm while the nation destroyed the enemy with its superior might.

With the exception of a small number of dissenters, Americans did not object to the amassing of nuclear arms during this period. Antigovernment types who opposed large government-funded domestic programs threw their weight behind the largest government project of all: military buildup. They asserted that national defense was the government's primary responsibility. Protecting the nation from attack required massive weapons and a strong military. If the strategy of deterrence failed, and if an enemy nation attacked, the United States would need to fight back.

While the government continued the arms buildup, citizens contemplated the impact of an atomic attack. Civil defense authorities saturated the public with graphic details about blasts and radiation, apparently in the belief that knowledge of nuclear weapons could make them safe. The information provided was questionable, however, and it was not likely to reassure anyone. In 1950, an article on the front page of the *Los Angeles Times* assured the public that "you are apt to survive" if you don't panic. To help readers figure out their own likelihood of being incinerated, the paper carried helpful illustrations that mapped the impact of a possible bombing on the city. One depicted the "radius of danger," with concentric circles emanating from city hall, which was the ground zero of this hypothetical bombing. Each circle represented "survival chances at various distances." In the first circle, around ground zero, "only the strongest shelters will prevent death by flying wreckage." But for those lucky enough to be in the fourth circle, two miles from the blast, "probably less than 1 in 100 of persons . . . will lose [their] lives."[54] Government officials joined scientists in trying to provide information that would keep citizens alert and informed. US Secretary of State Dean Acheson summed up the official position in 1950: "We must hope for the best while preparing for the worst."[55]

Whether these officials were trying their best to inform the public or cynically deceiving people into believing they could protect themselves, their civil defense programs were training Americans in a new mind-set: that of being ready for a nuclear attack. Citizens faced warnings almost everywhere they turned. Public screenings of films, such as the documentary *You Can Beat the A Bomb*, asserted that individual efforts could assure survival. In Los Angeles, the fire department developed plans to distribute 600,000 copies of the booklet *Survival Under Atomic Attack*, and colleges offered civil defense classes.[56]

Schools and communities provided a wide range of training films and exercises to instruct children on how best to protect themselves. There were "drop drills," when teachers, in the midst of their lessons, shouted "drop." Children responded by diving under their desks and curling into a fetal position, with their hands folded over their heads to protect their brains from flying debris. Instructional films, like the widely viewed *Duck and Cover* (1951), starring Bert the Turtle, were shown in schools, libraries, and other public places. The film taught children not only to run for shelter and curl up next to a wall, but also to follow rules, obey authority, and turn to older people for wisdom and advice. It is not clear whether the cheerful turtle who pulled his head under his shell was reassuring to children, who had no protective shells; nonetheless, they were told that when the bomb suddenly fell, they would be responsible for their own protection.

The movie informed children that an attack could happen at any time, without warning, perhaps when they were riding their bikes to school, or on the playground, or anywhere. Their parents might not be there to protect them; nor would their teachers. It was up to each child to remember how to behave when the flash of blinding light appeared. If they panicked, or forgot to contort themselves into the right position, or failed to face away from the blast, they could be blinded by the light, or burned by the fire, or their skulls could be crushed by falling debris. Even if they followed all the directions perfectly, would their frail little limbs and fingers really make them safe from the ferocity of an atomic bomb? And what would their world be like after the "all clear" sounded? Would things really be "all clear"?[57]

As if the idea of an atomic bomb blast was not frightening enough, civil defense officials warned that communists operating in plain sight might carry out germ warfare attacks. Public awareness campaigns proliferated, such as the 1952 educational film *What You Should Know About Biological Warfare*.[58] Regardless of the particular threat, the message was the same: an attack could occur at any time, from afar or from someone nearby, and individuals were responsible for their own protection.

Whatever reassurance these messages may have offered was undermined in 1952, when the United States detonated the first hydrogen bomb in a test on the Enewetak Atoll in the Pacific Ocean. The explosion vaporized the entire island, leaving behind a crater more than a mile wide. The power of the hydrogen bomb rendered most guidelines for civil defense obsolete. In 1956, Eisenhower acknowledged that the perils of nuclear war had reached a new level: "With such weapons, there can be no victory for anyone. Plainly the objective now must be to see that such a war does not occur at all."[59]

The possibility of war involving hydrogen bombs only highlighted the paradox of national security in the nuclear age.[60] By building more and more powerful weapons, the nation's leaders heightened the danger and increased the vulnerability of civilians. But few Americans objected to the military buildup. Most supported the arming of the nation and accepted the possible consequences.

By THE MID-1950S, with the advent and proliferation of the hydrogen bomb, civil defense plans appeared increasingly absurd. But government officials had nothing else to offer, so they continued to urge civilians to protect themselves. The Soviet Union detonated its first hydrogen bomb in 1955, ending the brief second period of supremacy held by the United States. The only other country with nuclear capability in the 1950s was Great Britain, an American ally, which tested the hydrogen bomb in 1958. While citizens worried, the arms race continued, with the production, stockpiling, and testing of weapons.

Hydrogen bombs were too destructive to test on American soil. But the government assumed that the A-bomb would still be a weapon of choice in the event of a nuclear exchange—Eisenhower believed that it could be used as a "tactical" weapon, against another nation's armed forces—so testing of the smaller device continued in the Nevada desert. These tests were intended not only to make sure that newer weapon designs worked, but to determine how effectively private shelters would protect civilians. In a 1955 A-bomb test explosion, civil defense officials constructed small houses in the test area and placed mock families of mannequins inside. Observers witnessed the tests in trenches and military vehicles from distances that were presumed to be safe.[61]

The test obliterated the houses and mock families and unleashed a cloud of radioactive dust that wafted far beyond the artificial civil-defense domiciles. People living downwind from the Nevada tests complained that fallout from the explosions threatened the health of their families and sickened and killed their livestock. A seven-year-old boy caught in the fallout died of leukemia; a priest who drove through the unsecured bombing range contracted face cancer; and other people in the area developed mysterious illnesses. The Atomic Energy Commission (AEC) refused to acknowledge any danger posed by the tests, asserting that "test fall-out has not caused the illness or injured the health of anyone living near the test site." When ranchers complained about beta burns on the backs of their cattle, AEC representatives claimed that the burns were "much like sunburn" and would not affect the cattle or their reproductive ability. The priest with cancer, however, accepted his fate as punishment for his failure to protect himself, saying, "If I got it from radiation, it was my own fault." He still trusted the government and accepted the risks: "I think the AEC knows what it's doing. When we have enemies like the Russians we should be prepared."[62]

Although the cancer-stricken priest trusted the experts, the AEC continued to mislead the public and offer worthless information. One AEC scientist told anxious Americans that if they happened to be caught outside and were dusted with radioactive fallout, they should take off their clothes and bathe with soap and water, and then hose down their home. But he added that the water would by that point be contaminated, so they should use water they had previously stored. But where would alert and responsible citizens find and stockpile enough uncontaminated water for all those baths and for hosing off houses? Supposedly scientific advice like this was more likely to encourage skepticism than confidence.[63]

Civil defense messages like these did little to ease fears of nuclear attack. Along with unsettling messages from experts, the popular media contributed to Atomic Age anxieties. Films and television shows that took up the question of nuclear dangers often contained terrifying images. A powerful example appeared in the middle of a popular TV show on May 27, 1956, when families watching *The Ed Sullivan Show* encountered an unexpected broadcast. The variety show typically featured family fare, including a wide range of entertainers. By this point, Sullivan had introduced viewers to a number of popular musicians and other performers, though Elvis Presley would not appear on the show until later that year, and the Beatles did not make their famous debut until 1964. With an estimated 15 million people watching the May 27, 1956, show, Sullivan offered his viewers a terrifying message about the danger of nuclear weapons. With no warning to his audience about the disturbing images they were about to see, he introduced a short film, called *A Short Vision*, with these reassuring words: "Just last week you read about the H-bomb being dropped. . . . I'm gonna tell you if you have youngsters in the living room tell them not to be alarmed at this 'cause it's a fantasy, the whole thing is animated. . . . It is grim, but I think we can all stand it to realize that in war there is no winner."

Although Sullivan said children should not be "alarmed," what he showed would be alarming to viewers of any age. The haunting six-minute animated film, accompanied by eerie music and a first-person narrator, traces the arrival and impact of a flying "thing" that streaks across the dark sky at night, silently and "uninvited." No one knows what it is or where it has come from. Animals see it and "hid[e] in fear." It flies over a city where men, women, and children are sleeping peacefully. Some men, wide awake, lift their heads skyward as the narrator intones, "But their leaders looked up, and their wise men looked up, but it was too late." Then a huge fireball fills the sky as the "thing" explodes, killing everything on earth.

At this point in the film, peaceful faces turn to expressions of horror and then bleed and melt as eyes ooze and skin evaporates, leaving charred, skeletal remains. Humans and animals, prey and predator, all suffer the same fate, until the whole world is destroyed. When "THE END" appeared on the dark screen, viewers were left with unanswered questions. In the film, there were no identified enemies, other than "the thing" itself, and there was no suggestion that there might be any political or other means to ward off the impending catastrophe. This was an early evocation of terrorism: an enemy that could strike civilians at any time, in any place, without any warning.

One viewer who watched the show as a child later remembered the "images of peoples' flesh melting from their faces to reveal bare skulls."

Another had "nightmares based on it," remembering that "for years it added an air of horror and fear to anything concerning nuclear war or bombs." One who was only eight years old at the time remembered vivid images, such as the woman whose "flesh simply melted from her face. Her liquefied humanity receded slowly from her cheeks, dripping down off the hollows, exposing more and more of her sculptured skull." The film left a "feeling a hopeless vulnerability that I can summon up with little effort to this day," this viewer added. Another said the film "haunted my childhood," and that "the ghastly visions continued to replay in my impressionable, juvenile mind." A nine-year-old girl "sat and watched in frozen horror as the film showed the mushroom cloud and the decaying faces." One young boy who saw the film "added a line to the prayer I recited every night when I went to bed," he later reported. "After the traditional 'Now I lay me down to sleep' invocation, I ended the prayer each night with, 'And don't let the Russians come and get us.'"[64]

A year after Sullivan's program, the Soviet Union launched Sputnik, the first satellite to orbit the Earth. Documentary footage from the time shows large gatherings of awestruck Americans gazing skyward as the small beeping communications satellite—"the size of a beach ball," according to a later description by the National Aeronautics and Space Administration (NASA), and weighing less than two hundred pounds—traversed the night sky.[65] Fear quickly set in across the country, fueled by politicians and the news media. Sputnik demonstrated that the Soviets had gained superiority in the arms race; similar technology could be used to carry nuclear weapons. Senator Lyndon B. Johnson from Texas unleashed panic when he called the launch of Sputnik "the second Pearl Harbor."

The response to Sputnik, like the response to the Ed Sullivan film, revealed the power of the media to provoke and channel fear. Political leaders, including Johnson, made use of their access to news outlets to drive home their message that the United States was in danger of losing the Cold War. Media reports helped to whip up fear that the United States was falling behind the Soviet Union in both the space race and the arms race. When the United States rushed to launch its own satellite, the rocket exploded on the launching pad. Television stations broadcast the humiliating moment live to a global audience. Many Americans saw these events as evidence of the nation's vulnerability in the face of the power of the Soviet Union. In an effort to catch up with the Soviets, within a year of Sputnik's launch the United States established NASA and enacted the National Defense Education Act (NDEA), providing funding for higher education, especially in the fields of science and technology.[66]

The public and official responses to Sputnik all contributed to widespread anxiety that the United States was vulnerable, and so were its citizens. By the end of the 1950s, nearly 70 percent of American adults believed that nuclear war was imminent. Regardless of whether they thought it was possible to survive a nuclear war, Americans had grown accustomed to living with fear.[67] The widespread media attention to shelter building, civil defense preparedness, and the threat of subversion and attack sensitized citizens to the presence of constant danger and the inability of the government to provide protection. Assurances from officials that citizens could protect themselves, which were meant to ease apprehension, actually heightened fears. The message was clear: you are on your own.

Not all Americans accepted the premise that the best response to the threat of an attack was to support the nuclear buildup and prepare for the worst. There were dissenters who organized and protested, calling for an end to the arms race. Pacifists and antinuclear activists founded the National Committee for a Sane Nuclear Policy (SANE) in 1957. Civil rights leaders added antinuclear activism to their fight against racism. They were among the first to oppose Truman's use of atomic bombs against Japan, and as the years went by, they continued to see connections between the buildup of nuclear weapons and the black freedom struggle. Why, they asked, was the nation pouring so much money and brainpower into the development of destructive weapons, rather than trying to improve life for the nation's underprivileged? Dr. Martin Luther King Jr., along with former First Lady and human rights activist Eleanor Roosevelt, bestselling child-care authority Dr. Benjamin Spock, author Norman Cousins, and civil rights and labor leaders A. Philip Randolph and Walter Reuther were among the best-known early members of SANE. SANE's growth and visibility marked the beginning of a national conversation about the wisdom of the arms race. But to get its message across, the group also fanned fears. SANE ran a full-page advertisement in the *New York Times* warning Americans, "We Are Facing a Danger Unlike Any Danger That Has Ever Existed." A year after running the ad, SANE had 130 chapters and 25,000 members.[68]

Dissenters became bolder and more numerous as the 1960s brought new fears to the fore.[69] But Americans were divided between the increasing numbers of vocal opponents to the arms race, on the one hand, and those who supported the buildup of weapons to defeat the Soviet Union, on the other. Two major international crises early in the decade strengthened both positions. Heightened tensions between the two superpowers made the possibility that a nuclear war could erupt at any time seem even more tangible.

The first crisis occurred in Berlin. After World War II, the four victorious Allied countries divided the German capital, with the Soviet Union in control of East Berlin and the other Allies occupying West Berlin. In 1961, the Soviet Union demanded the withdrawal of Western armed forces from the city altogether. When President John F. Kennedy refused, the Soviets built a wall dividing East and West Berlin, preventing any passage between the two halves. A military standoff ensued, and Kennedy warned that any escalation could lead to nuclear war.

The Berlin crisis reverberated within American civil defense. Major journals and magazines ran stories on shelter construction. Kennedy called for $207 million for a new civil defense program and urged citizens to build shelters in their homes. Speaking to the patriarchs of the nation's idealized nuclear families, the president said, "I hope to let every citizen know what steps he can take without delay to protect his family in case of attack."[70] Kennedy's speech led to a flurry of shelter construction.

The vast majority of Americans polled in 1961 believed that nuclear war was likely. Much as they feared a nuclear attack, they were willing to go to war to defeat communism. Fully 81 percent preferred "all-out nuclear war" to "living under communism." (The reverse was true in Britain, where only 21 percent said they would opt for war over communism.)[71] Back-channel negotiations between the United States and the Soviet Union headed off a direct confrontation, but the Berlin Wall remained in place until 1989.

Shortly after the Berlin Crisis, in the fall of 1962, the Cuban Missile Crisis sparked a new burst of fear as the United States and the Soviet Union faced off over the installment of Soviet missiles in Cuba. The episode brought the two nations to the brink of nuclear war. Kennedy alerted Americans to the missiles with a national television broadcast, while putting the military on alert. The president warned Americans that the nation would go to war if necessary: "We will not prematurely or unnecessarily risk the costs of worldwide nuclear war in which even the fruits of victory would be ashes in our mouth; but neither will we shrink from that risk at any time it must be faced."[72] Kennedy and Soviet Premier Nikita Khrushchev managed to avert a war, and the crisis led to a limited nuclear test ban treaty in the following year. But moving so close to the brink only heightened fears that nuclear war could erupt at any time.

In the wake of the two crises, shelter building peaked, from a total of about 1,500 home fallout shelters in 1960 to an estimated 200,000 by 1965.[73] Although the increase in shelter building was substantial, representing one response to the fear of an imminent nuclear war, the number of shelters was still small relative to the US population.[74]

The crises in Berlin and Cuba also inspired more attempts to achieve security by ending the arms race altogether. Women took the lead in this new burst of antinuclear activism. On November 1, 1961, 50,000 suburban homemakers in more than sixty communities staged a protest, Women Strike for Peace (WSP). Participants lobbied government officials to "End the Arms Race—Not the Human Race." The strikers were mostly educated, middle-class mothers; 61 percent did not work outside the home. According to *Newsweek* magazine, the strikers "were perfectly ordinary looking women. . . . They looked like the women you would see driving ranch wagons, or shopping at the village market, or attending PTA meetings. . . . Many [were] wheeling baby buggies or strollers." Within a year, support for Women Strike for Peace grew to several hundred thousand.[75]

Although there was nothing subversive about Women Strike for Peace, protests of any sort during the Cold War raised suspicions of disloyalty. The FBI kept the group under surveillance, and in 1962 the leaders were called before the House Un-American Activities Committee. Under questioning, these women spoke as mothers, claiming that saving American children from nuclear extinction was the essence of "Americanism." They brought their babies to the hearings and refused to be intimidated by their congressional inquisitors. During the hearing, supporters cheered and threw flowers from the gallery.[76]

While protesters took to the streets and the halls of Congress, the expansion of the media, especially television, gave artists and critics the opportunity to reach vast audiences with messages critical of the arms race. Ed Sullivan was the first to make use of the reach of television when he aired his antinuclear broadcast in 1956. Throughout the early years of the Cold War, many other apocalyptic scenarios depicting the end of American civilization permeated the popular culture.[77]

Sensitive artists and critics explored the impact of Atomic Age fears on Americans' social and psychic lives. Many believed that the mentality of "preparedness" was as destructive to the nation's social fabric as an actual attack. They pointed to debates about "shelter morality." Even though few Americans actually built shelters, the possibility of a private refuge from atomic attack raised a number of troubling issues. Some people built shelters but kept them a secret, for fear that, in the event of an actual attack, neighbors who did not have shelters would try to crowd in, using up resources meant for the family. In 1961, *Time* magazine ran a story that sparked considerable discussion. In "Gun Thy Neighbor," a Chicago suburbanite promised "to mount a machine gun at the hatch to keep the neighbors out if the bomb falls." He added, "I'm not going to run the risk of not being able to use the shelter I've taken the trouble to provide to save my own family." One civil defense coordinator, speaking to police reservists, held up a pistol and said, "Get one of these and learn how to use it."[78]

Rod Serling explored these questions in his insightful, eerie, psychologically probing television series *The Twilight Zone*. Most episodes had a familiar setting: middle-class American suburbia. But the stories were edgy, often mixing everyday family life with science fiction. Serling's strong political views shaped his writing. In addition to his civil rights advocacy, opposition to McCarthyism, and support of other liberal causes, he was the most active member of the Hollywood chapter of SANE. In one episode, "The Third Planet from the Sun," a family escapes from an impending nuclear disaster in a newly designed spaceship, heading for a safe haven on another planet. At the end of the episode, the characters—and the audience—learn that the planet they are approaching offers no refuge from atomic danger: it is a planet called Earth.

In an episode from 1961, titled "The Shelter," a neighborhood party of close friends is interrupted by an announcement that a UFO is approaching and believed to be a missile with an atomic bomb. The doctor hosting the party is the only one with a bomb shelter. He and his family barricade themselves in it, while the other neighbors desperately beg him to open the door and let them in. As the neighbors furiously destroy the door to the shelter, an announcement declares that the warning was a false alarm. But the damage has already been done. There was no attack, but there were casualties nevertheless: friendship, generosity, and individual sense of self. The former friends have, in essence, destroyed themselves.

Serling's insight was prophetic. The do-it-yourself ethos of privatized protection gave rise to fear and distrust, not only of distant enemies, but of one's own neighbors and friends. When danger seemed to approach—even if there was in fact no real threat—people who were instructed, conditioned, and socialized to take responsibility for their own safety and protection and that of their families were likely to lose sight of the common good. Neighborliness evaporated, and citizenship withered. Even if the expected attack never materialized, nothing would ever be the same.[79]

A few years after the *Twilight Zone* episodes, the widely popular and critically acclaimed film *Dr. Strangelove: Or How I Learned to Stop Worrying and Love the Bomb* appeared in theaters. A darkly humorous satire, it portrayed what might happen if a crazed American general launched a nuclear attack on the Soviet Union without authorization. The film follows the frenzied efforts of military and political leaders, including the bumbling president of the United States and his equally bumbling Russian counterpart, to stop the planes and hence the attack, but they are unable to do so. In the process of trying, they learn that the Soviet Union was about to announce a "doomsday machine" that would set off a chain reaction of nuclear explosions if any bomb fell on Russian soil. The device was intended as "deterrence," but it cannot be disarmed. As the bombs fall and explode, the American leaders, all of them men, decide to save themselves by retreating to a government shelter. Dr. Strangelove advises them to bring along enough sexually attractive women to provide for the future of the human race.

The absurdity of the film underscored the absurdity of the arms race itself: that the policy of deterrence, based on a buildup of nuclear weapons intended to make Americans safer, actually created more danger. The whole idea of preparedness, with all the civil defense plans that came with it, did nothing to protect Americans. It simply made Americans more afraid.[80]

By the early 1960s, Americans had absorbed the dangers and realities of the Atomic Age into their psyches and sensibilities. Reminders of the arms race permeated the media and dotted the landscape. Missile silos, mounted rockets, sculptures of missiles pointing skyward, and other Cold War artifacts appeared in uncanny settings, including open fields, churchyards, and public buildings. The presence of atomic bombs, and the nuclear arms race, had become so much a part of the culture that references to "atomic" anything appeared in advertisements, menus, and billboards. A young starlet posed in a swimsuit as the "Anatomic Bomb" in a magazine photo spread. A popular eatery called the Atomic Cafe emblazoned its name in neon. It seemed that wherever anyone looked,

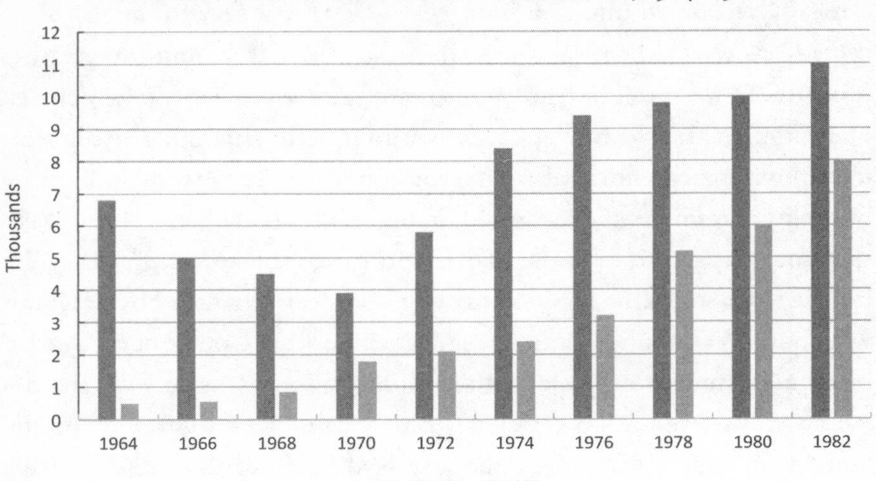

Source: Gerald Segal, The Simon and Schuster Guide to the World Today *(New York: Simon and Schuster, 1987), 82.*

in cities or in the countryside, on TV or at the movies, they encountered the threat of nuclear war.[81]

With the exception of antinuclear artists and activists, few objected when alarmists decried a "missile gap" and insisted on more and larger nuclear weapons. As a result, the United States' nuclear stockpile consistently outnumbered that of the Soviet Union from 1964 to 1982. Each superpower possessed enough nuclear weapons to destroy the world several times over.[82]

Although nuclear war did not erupt during the Cold War era, Atomic Age fears unleashed plenty of political and social fallout. Americans worried that subversives within the United States would aid the Soviets, making an attack more likely. They put their faith in the government to amass nuclear weapons, and to root out communist sympathizers from key institutions, in order to keep the communists at bay. While some dissenters protested, most people accepted these activities as necessary to defeating communism.

At the same time, Americans learned that the government could do little to protect them. Government policies heightened the danger of nuclear war but offered no realistic plans to shelter them in the event of an attack, which, especially with the appearance of the hydrogen bomb, would be utterly devastating. While the government debated public shelters and provided meager plans for duck, run, and cover, citizens had to provide their own physical and ideological fortifications.

What, then, did all of the civil defense efforts, the anticommunist crusades, and the nuclear arms buildup achieve? What was the effect of encouraging homeowners to build shelters, or training children to dive under their desks, or warning citizens, through public education campaigns, that an atomic attack was practically inevitable, and even imminent? There is no evidence that any of these programs and policies provided any real security or peace of mind.

These responses to the perceived danger did, however, cause harm. Anticommunist hysteria caused thousands of loyal Americans to lose their jobs; many went to prison. The nuclear arms race led to bigger and more dangerous weapons. Tests of those weapons harmed people, animals, and the environment with the effects of the blasts and the fallout. Civil defense programs frightened people, but did not protect them. And that fear would not go away.

In the years ahead, as the Cold War continued, as the crime rate crept upward, and as the nation became embroiled in an unpopular war, citizens became fearful of new alleged threats. The exaggerated fears of communism expressed by the majority of Americans transferred to other perceived dangers, especially violent crime. Those fears were far out of proportion to any danger posed by the small number of communists—and the small number of violent criminals—in the country. The Vietnam War, meanwhile, led many Americans to lose faith in, and even fear, their own government. In the first half of the 1960s, 75 percent of Americans polled said they trusted the government in Washington to do the right thing most of the time. That trust plummeted over the next fifteen years, and it was down to 27 percent in 1980.[83]

Many people and institutions contributed to that steep decline. Among them were the politicians and business leaders who continued to insist that every government program amounted to socialism, and that "outside agitators" with communist sympathies were responsible for urban unrest and social upheaval.

During the next several decades, Americans' new fears would be mobilized against ever expanding perceived dangers. In the face of peril, Americans did not reach out; they hunkered down in their private domiciles. Over time, a domestic arms race developed parallel to the nuclear arms race: citizens responded to alleged threats by fortifying their homes and arming themselves. Soon Americans could boast that they had more missiles, and more pistols, than anyone else.[84]

Chapter 2

THE COLOR OF DANGER: FROM RED TO BLACK

The eruption of violence and disorder directed at society's symbols of authority could be more devastating to America's hopes for the future than rockets and the 100-megaton bomb.

—*Los Angeles police official, 1961*[1]

By the early 1960s, the Atomic Age had seeped into the American psyche, and fear had become a national state of mind. The Cold War created an "us versus them" mentality that shaped attitudes not only about foreign threats but also internal ones. Once the fear of communist subversion took hold, it could readily spread to encompass other perceived dangers. In addition to the anxieties born of the escalating arms race between the United States and the Soviet Union, the social upheavals of the 1960s generated fears, not only of personal vulnerability, but of a world where previous certainties no longer prevailed.[2] Americans shifted the focus of their fears to perceived dangers even closer to home: from communist subversion and atomic attack, to social upheaval and crime.

In the process, the color of danger blended and morphed from the red of communism to the black of African Americans.

Fears of crime and chaos called for new approaches to personal protection. In the early Atomic Age, government officials could not protect civilians from nuclear attack—that responsibility fell to individuals and their families. Yet civil defense efforts did little except exacerbate fear. Crime was different. Government officials had both the responsibility and the capacity to protect citizens from crime, and citizens themselves could take reasonable and realistic steps to minimize the possibility of becoming a crime victim.

Nevertheless, there were parallels between the responses to nuclear attack from abroad and crime at home. In regard to foreign threats, government officials adopted a strategy of arms buildup and deterrence, rather than diplomacy aimed at alleviating tensions and reducing the danger of a potential nuclear conflict. Reciprocating the threat rather than diffusing it, national leaders amassed a huge nuclear arsenal that signaled to the Soviets that any hostile move on their part would result in devastating retaliation.

By the 1960s, when fears shifted to crime, national and local officials adopted a similar strategy. Just as in foreign policy, where leaders took a militaristic approach instead of a diplomatic one, in domestic politics the government abandoned social programs and rehabilitation as crime control strategies, turning instead to a buildup of militarized police forces across the nation along with punitive measures and mass incarceration, presumably to deter would-be criminals. This was the domestic version of the arms race and deterrence. And just as few citizens opposed the buildup of nuclear arms, most acquiesced in the buildup of militarized policing. Yet similar to the impact of civil defense measures, extreme policing and punishment efforts did not make for a safer society. Rather, the official overreaction to the dangers posed by crime fueled new fears, ultimately encouraging individuals—especially, but not only, white people—to distrust anyone whom they did not know, particularly people who were black.

In the 1960s, as the crime rate began to rise, cities across the country erupted in riots. These upheavals emerged just as long-standing hierarchies of race and gender began to crumble. African Americans and women, along with other marginalized citizens, began to assert their rights. As the "rights revolution" expanded, other minority groups—Latinos, American Indians, and other people of color, along with gays and lesbians—demanded equality and respect. Many Americans celebrated these changes. But many others found them unsettling, and a backlash began as the rights revolution gained momentum. Combined with the violence engulfing so many cities, many people, particularly white Americans, felt that the social order was collapsing.

The civil rights movement had been roiling the South throughout the 1950s. Peaceful protesters boycotted buses, lunch counters, and shops, hoping to topple the Jim Crow system of racial segregation. Often, they met with violence at the hands of whites who were determined to maintain the racial status quo. Activists were injured, arrested, and even murdered. Images of police attacking peaceful protesters with clubs, fire hoses, and dogs saturated the media, including on television, where a national audience watched in horror. The violence unleashed against dignified black protesters moved many citizens, above all in the North, to support the civil rights movement. But most whites in the South equated the protesters with criminals, insisting that they were "lawless" for violating the Jim Crow laws mandating racial segregation.

White antipathy toward black citizens spread north and west in the mid-1960s, when riots erupted in cities across the country, and the news media shifted its focus. The first major urban disturbance occurred in 1965 in Watts, a neighborhood of Los Angeles; others followed over the next five years in such places as Detroit, Newark, and Washington, DC. The massive uprisings stemmed from the frustrations of pervasive poverty, police brutality, and lack of opportunity. Rioters burned, vandalized, and destroyed buildings in largely black areas, devastating those communities and raising fears among whites that violence would engulf entire cities.

Danger had a location: the city. And it had a face: young black men. Popular media—including novels, movies, and news reports—began to portray cities as dangerous.[3] A number of factors contributed to this development. The flight of large numbers of white people from urban centers to the suburbs in the late 1940s and 1950s—a process subsidized by the government in the form of favorable mortgages and generous loans made available to white families, but rarely to people of color, through the GI bill—had eroded the tax base in cities. Over time, falling municipal revenues meant that urban leaders could no longer pay for the maintenance and improvement of their cities.

At the same time, millions of African Americans moved from the South to northern cities in hopes of greater economic opportunities and an escape from lawful segregation and extralegal, but tolerated, violence against them. But it was difficult for black migrants to find good jobs in the North, where deindustrialization as well as economic hardship in urban areas limited their opportunities. Out of desperation, some turned to crime. Between 1960 and 1965, the incidence of violent crime rose from 161 to 200 per 100,000 people. This represents an increase of just under 0.04 percent—noticeable but modest (or, in other words, one additional violent crime for every 2,500 people in the population). At the time, fewer than 1 percent of Gallup poll respondents identified problems related to crime as the nation's most important problem.[4] Nevertheless, African Americans as well as whites feared being victimized, and they, too, called for law and order. As civil rights activist A. Philip Randolph noted in 1964, "while there may be law and order without freedom, there can be no freedom without law and order." Although whites as well as blacks committed crimes, African Americans became the primary targets of law enforcement. By the late 1960s, black men were seventeen times more likely than white men to be arrested for robbery.[5]

The black freedom struggle turned more militant with the founding of the Black Panther Party in Oakland, California, in 1966. Although much of the Panthers' program focused on strengthening the black community through solidarity and self-help, their confrontational style alarmed many whites. As civil rights gave way to Black Power, images of armed Black Panthers in military formation led many whites to wonder if a race war was about to tear apart the nation.

As the crime rate rose, the national media brought scenes of burning cities and violent crime rate into homes across the country, fanning fears of social chaos. Sensationalized stories of violence drew large audiences and readerships. Media outlets expanded and television now reached millions of viewers in their living rooms; many Americans came to fear that their homes, their personal security, and their entire way of life were under siege. The assassinations of President John F. Kennedy in 1963 and of Martin Luther King Jr. and Robert F. Kennedy in 1968 contributed to the sense of danger and uncertainty.

In addition to the violence, cultural upheavals challenged longstanding values and social relations. Young people forged a sexual revolution, rejecting the double standard that had shamed and punished sexually active unmarried women. Students violated rules at schools and colleges that dictated hair length, clothing styles, and dormitory visiting hours, and major demonstrations for free speech, civil rights, and the like, and against the Vietnam War, erupted on campuses across the nation, including, notably, the University of California at Berkeley, Columbia University, and Kent State in Ohio, where four unarmed student protesters died after being shot by members of the Ohio National Guard on May 4, 1970.

On the domestic front, married women chafed at the constraints of domesticity. The marriage rate began to decline, and the average age of marriage rose. The entry of increasing numbers of women into the paid labor force, along with the feminist movement, began to alter domestic gender arrangements. The divorce rate, which had been stable during the 1950s, more than doubled between 1960 and 1975, prompting many to wonder whether the nuclear family would survive.

College campuses were not the only sites of protest against the disastrous and unpopular war in Vietnam. Antiwar protests raged in a number of US cities, including Washington, DC. In the 1950s, the United States had come to the aid of France in its effort to maintain control of its colony of Indochina in Southeast Asia. When the French were defeated, the United States established a puppet government in South Vietnam and went to war against communist North Vietnam. The tiny country posed no threat to the United States, but, according to the "domino theory" that guided foreign policy, if any small country was taken over by communists, others would fall like dominos. The result, eventually, would be victory for the Soviet Union in the Cold War.

The fateful decision to prop up an anticommunist government in South Vietnam cost the lives of more than 50,000 Americans and well over 1 million Southeast Asians. President Lyndon Johnson's escalation of the war polarized Americans into "hawks" and "doves"—those who favored the war and those who did not. Authorities expanded their lists of suspected internal enemies, and the FBI and other official agencies began to investigate antiwar activists as subversives. Americans who were already frightened by urban riots and rising crime rates now saw the massive antiwar protests as a further indication of the unraveling of the social order. Fears of communist infiltration persisted as politicians and law enforcement officials blamed alleged communist-inspired "outside agitators" for a wide range of protests, not just those against the war but also those for civil rights.

Indeed, communism and crime became intertwined in politics at both the national and local levels. Conservative politicians increasingly blamed liberal politicians for being "soft" on both communism and crime as well as for promoting social welfare programs that they considered socialistic. They believed these programs subverted the free enterprise system, undercut the American work ethic, and created what they saw as a dependent criminal class. Politicians were not alone in this thinking: public support for social welfare programs also declined. If citizens were responsible for their own behavior, then criminals—not social conditions—were responsible for crime.

In keeping with this ethos of individualism and punitiveness, increasing numbers of Americans embraced "law and order" as the appropriate response to crime. Executing or locking up criminals appeared to maintain order while getting the government out of the business of rehabilitation. Politicians from both major parties abandoned the rehabilitation model in accord with popular sentiment. Both parties embraced tough-on-crime positions, with the Republicans prevailing as the standard-bearer.

THE PRESIDENTIAL ELECTION of 1964 brought the issue of "law and order" into the center of national politics for the first time in the postwar era. Public opinion polls showed that concern about crime did not follow the actual reported crime rate; rather, concern spiked in the wake of political and media attention to the issue. When Senator Barry Goldwater, a Republican from Arizona, made law and order the centerpiece of his campaign for president in 1964, public opinion shifted, going from virtually no concern to "a great deal." Goldwater asserted, "Security from domestic violence, no less than from foreign aggression, is the most elementary form and fundamental purpose of any government."[6]

As the 1964 presidential campaign demonstrated, fears of nuclear war were fusing with fears about street crime, urban unrest, and political protest to produce widespread general anxiety. If foreign military threats were not enough, American society seemed to be exploding from within. The Cold War still loomed large. Goldwater, rattling the Atomic Age saber, said he would not rule out using tactical nuclear weapons in the event of a war. But candidates vied over the greatest dangers facing citizens as well as over who would offer the best protection from them.

Democratic incumbent Lyndon Johnson aired a powerful television ad suggesting that his opponent would unleash nuclear war. In the ad, a little girl in a meadow counts as she pulls petals off of a daisy. As a freeze frame captures her innocent face, a man's voice-over begins an ominous countdown, followed by sounds of a blast and horrific scenes of a nuclear bomb exploding. Johnson's voice is then heard: "These are the stakes: to make a world in which all of God's children can live, or go into the darkness. We must either love each other, or we must die." The ad was so controversial that it only aired once as a campaign advertisement. But it received tremendous attention. News programs aired the ad over and over again in their coverage of the controversy. The "Daisy

Girl" appeared on the cover of *Time* magazine, and two major networks did stories on the ad. Many analysts claimed that this ad ushered in the era of television attack-ad campaign strategies.[7]

Goldwater responded with his own fear-mongering, not about atomic war but about crime, political protest, moral decay, and social chaos. In a television advertisement with jarring images and discordant music, he drew connections between dangers from abroad and dangers at home. Above scenes of crime and rioting youths appeared large bold words, echoed by a booming male voice-over suggesting that Johnson was "soft" on the dangers facing the nation: "Graft! Swindle! Juvenile Delinquency! Crime! Riots! Hear what Barry Goldwater has to say about our lack of moral leadership."[8]

One twenty-seven-minute Goldwater campaign film, called *Choice*, contrasted the "two Americas." The narrator, actor Raymond Massey, explained that one America is "an ideal, a dream. The other America . . . is no longer a dream but a nightmare. Our streets are not safe. Immorality begins to flourish." The images on the screen contrasted the "dream"—scenes of white, clean-cut American children, churches, and patriotism—with the "nightmare" of rioting, looting, violence, crime, sex, pornography, and parading in the streets by female strippers and near-naked men. The film depicted African Americans as particularly lawless. One scene showed a nonviolent black leader urging a crowd to remain calm and support the police, but the rioters ignore him. Another scene portrayed white, middle-class teenagers as reckless, delinquent, immoral, and sexually loose, laying the blame on parents who "expect schoolteachers, the clergy and police to take their place."

The film articulated many of the themes that would gain ground by the end of the 1960s and propel the rise of the New Right: distrust of liberal authorities, a turn to a more punitive approach to crime, and a backlash against civil rights, feminism, and the counterculture. It called upon individuals to take law enforcement into their own hands. Because "the police aren't allowed to guarantee them safety, they take steps to protect themselves," the narrator said. "Radio cars, citizen patrol sidewalks, vigilante committees. Good citizens grope for a solution. Others, however, do nothing. They only stand by and watch." Near the end of the film, John Wayne stands in front of a large rifle mounted on a wall and says, speaking directly to the viewer, "You got the strongest hand in the world, that's right, your hand, the hand that marks the ballot. The hand that pulls the voting lever. Use it, will ya? Use it."[9]

Like Lyndon Johnson's "Daisy" campaign ad, *Choice* created a media firestorm. Warned of the controversy, Goldwater pulled the film in October 1964, just before it was scheduled to air, saying it was "nothing but a racist film," but word of the film leaked to reporters. Newspapers across the country published front-page articles about the film with banner headlines, such as "GOP Film to Deplore Rioting, Sexy U.S.A." in the *New York Daily News*. Publicity continued even after the campaign decided against airing the film. The *Washington Post* announced, "Goldwater Scraps Morals Film"; the *Los Angeles Times* ran the headline "Film On Morality Held Up by Barry." Meanwhile, during the brief period the film was shown at campaign headquarters, crowds gathered in front of the office in San Francisco, hoping to get a glimpse of the film. Much of the furor resulted from the sexually titillating scenes: a stripper actually sued Goldwater for using her image in the film without her permission and without payment.[10]

The Goldwater supporters who made the film had intended the scenes of sex and mayhem to horrify viewers and persuade them to vote for Goldwater, who promised to crack down on crime and immorality. The film had been the brainchild of a political consultant, F. Clifton White, who had urged Goldwater to make domestic issues as important as foreign policy in order to appeal to blue-collar white ethnic voters. In a memo to Goldwater a month before the 1964 election, when Johnson was far ahead in the polls, White wrote, "The big issue . . . is the moral crisis in America today. It is made up of several components, crime, violence, riots (the backlash), juvenile delinquency, the breakdown of law and order, immorality and corruption in high places, the lack of moral leadership in government, narcotics, pornography—it all adds up to the picture of a society in decay. This issue—morality—can be the 'missile gap' of 1960."

White understood that Atomic Age fears could easily morph into fears of domestic upheaval. The media, especially television news programs, were already reaching millions of viewers in their living rooms with vivid scenes of social chaos. These frightening scenarios served as free campaign advertising for Goldwater: "Every day the front pages of the nation's newspapers are filled with stories of crime and violence, ranging from rape to riots, from juvenile delinquency to embezzlement. We have, in fact, the built-in, national reservoir of hundreds of millions of dollars' worth of publicity working for us."

Goldwater had given White the green light to produce the film. With only a week for production, White had formed a front group called Mothers for Moral America, recruiting Republican activist women, including Nancy Reagan and Aloise Steiner Buckley (mother of conservative commentator William F. Buckley Jr.) to raise money for the project. The group brought in $65,000, and the women remained active supporters of Republican candidates and advocates for the issues that Goldwater had promoted.[11]

Goldwater was not the only candidate for president in 1964 raising the specter of moral decay, crime, and racial conflict. George Wallace, then governor of Alabama, lost the Republican nomination to Goldwater, but he gained a following during his campaign with his claim that liberals were soft on crime: "If you are knocked in the head on a street in a city today," he said, "the man who knocked you in the head is out of jail before you get to the hospital."[12]

Wallace was best known as an unapologetic segregationist. He saw himself as a defender of the Jim Crow system in the South, and his message resonated not only with southern whites, but with northern whites who blamed black Americans for crime and unrest. White and black Americans agreed that black people were the ones who suffered the most from urban riots. But explanations for the violence differed dramatically by race. According to polls, whites were twice as likely as blacks to believe that the riots were being organized by communist agitators or militant black leaders; blacks were twice as likely to see them as spontaneous responses to racism, poor housing, and unemployment.

By a factor of two to one, blacks blamed police brutality for the unrest, but whites rejected that explanation by an eight-to-one margin.[13] Wallace appealed directly to northern whites by playing to these racial fears and hostilities.

"Law and order" became the vehicle for reinforcing the racial hierarchy that the black freedom struggle had challenged.[14] The framing of crime as a racial issue by politicians and the media represented the reemergence of the myth of black male violence and criminality that dated back to the nineteenth century. By the early twentieth century, decades of discrimination and the incarceration of black Americans had resulted in an overrepresentation of blacks in the criminal justice system. Although African Americans were unfairly targeted and arrested, crime statistics gathered and published in the years after 1890 seemed to give credence to the notion that black people were inclined to criminality. Many black leaders and other reformers pointed to those statistics as evidence of widespread racism and oppression. Nevertheless, social scientists, journalists, and political leaders accepted and promoted the idea of innate black criminality. By the 1960s, that association was firmly established, and conservative politicians were able to revive, highlight, and capitalize on it.[15]

Although Johnson easily defeated Goldwater, his election was the last hurrah for the Democrats until the 1990s. With the exception of Jimmy Carter's 1976 election to a one-term post-Watergate presidency, no Democrat won more than 43 percent of the popular vote in a presidential election until Bill Clinton in 1992. In spite of losing in 1964, Goldwater and Wallace brought the law-and-order view from the margins to the mainstream of political discourse—and it went on to shape American politics for decades.

In the 1966 midterm congressional elections, the Democrats lost forty-seven seats to Republicans in the House and three in the Senate. Much of the shift to the right was fueled by racial anxieties. Republican candidates had exploited fears of crime and disorder with campaign messages conveying thinly veiled racist warnings. Republican candidates, for example, distributed handbills in Chicago's white neighborhoods that included coded language against racial integration:

> *VOTE STRAIGHT REPUBLICAN IF YOU ARE:*
> *AGAINST—violence, riots, and marches in the streets;*
> *AGAINST—disregard for law and order;*
> *AGAINST—The 3 Rs of today—Riots, Rape & Robbery . . .*
> *This is your chance to show where you stand on FORCED HOUSING . . . [T]he law applies everywhere, including the suburbs.*
> *WHERE WOULD YOU GO TO BE SAFE?*[16]

A similar flyer circulated in Detroit's white neighborhoods exhorting residents to "defend your home or neighborhood against bands of armed terrorists who will murder the men and rape the women." In California, Ronald Reagan, who had switched from the Democratic Party to the Republican Party in 1962, swept into the governorship with a landslide, largely as a law-and-order candidate. Appealing to white Americans' racial fears, he warned that when night approached, "the jungle comes a little closer. . . . There isn't a city street that's safe for our women after dark."[17]

The trends that fueled the 1966 elections escalated in 1967. Racial violence erupted in cities across the country, the most devastating in Detroit where forty-three people died. Yet racial tensions did have a silver lining: they motivated other minority groups to organize for equal rights. Mexican Americans in San Antonio, Texas, for example, formed the Mexican American Youth Organization, which later became La Raza Unida, the first Chicano political party. The following year, activists in Minneapolis founded the American Indian Movement (AIM). These and other groups would challenge the conservative message that all people of color were suspect in one way or another.

By the late 1960s, public opinion polls indicated that Americans believed urban riots were the nation's most pressing problem. In 1967, President Johnson appointed a commission to study the causes of the riots and recommend solutions. Overseen by Chairman Otto Kerner, the Democratic governor of Illinois, and Vice Chairman John Lindsay, the Republican mayor of New York City (who became a Democrat in 1971), the Kerner Commission issued its report in 1968. It famously declared, "Our nation is moving toward two societies, one black, one white—separate and unequal." It called for a recognition of the devastating effects of racism and "a commitment to national action," adding, "It is time to make good the promises of American democracy to all citizens."[18]

But the Kerner Commission's recommendations fell mostly on deaf ears. Johnson was already under attack by political opponents for the liberal civil rights and social welfare policies of his Great Society program. Although Johnson believed that the causes of crime were rooted in poverty and social circumstances, and was committed to liberal social programs, he felt he had to respond to his conservative critics, who claimed he was soft on crime.

In fact, a few years previously, in 1965, Johnson had launched the "War on Crime" in the form of the Law Enforcement Assistance Act, which brought the federal government into state and local policing. The Department of Justice provided local police departments with military equipment designed for foreign wars to use in the domestic initiative. The act gave the police new powers, training, and equipment and led to aggressive crime-fighting tactics and punitive laws and minimum sentencing measures, which resulted in rising rates of incarceration.[19]

In response to growing public fears and political pressures, and despite the conclusions of the Kerner report, Johnson oversaw the passage of the draconian Omnibus Crime Control and Safe Streets Act, enacted on June 19, 1968, expanding the role of the federal government in policing. The law assigned more than $400 million to a new federal agency that would distribute crime-fighting funds to state and local governments, allow wiretapping and other forms of eavesdropping without a warrant, and permit new interrogation tactics.[20] Congressional opposition to the bill was minuscule, since most Democrats were fearful, like Johnson, of looking soft on crime: only four Senators and seventeen Representatives voted against it.

By that point in 1968, Americans had already experienced a series of new crises. The year opened with the Tet Offensive in Vietnam, a massive attack by the North Vietnamese and their South Vietnamese allies that included the takeover of the US embassy in Saigon, which they held for eight hours. Television news covered the fighting, and many Americans were shocked; they had thought the communist forces in Vietnam were incapable of such a brazen attack. Although the US forces eventually prevailed, the Tet Offensive marked a turning point in the war as well as in popular support for it. Facing increasing criticism, on March 31, 1968, President Johnson announced that he would not seek reelection.

Meanwhile, the month after the Kerner Commission released its findings, Dr. Martin Luther King Jr. was assassinated, sparking civil disorder in 124 cities. In June, Robert Kennedy was assassinated just after winning the Democratic presidential primary in California. In August, tens of thousands of antiwar protesters battled police outside the Democratic National Convention in Chicago. The divided delegates inside, meanwhile, nominated Johnson's vice-president, Hubert Humphrey, as the Democratic candidate for president. The mayhem and protest, all of it broadcast into Americans' living rooms, provided fodder for Richard Nixon, the Republican candidate for president, who blamed Johnson and Humphrey for the disaster of the war as well as the chaos within the country's borders.

Although the social turmoil and rising crime rates were real, the fear they generated among white people was out of proportion to the reality. In fact, throughout the decade, the rate of white victimization remained constant. But that fact was not widely publicized. The FBI continually raised alarms about the rising crime rate without noting that black people were far more likely than whites to be victimized.[21]

Whites expressed fear of blacks even though very few white people were victims of crimes committed by blacks. "You just never know what's going to happen. I'm afraid to go downtown anymore," a white suburban mother in Michigan told a researcher in 1967.[22] Others assumed that riots would spread from black neighborhoods to white ones, although that never happened. A "working girl" wrote to President Johnson, in response to a violent protest that erupted in Harlem, when a police officer killed a black teenager: "I'm afraid to leave my house. . . . I feel the Negro revolution will reach Queens. . . . Please send troops immediately to Harlem." In August 1967, polls showed that the percentage of whites who feared for their personal safety increased from 43 percent to 51 percent over the previous year.

African Americans reported an even greater increase in fear than whites. They had good reasons to be afraid. Blacks were the most likely victims of violent crime. In the South, white racists routinely attacked, beat, and killed civil rights activists. In the North, police brutality was rampant against black citizens. When riots erupted in cities, they did so in black neighborhoods and businesses. White fears of attacks by blacks were misdirected. Perpetrators of most violent crimes were of the same race as their victims: whites victimized other whites, and blacks victimized other blacks. One young black man from Philadelphia said, "On Fridays and Saturdays I don't walk the streets."[23]

Politicians both generated and exploited these fears. Nixon latched onto the theme of law and order, which had first been highlighted by Barry Goldwater four years before, as a centerpiece of his 1968 campaign. Along with his promise to end the war in Vietnam "with honor," he attacked the Democrats for being soft on crime. Nixon, along with the news media, pundits, and officials, blurred the distinctions among street crime, political protest, and urban riots, casting blame on civil rights activists, rebellious youth, and protesters who they said were being egged on by "outside agitators" with subversive ideas.[24]

Nixon also fueled the perception that liberal policies "coddled" criminals. The Supreme Court's decisions in *Escobedo v. Illinois* (1964) and *Miranda v. Arizona* (1966), requiring that defendants in police custody be informed of their rights to remain silent and consult an attorney before being questioned by police, reinforced the widespread belief that the government cared more about criminals than their victims. While liberals hailed those decisions, critics claimed that they further hampered the police from doing their jobs.

Politically, the nation was profoundly divided. Liberals had not abandoned their calls for government programs to alleviate poverty, and they overwhelmingly supported the movements for equality for women and minorities. Conservatives opposed government social welfare programs, as they had for decades. But in the late 1960s they began to draw support from new constituencies, particularly working-class white men, who had voted Democratic for decades, but who now resented the gains made by minorities, often, they felt, at their own expense. Many of these voters believed that crime and social disorder resulted from permissive welfare policies and lenient treatment of criminals.

Nixon's law-and-order campaign reached out to these formerly Democratic voters, whom Nixon called the "silent majority," and they propelled him to the White House. Nixon already had a well-earned reputation as a fierce anticommunist; in 1968, he turned his attention to street violence and political protest, running a television ad that centered on the need for law and order. Amid scenes of urban chaos and violence, with a soundtrack of snare drums and dissonant piano chords, Nixon says, "It is time for an honest look at the problem of order in the United States. Dissent is a necessary ingredient of change, but in a system of government that provides for peaceful change, there is no cause that justifies resort to violence. . . . So I pledge to you, we shall have order in the United States." Nixon was well aware of the racial message he was sending. He is reported to have said that the ad "hits it right on the nose. It's all about those damn Negro–Puerto Rican groups out there."[25]

Nixon linked his law-and-order message to a critique of liberal social welfare programs. In his acceptance speech for the Republican Party's nomination, he declared:

> For the past five years we have been deluged by Government programs for the unemployed, programs for the cities, programs for the poor, and we have reaped from these programs an ugly harvest of frustrations, violence and failure across the land. And now our opponents will be offering more of the same—more billions for Government

> jobs, Government housing, Government welfare. I say it's time to quit pouring billions of dollars into programs that have failed. . . . America is a great nation today, not because of what government did for people, but because of what people did for themselves over 190 years in this country.[26]

Nixon's statement was a telling shift from Kennedy's inaugural plea to "ask what you can do for your country." Nixon, by contrast, insisted that Americans should do what they can "for themselves."

Nixon was not the only candidate in 1968 who attacked liberal programs and used "law and order" as a code for race. Alabama governor George Wallace, who had lost the Republican primary to Goldwater in 1964, ran as the candidate of the American Reform Party in 1968. Wallace set out to play on northern whites' racial fears. In one television ad, he combined a message against busing children to achieve racial integration in the public schools with a warning about the dangers of city streets, especially for women. As a school bus drives off, the narrator says, "Why are more and more millions of Americans turning to Governor Wallace? Follow, as your children are bused across town." Wallace responds, "As President, I shall—within the law—turn back the absolute control of the public school systems to the people of the respective states." The ad then cuts to a darkened street with a woman walking, only her feet and the hem of her skirt visible. The narrator says, "Why are more and more millions of Americans turning to Governor Wallace? Take a walk in your street or park tonight." Viewers see a streetlight that is shot and goes dark. Wallace says, "As President, I shall help make it possible for you and your families to walk the streets of our cities in safety." Wallace did not need to mention race directly. His message was clear.

Hubert Humphrey was the only candidate in 1968 to address crime as a social problem. In one campaign ad he tells an assembled crowd, "You're not going to make this a better America just because you build more jails. What this country needs are more decent neighborhoods, more educated people, better homes. . . . I do not believe that repression alone builds a better society." But his message did not resonate with voters. Nearly 12 million people who had voted for Johnson in 1964 voted for Nixon in 1968.[27]

Nixon's 1968 victory marked a major shift in national politics. Humphrey was the last twentieth-century candidate of either party to articulate an approach to crime that addressed its underlying causes. The combined votes for Nixon and Wallace equaled 57 percent of the total. Although Humphrey's loss was in large measure due to his association with Johnson and the Vietnam War, the election results taught the Democrats a lesson. Four years later, Democratic candidate George McGovern embraced law-and-order rhetoric that echoed the Republican candidates during the 1960s. From that point forward, "law and order" became a political necessity, and a more palatable alternative to explicit racial messages.[28]

During his presidency, Nixon made crime control a top priority. He noted proudly in 1970 that "at a time that we are cutting budgets, . . . there is one area where we are drastically increasing budgets." Aid from the federal government to states and cities for law enforcement rose from $60 million in 1969 to $280 million the following year, with plans to increase the amount to $500 million. "We feel that this is the correct priority . . . because the cost of crime to the country, not just in human terms but also in terms of the billions of dollars that the criminal elements take out of our society, justifies this kind of investment, an investment not only in law enforcement but in crime prevention."[29]

Nixon ramped up his crime-fighting efforts when he declared a "War on Drugs" in 1971. First he created the Office of Drug Abuse Law Enforcement (ODALE), which created task forces to fight the drug trade at the federal and local levels. According to former Nixon aide John Ehrlichman, the War on Drugs was a cynical political ploy for Nixon to go after blacks and antiwar activists: "We knew we couldn't make it illegal to be either against the war or black, but by getting the public to associate the hippies with marijuana and blacks with heroin, and then criminalizing both heavily, we could disrupt those communities." Using drug busts to target activists, Ehrlichman explained, "we could arrest their leaders, raid their homes, break up their meetings, and vilify them night after night on the evening news. Did we know we were lying about the drugs? Of course we did."[30]

Nixon had a willing ally in the FBI director, J. Edgar Hoover, who used drug enforcement as a means to pursue political foes involved in radical politics and the counterculture. Hoover instructed the FBI's field offices, in 1968, that "since the use of marijuana and other narcotics is widespread among members of the New Left [a reference to a broad coalition of left-leaning activists] . . . you should be alert to opportunities to have them arrested by local authorities on drug charges."[31] He mobilized the Counterintelligence Program (COINTEL), which had originally been established to disrupt the activities of the Communist Party in the United States, to target black activists, particularly civil rights leaders, including Martin Luther King Jr. and the Black Panthers. Here we see a clear example of the danger of red shading into the danger of black.[32]

Nixon resigned the presidency in 1974 in the wake of the Watergate scandal, when the law-and-order president himself flagrantly broke the law. But his resignation did little to derail the wars on drugs and crime, which continued to escalate.

As IN NATIONAL politics, the red menace and the black menace merged at the local level, as communism and crime came to be seen as two sides of the same coin. In 1961, a headline in the *Los Angeles Examiner* claimed that teen violence was "as Bad as [the] H-Bomb"; the article reported that the FBI saw a "deliberate Communist pattern of attack." A police official asserted that youthful disregard for authority could be more devastating than "rockets and the 100-megaton bomb." Across the country, the effort to control youth disturbances involved local police and sheriff's departments, state troopers, civil defense officials—and trained police dogs.[33]

Throughout the 1960s, protests and urban disruptions brought accusations of communist infiltration. In the summer of 1960, when young working-class whites demonstrated to demand a drag racing strip in San

Diego, the *San Diego Union* described the demonstration as a "riot" and blamed it on a communist conspiracy: "Just as at another period, the Communist Party of the United States devoted itself to infiltrating the Negro population, so, for 1960, the program is youth. The Communist party, which went underground during the early years of the cold war and peaceful competitive coexistence, is now coming out into the open again."[34] This was a common line of attack: the claim that the black freedom struggle was merely a pretext for a communist takeover.

In Los Angeles, Chief of Police William H. Parker provided a bridge between the era of rampant fear of communism and the years when crime began capturing the headlines. Parker, police chief from 1950 to 1966, wielded immense influence over the city and its officials. He had risen through the police ranks to prominence as a reformer who would rid the Los Angeles Police Department of corruption and establish it as a modern professional organization. His public statements as chief demonstrated the merging of the two fears of the day—fear of communists and fear of criminals—which together now posed a double threat to society. In the early 1960s, Parker declared a "war on narcotics" and claimed that "the Communists furthered the heroin and marijuana trade, because drug use sped the moral degeneration of America." He weakened the oversight authority of the civilian Police Commission, cultivated the support of the business community, and used the media to rail against communists, lax morality, and drugs.[35]

Local news reports echoed Parker's claims of connections between crime and America's Cold War enemies. Parker was known for his opposition to "socialistic" public housing and for his use of racial slurs. He made reference to "jungle life" in housing projects, and he described Mexican Americans in the barrios as "one step removed from 'the wild tribes of Mexico.'" He claimed that the police were doing their best despite being outnumbered by blacks and Latinos, who he claimed were much more likely to commit crimes than whites.[36] Civil rights leaders and others criticized Parker for the way the LA police treated racial minorities, and blamed him for the Watts riot in 1965. Nevertheless, Parker maintained his grip on power until he died in office in 1966.

Across the country, being "tough on crime" became the quickest way to gain local power. In the relatively small and mostly white city of Minneapolis, Charles Stenvig was elected mayor in 1969. Stenvig, a forty-one-year-old police detective and president of the Minneapolis police federation, ran as an independent candidate pledging to "take the handcuffs off the police" and crack down on "racial militants," criminals, and student protesters. His landslide victory shocked the local liberal political establishment.

Stenvig was just one of several law-and-order mayors elected in the wake of the upheavals of the mid-1960s. Sam Yorty in Los Angeles and Frank Rizzo in Philadelphia also won mayoral elections by blaming liberals for crime and targeting racial minorities. Rizzo, like Stenvig, had come out of the police force. He had run as a "supercop," pledging to crack down on the Black Panthers. Yorty ran as a law-and-order candidate using the Watts riot as his platform.

Disdainful of educated technocrats, Stenvig claimed to speak for the "little people." When antiwar demonstrations erupted at the University of Minnesota in 1972, Stenvig refused to communicate with university officials, who were calling for police restraint. Instead he called in the National Guard, which quelled the protest with tear gas.

After the protests, a commission appointed by university leaders accused the police of instigating violence during the demonstration, asserting that "the Minneapolis police performed in an abominable fashion." But Stenvig, who refused to participate in the commission's investigation, gained broad public support for his handling of the protest. In a poll conducted by the *Minneapolis Tribune*, 78 percent of the Twin Cities' residents approved of his crackdown on the students.[37] Although university officials saw the student protest as an expression of opposition to an unpopular war, Stenvig and his supporters simply saw the protesters as lawbreakers.

Stenvig also capitalized on the strong antigovernment sentiment that prevailed in the 1970s. Like other law-and-order candidates, he painted liberals as misguided meddlers who spent money on useless government programs, and as coddlers of criminals who undercut police authority.

He promised that as long as he was mayor, no civilian review board would provide oversight of the police. He proposed very few government programs and vetoed nearly every bill that came to his desk from the city council, stating that "the people have had it up to here with government and it [is] time to put a stop to it." One reporter noted that "a policeman-mayor can give a city confronted with change a feeling of security, even while temporizing on important issues." A cab driver quoted in a 1971 *Newsweek* article on Stenvig said, approvingly, that "Stenvig hasn't done much. He hasn't done much right and he hasn't done much wrong. But it's nice to know that if anything happens we've got a tough guy who can handle it in City Hall."[38]

THROUGHOUT THE 1960s and beyond, fear began to take on a life of its own, fueled largely by politicians and media coverage. By focusing on rare but heinous crimes to an extent far out of proportion to their frequency, television news programs and newspapers fed exaggerated fears of random violence. Crime coverage in the United States far exceeded that in Europe, particularly England and Scandinavia, where reporting of crime statistics was routine and available, but not sensationalized.[39] Although most violent crimes occurred between people who knew each other, a 1974 study found that fear was directed at strangers.[40]

More than anything else, people feared for their personal safety. In 1964, 61 percent of those polled said they were more worried about their safety than they had been a year earlier. By 1979, 85 percent felt that over the previous twenty years, their risk of becoming a crime victim had increased.[41] But the level of fear was out of proportion to the actual risk. Although crime increased during the 1960s and early 1970s, even at its peak in the second half of the twentieth century the rate of violent crime barely exceeded its highest point in the first half of the century. In the mid-1960s, violent crime affected fewer than 2 people in 1,000. At its height, the rate of all violent crimes remained consistently below 1 percent of the population.[42] By contrast, people were twice as likely to die in an automobile accident than to be harmed by a stranger. Walking on the street was much safer than driving in a car.

Fear had little to do with actual dangers, but it generated destructive assumptions. *Time* magazine asserted that "the universal fear of violent crime and vicious strangers . . . is a constant companion of the populous. It is the cold fear of dying at random in a brief spasm of senseless violence—for a few pennies, for nothing."[43] Much of the fear-mongering was over the supposed dangers to women. At a time when African Americans and women were asserting their rights as full citizens, participating in jobs and public life in new ways, the news media revived the age-old trope that black men were dangerous and that women—especially white women—were vulnerable.[44] The popular press saturated readers with the message that attacks on city streets, and particularly attacks on women, were practically inevitable.

As early as 1963, *U.S. News and World Report* exhorted women, "First Scream, Then Scram. . . . [M]uggings, rapes and assaults have become common." The *Washington Post* warned women not to "walk around alone at night," to keep all doors and windows locked, and to install burglar alarms.[45] These messages exhorted women to stay home, where they were presumed to be safe, even though women were more likely to be assaulted by relatives in their own homes than by strangers out in the streets. According to a Chicago study, from September 1965 to March 1966, 46 percent of the major crimes against women took place in the home. The number of police responses to domestic disturbances exceeded the combined responses for murder, rape, aggravated assault, and other violent crimes against women.[46]

Who were these alleged attackers? In 1970, *Time* magazine made it clear that innocent citizens should fear young black men, "the most crime-prone segment of the population," whose numbers were increasing.[47] *Time* gave the impression that the nation's city streets were swarming with young blacks eager to commit "interracial crime." The police chief in Washington, DC, trained his officers "to treat blacks decently mainly as a matter of self-protection. A mistreated kid, for example, may hurt a cop when he gets big and dangerous."[48]

The term "black militant" carried the most ominous resonance, evoking power, violence, and danger. And it was used indiscriminately, encouraging greater fear. For example, in August 1970, *Time* quoted Julius Hobson, a critic of the city government of the District of Columbia, and identified him simply as "a local black militant." *Time* failed to mention that Hobson was a longtime civil rights activist and World War II veteran who had attended Tuskegee, Columbia, and Howard Universities, held a master's degree in economics, was a member of the Washington, DC, school board, and taught at three universities.[49] To *Time*, and very likely its readers, he was just one more dangerous black man.

Fear continued to rise even as the crime rate leveled off. The rate of most violent crimes actually declined after 1973. Yet a poll taken in 1981 showed that while the chance of being murdered was a mere 1 in 10,000, and becoming a victim of violent crime was just 60 in 10,000, fully 40 percent of Americans polled reported that they were "highly fearful" of assault. According to public opinion polls taken throughout the 1990s, when the crime rate was declining, a majority of Americans were more fearful about their personal safety than they had been the previous year.[50]

Fear of crime affected the way people lived. More than half of respondents to polls said that they dressed plainly to avoid attracting the attention of attackers. A majority reported that they kept a gun for protection.[51] In 1984, a third of all respondents said they feared going out after dark in downtown areas, and 14 percent feared going out in their own neighborhoods. A 1983 study concluded that fear of crime was "growing and . . . slowly paralyzing every level of society." A New York City advertising executive explained how fear shaped his life: "I've changed. I'm defensive, watchful, cautious, and it takes very little to activate my 'fight or flight' instincts." Although he had never been a victim of crime or felt personally threatened, he had become generally afraid. "I check for teenagers wearing sneakers, I cross the street to avoid potential confrontations with groups of strangers, I constantly swivel my head to scan the area around me even during the day." He didn't like "the feeling of inhibition this attitude imposes on me and on my attitudes about people," yet he didn't know why he was so fearful, and he was unable to control it.[52]

Throughout the 1980s, public officials encouraged the panic by warning that the worst was yet to come, basing their predictions on unfounded assumptions. In 1980, when the chance of becoming a murder victim was 1 in 10,000, researchers at the Massachusetts Institute of Technology made the absurd claim that 1 out of every 61 babies born in New York City in that year would become a murder victim. The following year, the former director of the Bureau of Justice Statistics, at the US Department of Justice, predicted that "within 4 or 5 years every household in the country will be hit by crime."[53]

The ongoing War on Drugs fed these baseless predictions and accelerated the expansion of policing and incarceration. Launched by Nixon, the war was continued by Ronald Reagan. When Reagan became president in 1981, he set about slashing government welfare programs while at the same time expanding funding for the military and law enforcement. During his first term in office, antidrug funding for the FBI increased from $8 million to $95 million. The Department of Defense also received a major boost in antidrug funds during Reagan's presidency, from $33 million to just over $1 billion. The Drug Enforcement Administration (DEA) saw similar increases in congressional largess. During those same years, funding for drug treatment, prevention, and education was cut dramatically. The 1986 and 1988 Anti-Drug Abuse Acts (and the 1994 Violent Crime Control and Law Enforcement Act, under President Bill Clinton) further intensified anticrime measures, targeting minorities and the poor.[54]

Before 1988, the prison sentence for possession of any drug, in any amount, was a maximum of one year. The provisions of the 1988 Anti-Drug Abuse Act ramped up punishment for all drug crimes, including minor nonviolent offenses such as drug possession. The law expanded the death penalty for serious drug crimes and established mandatory sentences even for less serious ones, including five years in prison for simple possession of cocaine base with no intention to sell, even for first-time offenders. The act passed Congress 346 to 11—six of the opponents came from the Congressional Black Caucus. In cities such as New York, "zero-tolerance" policies led to arrest and incarceration for trivial crimes, especially for blacks.

As a result of these policies, large numbers of young African Americans came through the prison system and were unemployable after their release, marked forever as felons. Often their crimes were petty, victimless, and nonviolent—crimes that had been reclassified from misdemeanors to felonies. Most devastating to the black community were the new punitive federal sentencing guidelines put into effect in 1987, mostly for drug offenses, which imposed long sentences and often ruled out probation.

The new guidelines imposed a 100-to-1 differential in penalties for cocaine possession. One hundred grams of powdered cocaine (preferred by whites) carried the same sentence as one gram of crack (the form of the drug commonly used by African Americans). Partly as a result of these new guidelines, the number of federal prisoners nearly tripled between 1984 and 1993. This racial disparity in sentencing was not addressed until 2010, with the Fair Sentencing Act, which reduced the 100-to-1 disparity to 18-to-1. In other developed countries, the victimless offense of drug possession usually merits less than six months in jail, or no jail time at all.[55]

The War on Drugs did more than beef up the penal system and snare millions of nonviolent, mostly minority offenders. It also eroded virtually all constitutionally protected civil liberties. New laws led to numerous violations of Fourth Amendment protections against unreasonable searches and seizures, including mandatory drug testing of employees and students, random searches, sweeps of public schools, search warrants based on anonymous tips, "no-knock warrants," expanded government wiretapping authority, the use of paid unidentified informants, and helicopter surveillance of homes without a warrant.

The US Supreme Court, dominated increasingly by conservative Republican appointments, upheld measures such as preventive detention, which allowed judges to deny bail to defendants deemed to be potentially dangerous. Preventive detention was first passed by Congress in 1970 and went into effect in Washington, DC. It was rarely used until the mid-1980s, when thirty-four states enacted similar laws. But like so many other tough-on-crime measures, preventive detention was based largely on fear and myth, had an insignificant effect on the crime rate, and focused attention away from more serious threats.[56]

Very few of those who were incarcerated for drug offenses ever posed a threat to anyone. Drunk driving was vastly more lethal—by the end of the 1980s, drunk drivers were killing more than 22,000 people every year, and all alcohol-related deaths totaled 100,000 per year. Due to the efforts of organizations such as Mothers Against Drunk Driving (MADD), many states enacted mandatory sentences for drunk driving—typically a few days in jail, fines, license suspension, and community service. In most cases, drunk drivers were charged with only a misdemeanor, not a felony. But possession of a small amount of crack cocaine carried a mandatory minimum sentence of five years in federal prison. Drunk drivers were typically white men, and they were vastly more dangerous to society than most of the people who were incarcerated for felony drug offenses.[57] Nevertheless, the War on Drugs continued to target relatively harmless offenders, clogging jails and prisons with people who should not have been incarcerated and distracting citizens and law enforcement from much more pressing public safety issues.

The War on Drugs also provided a rationale for militarizing the police. In 1981, Reagan persuaded Congress to pass the Military Cooperation with Law Enforcement Act, which encouraged the military to give local, state, and federal police access to military bases, intelligence, research, and weapons for drug interdiction. New policing strategies, such as the creation of Special Weapons and Tactics (SWAT) teams to control rioting, turned the police into a quasi-military force. SWAT teams were just one factor in the shift from "community policing" to "military policing." The militarization of the police began in the early years of the Cold War, when large-scale investments in defense fed the creation of new technologies and institutions. Military innovations quickly spread into civilian applications in both the public and private sector. Officials drew on techniques developed for use against foreign enemies to combat urban problems such as blight and urban unrest, and as a result, police forces began to emulate, and eventually resemble, the military.[58]

IRONICALLY, THE VAST amounts of money pouring into law enforcement and prisons did not make citizens feel safer. Among other factors, the ferocity of the police gave the impression that the nation was under siege. Americans continued to believe that crime was skyrocketing, even though it wasn't, and fear increased accordingly.

Although the police presence was expanding, the message from the government was clear: don't count on public officials or police to protect you. As in the early years of the Atomic Age, on the issue of international threats and the arms buildup, on the issue of urban crime government officials warned citizens that they were responsible for their own safety. It was true that the government could not protect citizens against an atomic attack. Citizens could not protect themselves, either, but the government tried to reassure them that they could survive such an attack if they took adequate precautions. Years later, when the dangers closer to home came to the fore, officials offered the same advice, in this case emphasizing that police could not be in every location where a crime might occur, so citizens needed to rely on themselves for protection.

A special report by the government's National Institute of Justice in 1982 offered urban residents "guidance on protecting themselves against crime by recognizing and handling dangerous situations, safeguarding their home, obtaining good training in self defense, and hiring a security guard for a block or organizing a citizens' patrol." Rather than encouraging people to work with their local police, the report urged them to hire private guards and maintain their own surveillance: "The single most important defense against being robbed or assaulted is to be alert. . . . [S]treet criminals, especially muggers and purse-snatchers, are essentially predators who spot victims, stalk them, and attack. They can sense vulnerability by noting the way a person walks, holds the head, and carries a handbag or package. Specific techniques can prevent crimes in the lobby of a building, in an automatic elevator, inside an apartment, in a car, and on bus or subway."[59]

In a 1985 *Newsweek* poll, half of the respondents said they had little or no confidence in the police to protect them against violent crime. Some individuals and neighborhoods began to hire their own private cops. Security companies provided armed guards, who began patrolling neighborhoods. A New Jersey security agency, for example, offered a "Family Protection Plan" that provided personal bodyguard service. Affluent customers began hiring bodyguards to take them into New York City, or to go shopping. During the 1980s, the number of people working in the private security industry increased dramatically, far outstripping the rate in law enforcement, which declined. By 1990, expenditures for private security reached $220 per capita, compared to $140 per capita for public law enforcement.[60]

Acknowledging citizens' reluctance to trust law enforcement to protect them, Houston's police chief, B. K. Johnson, lamented, "We have allowed ourselves to degenerate to the point where we're living like animals. We live behind burglar bars and throw a collection of door locks at night and set an alarm and lay down with a loaded shotgun beside the bed and then try to get some rest. It's ridiculous. Americans are arming themselves with guns as though they still lived in frontier days." But Chief Johnson himself kept several loaded guns in his own bedroom. Countless citizens did the same, arming themselves with guns, guard dogs, chemical mace, and burglar alarms.[61]

Ironies abounded. The police looked and acted increasingly like an army, but did not inspire confidence among fearful citizens. Officials warned citizens to protect themselves, yet politicians blamed each other for failing to protect the public. Racialized fear-mongering intensified during the 1980s, exemplified in 1988 with the infamous "Willie Horton" ad by Republican presidential candidate George H.W. Bush, which featured a black man on parole who had raped and murdered a white woman after being released from prison under the watch of Massachusetts governor Michael Dukakis, the Democrat running against Bush.

Dukakis responded not with a condemnation of Bush's race-baiting and fear-mongering but with a "Willie Horton" ad of his own, featuring a Latino parolee from a federal prison who had raped and murdered a woman during Bush's years at the helm of the Central Intelligence Agency.[62] Ironically enough, these dueling messages conveyed an idea to which neither candidate subscribed: that there was something government officials could do to keep dangerous criminals off the streets.

These ads also reinforced the idea that the "face" of violent crime was not white—a message reinforced by the media. A 2001 study in *Critical Criminology* found a correlation between time spent watching television and fear of crime. The study showed that for white viewers, fear of crime increased when the criminals portrayed on television were members of minority groups, but not when the criminals portrayed were white. For black viewers, the race of the criminals did not make a difference.[63]

By the 1990s, as crime rates declined, hardly anyone noticed—and fear continued to rise.[64] In 1992, nearly half of those polled said that they feared for their personal safety walking at night within a mile of their own homes.[65] In December 1993, sales of mace were ten times higher than in same month in 1991. Home burglar alarm sales were up 8 percent.[66]

By 1994, after more than a decade of declining rates of violent crime, public perception of crime as the most important problem in America soared to an all-time high.[67] Between 1989 and 1994, the percentage of those polled who said they were "truly desperate" about crime nearly doubled, from 32 percent to 62 percent.[68] One survey asked Americans what kinds of things they asked for when they prayed to God. Two-thirds of respondents said that they prayed for protection from threats to their personal safety.[69]

These exaggerated fears had an impact on how Americans viewed each other. Many people were wary of young men—especially young black men. In 1994, official crime statistics showed that juveniles committed only about 13 percent of all violent crimes. But according to public opinion polls at the time, Americans believed that juveniles

Americans That Are "Truly Desperate"
About Crime vs. Violent Crime Rate, 1989 and 1994

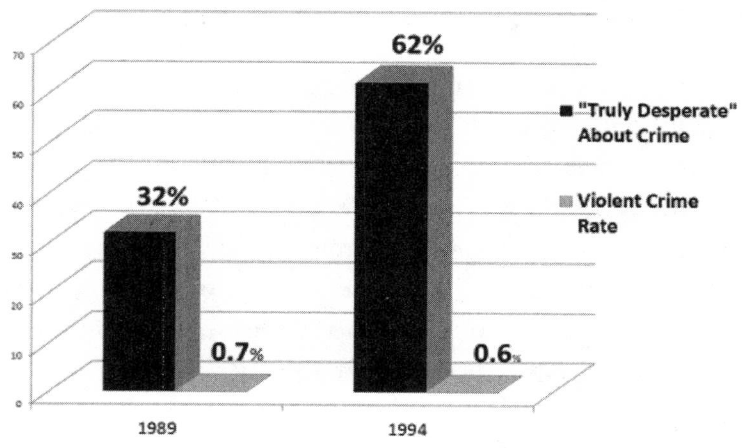

Source: Rorie Sherman, "Crime's Toll on the U.S.: Fear, Despair and Guns," National Law Journal, *April 18, 1994, A1, A19–A20.*

committed 43 percent of violent crimes—more than three times the actual proportion. Most of those polled wanted harsher punishment for young offenders.[70] Not simply afraid *for* their children, Americans were becoming afraid *of* the nation's youth.

Experts and officials asserted that black boys would soon become dangerous young black men, and that their numbers were increasing. These claims were patently false, but they spread like wildfire. In 1996, Princeton University political scientist John DiIulio Jr. made a startling prediction. Looking at demographic trends, he noted that by 2005 the number of fourteen- to seventeen-year-old males would increase by 23 percent, and that the rate would rise faster among black children than among white children. He assumed that black boys were more likely to become violent teenage criminals and coined the term "super-predators" to describe these youths, calling the trend a "ticking time bomb" that would unleash "a storm of predatory criminality" on the nation.[71] DiIulio blamed absent fathers as well as single mothers. Claiming that superpredators were "fatherless, godless and without conscience," he wrote, in the *National Review*, that "all that's left of the black community in some pockets of urban America is deviant, delinquent and criminal adults surrounded by severely abused and neglected children, virtually all of whom were born out of wedlock."[72]

DiIulio warned of the "thickening ranks of juvenile 'superpredators'—radically impulsive, brutally remorseless youngsters, including ever more preteenage boys, who murder, assault, rape, rob, burglarize, deal deadly drugs, join gun-toting gangs and create serious communal disorders." He predicted that by 2010, there would be approximately 270,000 more "superpredators" on the streets.[73]

Others quickly jumped on the bandwagon. Political scientist James Q. Wilson asserted that by the end of the 1990s there would be 60,000 more "young muggers, killers and thieves than we have now." He added: "Get ready." The conservative lobbying group Council on Crime in America warned in 1996 of "a coming storm of juvenile violence."[74]

The media latched onto and spread DiIulio's claims about "superpredators," which also echoed through government institutions. James Alan Fox, dean of the College of Criminal Justice at Northeastern University, predicted a "blood bath" by 2005. He prepared a report for the Bureau of Justice Statistics pointing to millions of children living in poverty. But he did not call for assistance for struggling families. Rather, he cast blame on parents who did not provide full-time supervision and guidance. Soon, he warned, these children would "reach their high-risk years," and a "wave of youth violence" would be unleashed that would "be even worse than that of the past ten years." Michael Petit, deputy director of the Child Welfare League of America, said that superpredators were "literally being manufactured, programmed, hardwired to behave in a certain way." An editorial in the *Omaha World Herald* described these children as "killing machines."[75]

These dire predictions never materialized and were thoroughly discredited. Juvenile crime was already declining in 1996. Instead of rising, the rate of juvenile crime continued to drop by more than half. In 2014, juvenile crime was at its lowest point in thirty years. "Superpredators" existed only in the fevered imagination of alarmists.[76] But the exaggerated fears of crime had real consequences, most of all for those who were viewed as being inherently criminal.

ALTHOUGH THE NATIONAL crime rate dropped 40 percent over the course of the 1990s, criminal justice became increasingly punitive. President Bill Clinton, a Democrat, just like the Republicans in the Oval Office who preceded him, exaggerated the danger of crime and furthered the punitive trends. In his 1994 State of the Union Address, he declared, "Violent crime and the fear it provokes are crippling our society, limiting personal freedom and fraying the ties that bind us." Instead of reassuring the public that violent crime was decreasing, he proposed legislation calling for more punitive measures.[77]

The 1994 Violent Crime Control and Law Enforcement Act authorized $30.2 billion to put 100,000 more police on the streets, build more prisons, and fund other crime prevention programs. The act made sixty federal crimes eligible for the death penalty, and mandated life sentences for offenders convicted of three violent crimes: the so-called three-strikes law. It also permanently banned drug offenders from welfare and food stamps. Drug-related convictions could now result in eviction from public housing and elimination of consideration for benefits such as student loans. These measures severely punished offenders who had already served their time by permanently closing off their opportunities for jobs and government programs, forcing many back into the drug trade.[78]

States also passed punitive three-strikes laws, and the state laws took inspiration from federal sentencing policies. In 1993, the state of Washington set a mandatory life sentence with no eligibility for parole for three convictions of any Class A felony, which included assault, controlled substance homicide, extortion, child molestation, "indecent liberties" (which also involve child sexual abuse), rape, robbery, vehicular assault, the promotion of prostitution, and a number of other crimes.

The next year, California passed a three-strikes ballot initiative, Proposition 184, a measure prompted by the Polly Klaas kidnapping and murder case. The crime was horrific. On October 1, 1993, twelve-year-old Polly was kidnapped at knife point during a slumber party at her home in Petaluma, California. She was later found strangled to death. The murderer, Richard Allen Davis, had been in prison several times for serious crimes before this murder. In the wake of this brutal crime, Proposition 184 quickly qualified for the ballot. Although many criminologists and members of the state's prison bureaucracy opposed the law, California governor Pete Wilson approved it and signed it into law. By a margin of 72 percent to 28 percent, voters put the law into the California state constitution, which meant that it could not be removed by an ordinary majority vote in the legislature. In this way, a heinous but very rare crime led to a law that inflicted long prison sentences on offenders, many of whom committed relatively minor crimes.[79] By 2004, 42,322 people had been incarcerated in California under the law. By 2012, twenty-five states had similar laws, and thousands of offenders were being locked up for lengthy sentences or life in prison—sentences imposed by mandate with no judicial discretion.[80]

These laws were driven by irrational fear, not a sure grasp of reality. By the end of the century, the murder rate had fallen every year for eight years, and the rate of all violent crimes dropped by almost a third during the 1990s. But this dramatic and important news did not make headlines. The media continued to sensationalize crime: as the saying went, "if it bleeds, it leads."[81] As a result, the rights of possible future victims of violent crime took precedence over the rights of the accused, and even the rights of alleged offenders arrested for nonviolent, victimless crimes were abridged. The police often portrayed themselves as victims, claiming to be stymied by soft-on-crime judges, defense attorneys, and court-mandated requirements, such as the Miranda rights. But there is no evidence that protections of the rights of the accused ever "handcuffed the police."[82]

Draconian criminal justice policies continued to have a disproportionate impact on African Americans. Young blacks were much more likely than young whites to be arrested for such minor crimes as drug abuse, even though there was no difference in drug usage by whites and blacks. In fact, there is evidence that whites, especially white youths, were more likely to engage in drug crimes than people of color. Yet some states incarcerated black men on drug charges twenty to fifty times more often than they did white men. In the 1990s white people constituted 70 percent of those who were arrested for all crimes (in line with their percentage of the population), but only 30 percent of those who went to prison. The reverse was true for people of color, who represented 30 percent of those arrested but 70 percent of prison inmates.[83] In major cities, 80 percent of young black men had criminal records, which meant they would face legal discrimination for the rest of their lives.[84]

Laws such as "three strikes" and mandatory minimum sentencing filled prisons with offenders whose crimes were drug related. The vast majority of drug arrests were for minor, nonviolent offenses. Marijuana possession accounted for nearly 80 percent of the increase in drug arrests. Women incarcerated for drug offenses were the fastest-growing segment of the prison population.[85]

The War on Drugs, by criminalizing addiction rather than approaching it as a public health problem and providing treatment, fostered an underground criminal market for illegal drugs permeated with guns and violence. Official efforts to control the drug trade bred violence not only on the part of the offenders, however, but also on the part of the authorities. Police brutality, surveillance, racial profiling, and murder at the hands of law enforcement all increased with the War on Drugs. These patterns continued well into the twenty-first century. By 2014, young black men were twenty-one times more likely to be killed by the police than their white peers. Even children were not spared. From 1980 to 2014, two-thirds of the teenagers and children who were killed by police were African American.[86]

Punitive measures like the 1994 crime bill led Americans into a nightmare of incarceration. The numbers are staggering. In 1975, there were 240,593 prisoners in the United States. Over the next twenty years that number rose to over 1 million—an increase of more than 300 percent at a time when the US population grew by only 23 percent. At the end of the century, the United States had 5 percent of the world's population, but 25 percent of the world's prisoners. Indeed, imprisonment rates in the United States were far higher than in other developed nations, as well as in countries known for their repressive regimes, such as Russia, China, and Iran. As incarceration rates remained stable or declined in European countries, the rates in the United States quadrupled.[87]

The Cold War was over, but the War on Drugs had in many ways taken its place. Bringing Atomic Age fears full circle, in 1996 a TV ad for Republican presidential candidate Bob Dole began with footage of the little girl with a daisy taken from the 1964 ad for Lyndon Johnson. But this time, a female narrator says, "Thirty years ago, the biggest threat to her was nuclear war. Today the threat is drugs. Teenage drug use has doubled in the last four years. What's been done?" The ad continues with images of preadolescent children using various forms of drugs in a public park.[88] The ad linked the dangers of the atomic bomb with the dangers of drugs: both could strike your child anywhere—in a park, at home, in the neighborhood. The threat of subversive infiltration and communist attack had been replaced by the danger of criminal youths.

WHAT CAME OF all the new crime-fighting strategies of the 1980s and 1990s? Did these efforts make anyone safer? Consider mass incarceration, which was, of course, not the consequence of a single policy but of a wide range of tough-on-crime policies. It had catastrophic effects, and not only on those who were incarcerated. Funds assigned to the prison system left less money in state budgets for other spending, shifting money away from social welfare. Mass incarceration devastated entire segments of the population and disenfranchised millions of citizens. States with the highest incarceration rates had the least generous welfare programs, and those with more robust welfare programs had lower rates of imprisonment.[89] Above all, there is little evidence that mass incarceration made anyone safer. Although the rise in incarceration in the 1990s tracked with the decline in crime, the best analyses of these trends reveal that, in fact, there was little causal relationship between them.

There were some, however, who clearly benefited from mass incarceration. Although mass incarceration did more harm than good in American society, some private companies profited. The overcrowding of prisons with nonviolent offenders who were guilty of such crimes as drug possession and immigration violations eventually brought private enterprise into the criminal justice system. Starting in the mid-1980s, as public jails and prisons filled to capacity, for-profit prisons expanded across the country, holding increasing numbers of inmates.[90] Financial incentives, along with misguided and discriminatory sentencing policies, helped to fuel and expand the carceral state. By 2017, the nation was spending $182 billion every year on the penal system.[91]

Meanwhile, the most vulnerable individuals, families, and communities suffered the majority of the effects of mass incarceration. Pundits and observers often pointed to the alleged "pathology" of black families headed by single mothers. But in fact, female-headed households did not cause crime—they were often the result of mass incarceration. With millions of black men removed from their communities, families were torn apart. By the early twenty-first century, there were nearly 3 million more women than men in black communities. An unfairly punitive criminal justice system was the main reason why so many black children were raised by single mothers. While white men were rarely incarcerated for minor drug crimes, such as possession of small amounts of illegal substances, thousands of black fathers were imprisoned for such minor offenses and removed from their families and communities for years.[92]

As for the convicts themselves, regardless of the length of their sentences or the nature of their crimes, they were effectively banished from many areas of society upon release. In many states these offenders faced discrimination in employment, housing, education, public benefits, and jury service.[93] Ex-felons were left with few opportunities to make a living other than in the underground drug trade or other criminal activities.[94]

One of the harshest consequences of a felony conviction, in most states, was the loss of the right to vote. By the early twenty-first century, nearly 6 million Americans were unable to vote on account of their criminal convictions—one in every forty adults. Most states did not allow prisoners to vote. Many also disenfranchised those who were out of prison but still on parole or probation. Other jurisdictions prevented ex-felons from voting for life, even long after they had served their time in prison, on parole, or in probation. Voting is one of the most important rights of citizens—and losing that right can be devastating. Former felons who regain the right to vote often feel like they have regained a stake in society. They are more likely to become active in their communities and stay out of the criminal justice system in the future.[95]

Disenfranchisement not only holds individuals back from becoming fully empowered citizens and contributing to their communities, but also has a profound effect on elections. A robust democracy requires an engaged citizenry that votes. Keeping millions of citizens away from the polls distorts the electoral process. In 1976, 1.1 million Americans were disfranchised because of felony convictions. That number increased to 4.7 million by 2000, and to 6.1 million in 2016. The close elections in those two years, when the losing candidate won the popular vote and lost in the electoral college, might have turned out differently if former felons could have voted.

Most people of color vote Democratic, and the states with the largest numbers of incarcerated African Americans tend to have the most punitive disenfranchisement laws. Florida, for example, had the most restrictive laws preventing ex-felons from voting in 2000, and in that year 827,000 ex-felons were not allowed to vote. In the 2000 presidential election, if former felons in Florida had been allowed to vote, it is likely that Democratic candidate Al Gore would have won the presidency.[96] In the 2016 election, Republican Donald Trump's margin of victory in key states was minuscule, and if former felons had been allowed to vote in a few crucial states, Democratic candidate Hillary Clinton—who won the popular vote by nearly 3 million—might have won in the electoral college as well.[97]

Mass incarceration is not only ineffective as a law enforcement strategy; it actually produces more crime. For hundreds of thousands of ex-offenders, life after incarceration is little more than an extension of punishment, invisible and ongoing, forcing many back into criminal behavior, and then back into prison. The system fails ex-offenders in numerous ways. They are released from prison with little support or resources to rejoin society. Punitive incarceration policies result in the elimination of education and substance-abuse programs within prisons, and mandatory sentencing guidelines give judges no flexibility to consider individual circumstances.[98]

THE WAR ON Drugs and the War on Crime were failures. Those failures were in fact predicted. As early as 1973, the National Advisory Commission on Criminal Justice Standards and Goals issued a recommendation that no new prisons for adults should be built and that all such institutions for children should be closed. They found that "the prison, the reformatory and the jail have achieved only a shocking record of failure. There is overwhelming evidence that these institutions create crime rather than prevent it."[99] But those recommendations were ignored, and the carceral system exploded. Instead of reducing crime and violence, the policies that prevailed quickly backfired, actually creating more lawlessness and violence and destabilizing communities. After thirty years of the War on Drugs, illegal drugs were more readily available and more potent than ever, drug violence and killings were more common, and drug dealers were wealthier.[100]

Not only that, but the decades-long panic over crime, and the official policies that resulted, blunted many of the gains of the movement for racial equality. In 2015, *New York Times* columnist Charles Blow described a "distortion of perception" that fed erroneous and dangerous assumptions about crime. The majority of Americans believed that crime was rising, when in fact it had declined since the late 1980s. In the midst of the presidential campaign of 2016, Newt Gingrich, former Speaker of the US House of Representatives, responded to that perception. Although the rate of violent crime had been plummeting for years, Gingrich called upon leaders to respond to fear rather than fact: "The average American, I will bet you this morning, does not think that crime is down, does not think that we are safer. . . . People feel more threatened. As a political candidate, I'll go with what people feel."[101] And what people felt was tinged with racial assumptions. White Americans dramatically overestimated the percentage of crime committed by minorities by as much as 20 to 30 percent. Regardless of the facts, in large part because so many black men were being arrested and imprisoned, and also because news reports continued to associate crime with African Americans, crime remained overwhelmingly associated with black men in the public mind.[102]

As the color of danger shifted from red to black, two parallel trends developed. One was the vast expansion of the carceral state; the other was the increasing effort on the part of individual citizens to protect themselves from perceived danger. Both trends were responses to exaggerated fears, and neither strategy was effective. Mass incarceration did not increase public safety and did little to promote confidence in the criminal justice system. Even with increased investments in law enforcement and a militarized police force, Americans continued to fear for their personal safety. As in the early years of the Atomic Age, officials remained unable to assure the public that they could keep them safe from harm. At the same time, citizens turned to self-protection. Fear of crime gave rise not only to new prisons and well-armed police forces, but to a new citizen-hero: the vigilante.

Chapter 3

VIGILANTE VIRTUE: FANTASY, REALITY, AND THE LAW

Consider Your Man Card Reissued.

—*Advertisement for Bushmaster Semiautomatic Rifle, 2012*[1]

As Americans were growing more and more fearful of crime, many also became drawn to vigilantism. Vigilante violence is the epitome of "do-it-yourself defense." Its appeal reflected the public's growing disillusionment with law enforcement, its declining faith in the ability of the police to keep citizens safe, and a new belief by many that aggressive self-protection was the only way to achieve true security. Vigilante violence began to gain mainstream popularity in the 1970s and 1980s. We see evidence of this trend in the popular culture, in the response to certain notorious crimes, in the increasing attraction of guns and gun culture, and, ultimately, by the twenty-first century, in laws that sanction vigilante violence in the face of perceived danger.

Vigilante violence has a long history in American life. The most notable examples in the nineteenth century involved the Ku Klux Klan. The Klan first emerged during Reconstruction following the Civil War, when many southern whites believed that the rule of law had collapsed and that the freed slaves and their supporters had taken power from white authorities. Fearing the loss of white power, white vigilantes formed the Klan to terrorize black people and reassert white supremacy. One of their main claims to righteousness was their assertion that freed blacks were a threat to white women. False accusations of rape often resulted in lynching of black men by the Klan.

The Klan went through a revival in the North in the 1920s and gained widespread support, largely among small-town whites. The new Klan attracted followers not only because of its racism, but also as a result of its hostility to elites and outsiders and its affirmation of supposedly traditional American values.[2] In some locales, the Klan became so mainstream that its members were elected to local offices. Other white supremacist vigilante groups emerged in the following decades, such as the Posse Comitatus in the 1960s. In the post–World War II period, far right militias arose in response to what they saw as government overreach.

But vigilantism has not always been confined to the far right. One of the best-known nineteenth-century vigilantes was the radical abolitionist John Brown, who in 1859, along with his followers, seized the federal armory and arsenal at Harpers Ferry, West Virginia, with the goal of generating a revolt that would overthrow slavery. Brown was captured and hanged for his crimes, but many abolitionists considered him a hero. A more recent example is the Symbionese Liberation Army (SLA), which in 1974 kidnapped the heiress Patty Hearst and insisted on a massive distribution of food to the poor as her ransom. The SLA committed a number of violent acts, including murder, before six of its members died in a shootout; the remaining members were arrested. These groups, whether on the far right or the far left, typically operate outside the mainstream, but they reflect the extreme ends of the vigilante sentiments that many Americans have shared in different eras.

The vigilante spirit that emerged in the decades after World War II had a different tone and purpose. Rather than targeting specific groups or promoting a particular ideological position, the new vigilantes were primarily interested in protection. They emerged during a time of widespread belief that the dangers to personal safety were increasing, and law enforcement was powerless to keep citizens safe.

The first signs of this spirit of self-protection appeared in the early postwar years, when officials and experts began warning Americans that they were responsible for their own safety in the face of the possibility of internal subversion or an atomic attack. Individuals had to be on the lookout for communist infiltration, and they had to be prepared for the worst in the event of a nuclear war. Although the government was amassing a nuclear arsenal to deter potential adversaries from attacking the United States, individual safety depended on citizens protecting themselves. Deterrence could fail. That message continued as perceived danger shifted to crime and social upheaval: the government would expand and arm the police with military weapons, but citizens still needed to protect themselves.

By the 1970s, citizen self-protection had begun to take many forms. A relatively benign form of the vigilante spirit can be seen in the rise of neighborhood policing by civilians. Fear that law enforcement units were too overwhelmed to provide sufficient protection prompted many citizens to patrol the streets near their own homes. These efforts echoed some of the types of surveillance that had emerged in the Atomic Age, such as the citizen volunteers who watched the sky for approaching enemy planes, or snooped around their neighborhoods looking for people who seemed suspicious.

Some of these volunteers worked in partnership with the military; in later years they provided support to law enforcement. For example, the National Sheriffs' Association launched the National Neighborhood Watch Program in 1972 with the aim of "assist[ing] citizens and law enforcement" by focusing on residential areas and involving local residents.[3] Other neighborhood groups formed independently to address the problem of crime control. One study found that lack of faith in law enforcement prompted citizens to rely on volunteers or private guards to protect their homes and neighborhoods, but concluded that those efforts were generally ineffective and even dangerous.[4]

By the 1980s, the notion that the family, the home, the government, or law enforcement could keep people safe had diminished. Many people lost faith that those institutions could contain the dangers of the age. The sense that the nation's authorities could not protect the citizens persisted. The Watergate scandal that forced the resignation of President Richard Nixon, and soon after, the humiliating retreat from the war in Vietnam, struck blows to national pride and cast doubt on the effectiveness of the nation's leaders. Defeat in Vietnam led many Americans to question the ability of the military to support the role of the United States as the leader of the free world. At home, ongoing social and cultural upheavals fueled exaggerated fears of danger from criminals and outsiders.

Capitalizing on the dark mood of the country, Ronald Reagan ran for president in 1980 promising "Morning in America." He vowed to end the "Vietnam syndrome," which made Americans feel shame for the defeat. Many citizens believed that weak-willed leaders in Washington had tied the hands of the military, preventing US forces from winning the war. Reagan promised to restore pride to veterans and elevate soldiers to their rightful stature.

Reagan's message struck a chord with Americans who felt betrayed by their leaders. A 1985 poll taken by the *Los Angeles Herald Press* found that more than 80 percent of respondents believed that politicians, not the soldiers, had caused the defeat in Vietnam. One respondent asserted, "Our boys did not lose in Vietnam. They had it taken away from them by weak-kneed politicians and the cowardly kids protesting in the streets who were all afraid to do their duty." Another claimed, "Everybody knows that our military never lost a battle in Vietnam. We lost in Vietnam because we were afraid to win, and you can't fight like that."[5]

Reagan brought an image of toughness to his campaigns. Once a Hollywood actor, he had run successfully for governor of California in 1966, and he had a long history as an anticommunist cold warrior. He had won the governorship by calling for law and order and promising to clamp down on student protests, social upheavals, and crime. Before running for president, he served as governor for two terms.

As president, Reagan defined his political enemies as those liberals who were both soft on crime and weak on foreign policy, and thus responsible for both domestic disorder and defeat in Vietnam. They had left the nation vulnerable to internal and external enemies, Reagan said. By encouraging Americans to stand tall, he drew disaffected Democrats into the Republican fold.

Reagan revived early Cold War rhetoric and called for national vigilance in the face of numerous foreign enemies. Giving renewed attention to the nuclear arms race, he proposed a "star wars" nuclear shield program to keep the nation safe. Although the plan never came to fruition, it was a sign of his commitment to defeat the Soviet Union.

Even as Reagan called on Congress to spend more on law enforcement and prisons, the individualistic brand of politics that he embodied and espoused encouraged Americans to take protection into their own hands. One result was a vast expansion of the home security industry. Federal and state governments, for their part, passed laws that weakened gun control measures. Yet another consequence was the elevation of the vigilante into something of a cultural hero. Many Americans blamed bureaucrats in Washington for tying the hands of the soldiers in Vietnam, and they were not inclined to let officials at home prevent them from protecting themselves and their families.

At the start of the 1980s, faith in government was plummeting. According to public opinion polls, 77 percent of Americans had trusted the government in 1964; now, in 1980, only 27 percent did.[6] In this climate of distrust, vigilantism began to take hold in the public imagination as an antidote to the perceived weakness of official institutions.

One event in particular stands out in the rise of the vigilante hero. In December 1984, Bernhard Goetz, a white thirty-seven-year-old electrical engineer, was confronted in a New York City subway by four black teenagers. The young men demanded five dollars. Aside from the screwdrivers they held (which, it later turned out, they allegedly had planned to use to burglarize a video arcade), they were unarmed. Goetz pulled a gun and fired five rounds, wounding all four of the boys. As one of them lay wounded, Goetz said, "You don't look too bad, here's another," and fired into his torso. That bullet left Darrell Cabey paralyzed from the waist down. He almost died, but instead spent weeks in a coma. After fourteen months in the hospital he was released, but he suffered permanent brain damage, ending up with the mental capacity of an eight-year-old.

Goetz quickly became a folk hero. According to a *Newsweek* poll taken three months after the shooting, 57 percent of respondents approved of Goetz's actions. Half said they had little or no confidence in the police to protect them against violent crime. Some people wore T-shirts celebrating Goetz with slogans such as "Thugbuster," "Acquit Bernhard Goetz," or "Goetz Four, Crooks Zero."[7] *U.S. News and World Report* was quick to comment: a political cartoon in the magazine depicted the inside of a crowded subway car. All the passengers are armed to the teeth, including elderly women. One passenger reads a newspaper with the headline, "Muggings down." The message was clear: the way to stop crime was for citizens to carry weapons, become vigilantes, and protect themselves, like Goetz had.[8]

The response to the case revealed the fact that many citizens feared crime and had little faith in city institutions to address it. New York's mayor at the time, Ed Koch, said that "most people believe that the criminal justice system is broken down." US Senator Alfonse (Al) D'Amato, a Republican from New York, said that the Goetz case had "touched a raw nerve" and demonstrated "people's outrage to the criminal behavior that's taking place." People "understand the frustration of Goetz," he added. "They're not saying he did the right thing, but they understand him." D'Amato told a Senate committee that even his own bodyguards were afraid to ride the subway.[9]

Although Goetz was charged with attempted murder, assault, and several other crimes, a Manhattan jury acquitted him of all charges, except for one count of illegal possession of a firearm. In 1989, he was sentenced to one year in jail, one year of psychiatric treatment, five years of probation, two hundred hours of community service, and a $5,000 fine. At his sentencing, he told the judge, "I do feel this case is really

In the wake of the subway shooting by Bernhard Goetz, this cartoon suggests that now everyone has become an armed subway rider.

Source: "Behind Tough Public Stance on Criminals," U.S. News and World Report *98, no. 2 (January 21, 1985): 60. Courtesy of the artist, Dick Locher.*

more about the deterioration of society than it is about me. Society needs to be protected from criminals."[10]

By the time Bernhard Goetz became a folk hero, Americans were already cheering the heroic loner of popular culture who appeared in novels, television shows, and movies. The protagonist in these stories was usually a white man who had no use for the police or other officials and went after the villains himself.[11] The popularity of these fictional characters demonstrates the widespread distrust of authorities and admiration for the outlaw who triumphs over evil. Clint Eastwood, the star of many vigilante films, described the outlaw hero as "the loner operating by himself, without benefit of society . . . [who] takes care of the vengeance himself, doesn't call the police. Like Robin Hood. It's the last masculine frontier."[12]

Although the heyday of the vigilante film was the 1970s and 1980s, the vigilante genre first gained popularity in the early years of the Cold War. Following World War II, the author Mickey Spillane wrote a series of widely popular pulp crime novels featuring a vigilante private eye, Mike Hammer, whose mission it was to rid New York of communists and criminals. Spillane's most popular books appeared between 1947 and 1952. Although widely panned by critics, his books eventually sold more than 150 million copies.[13]

Spillane's stories illuminate the connections between Cold War fears of subversion and the public's fascination with the crime-fighting vigilante. In his 1951 thriller *One Lonely Night*, Spillane's hero foils a plot by evil women who try to use their seductive powers to steal atomic secrets. With murderous rage, he gloats over the carnage he has caused: "I shot them in cold blood and enjoyed every minute of it. I pumped slugs in the nastiest bunch of bastards you ever saw," he says, adding, "They were Commies. . . . Pretty soon what's left of Russia and the slime that breeds there won't be worth mentioning and I'm glad because I had a part in the killing. God, but it was fun!" With patriotic zeal, Hammer proclaims, "I want to make sure this country has a secret that's safe."[14]

In turning to violence, Spillane's vigilante aims to destroy the crime-and-communist-infested "monster" that the American city has become, but then he retreats to the peaceful suburbs. He fantasizes about destroying the threat at its source: "Some day I'd stand on the steps of the Kremlin with a gun in my fist and I'd yell for them to come out and if they wouldn't I'd go in and get them and when I had them lined up against the wall I'd start shooting until all I had left was a row of corpses that bled on the cold floors."[15]

Advancing a theme that would take root in the popular imagination, Spillane's hero had no use for the ineffectual police. In *I, The Jury* (1947), Hammer tells a friend who is a police detective, "I'm not letting the killer go through the tedious process of the law. . . . [T]his time I'm the law and I'm not going to be cold and impartial." Hammer sees the legal system as filled with loopholes that allow murderers to go free. In *The Big Kill* (1951), he explains to his police detective friend, "Tell me that I'm interfering in police work and I'll tell you how sick I am of what goes on in this town. I live here, see? I got a damn good right to keep it clean even if I have to kill a few bastards to do it. There's plenty who need killing bad and if I'm electing myself to do the job you shouldn't kick."[16]

The fictional Mike Hammer became the hero of a TV series that ran from 1958 to 1960, and several of Spillane's books were made into movies, joining a genre of popular films that featured vigilante heroes, many set in New York City. Early postwar films portrayed the city as glamorous. But in the mid-1960s, New York began to appear on-screen as gritty and dangerous. As the nation's largest city, it came to symbolize everything that was wrong with urban America. From 1966 to 1973, 366 movies were shot in New York. Film critic Vincent Canby noted that these films tend to show the city in a harsh and negative light, "run by fools" and taken over by criminals.[17]

Vigilante films increased in number and popularity from the 1970s onward. The first of the very popular *Death Wish* films, starring Charles Bronson, appeared in 1974, and the last sequel was released in the mid-1990s. As with Spillane's novels, critics panned the films, but audiences flocked to them. The first *Death Wish* grossed the equivalent of $100 million in 2017 dollars. The film's producer, Dino De Laurentiis, said the film was "an open invitation to the authorities to come up with remedies to the problem of urban violence, and fast."[18]

The plots of all five increasingly violent *Death Wish* movies follow a man named Paul Kersey. In the first film, Kersey's wife is murdered and their daughter is raped by a gang of thugs who break into their home. Kersey, a white New York City architect, had been a gentle, loving husband and father and a "bleeding heart liberal." But when the police turn out to be completely ineffective, he is transformed into a gun-toting vigilante out for revenge. The villains in the films are often, but not always, black men. They are joined in violent mayhem by members of other racial minorities as well as white hippies.

Kersey vows to clean up New York, "the most violent town in the world." He begins to roam the city's streets, killing muggers, who are

This poster for the movie *Death Wish* celebrates the vigilante hero, who serves as judge, jury, and executioner.

Source: Margaret Herrick Library, Academy of Motion Picture Arts and Sciences.

almost always black, at will. One scene prefigures Bernhard Goetz and the reaction to his vigilante moment. Kersey is on a subway when a black man with a knife tries to rob him. The hero pulls a gun and kills the would-be mugger. Viewers report that audiences in theaters stood and applauded the scene.[19]

The vigilante hero resonated with audiences, and the film broke box-office records. One critic described the "lunatic cheers that rocked the Astor Plaza" during the film; another noted that "every time Bronson dispatched one of his sleazy victims . . . the audience applauded wildly." One viewer remarked that "all his shootings were morally (if not legally) justified." Another described what he saw as the context for the film's popularity: "Just about everybody in New York felt angry, alienated and helpless. People were sick of it all, the terrible Vietnam War, the corrupt Richard Nixon, corrupt everything." Viewers merged the identities of the character (Kersey) and the actor (Bronson), bringing fantasy into the realm of reality. A young woman "thought what Bronson did was right, no one else is doing anything. Our system isn't working today. So you've got to protect your own self." An older male viewer agreed: "If we had more people like Bronson we would have less crime. I would like to do something like Bronson but I don't see how I would get away with it."[20] At least one fan of the movie boasted that he went out and bought a gun after seeing *Death Wish*.[21]

The appeal of *Death Wish* extended to its depiction of deranged hippies. In the midst of the violence committed against Kersey's wife and daughter, one of the long-haired intruders spray-paints a wall in red. Viewers at the time surely recalled the murderous rampage of Charles Manson, who, in 1969, masterminded a killing spree with a group of young women followers; the group left messages in blood on the walls of the victims' homes. Hippies in the 1960s were known for their belief in peace and love. Nevertheless, the long-haired Manson and his female devotees became associated with hippies in the popular mind.

A series of films starring Clint Eastwood also capitalized on the backlash against hippies and radicals. In the 1976 film *The Enforcer*, the criminals call themselves the "Revolutionary Strike Force," a clear reference to the Symbionese Liberation Army, the group of politically radical criminals that kidnapped heiress Patty Hearst in 1974. In this way, these films became much more than pure fantasies—they evoked notorious crimes that had saturated the media and captivated the public imagination. In the vigilante films of the era, one could tell the good guys from the bad guys just from looking at them. The bad guys included a variety of ethnic minorities, as well as white men stylized as hippies and marked with symbols of the antiwar movement. They also tended to be men with sexual proclivities outside the heterosexual norm. In one film, the villain was joined by a violent lesbian.[22] But the real culprits in nearly all of these films were the liberal politicians who promoted social welfare policies that, according to conservative critics, rewarded the undeserving.

Meanwhile, the good guys—in Clint Eastwood's five *Dirty Harry* movies, Charles Bronson's five *Death Wish* features, and Chuck Norris's three action films *The Delta Force* (1986), *Delta Force 2: The Colombian Connection* (1990), and *The Hitman* (1991)—were middle-aged white men. Clint Eastwood's Inspector Harry Callahan represents the apotheosis of this character type. Callahan is a San Francisco police detective who, owing to multicultural values and affirmative action policies, is saddled with minority or female partners. In the first movie, when he nabs a villain, his superiors force him to release the culprit because his Miranda right to stay silent was violated. The villain goes on to commit more violent crimes until finally he threatens to attack a busload of children. Callahan—violating protocol and acting on his own—kills the man with his trademark elongated Magnum .44 pistol, "the most powerful handgun in the world [that] would blow your head clean off."[23]

The vigilante films of the era featured heroic, individualistic, violent white men who operate on the edges or outside the law, but they are not overtly racist or sexist, except in a paternalistic fashion. Harry Callahan objects to the partners assigned to him, but he grudgingly comes to accept them when they prove their mettle. The placement of loyal minority or female partners or assistants signals that the filmmakers would like audiences to believe that the white male heroes—and the movies themselves—are not really racist or sexist. But the inclusion of subordinate women and minorities as tokens represents little more than a nod to the gains of the civil rights and feminist movements.

Well into the twenty-first century, vigilante values continued to inspire Americans in fiction as well as in real life. Superheroes have assumed the mantle of the modern vigilante hero in comic books, novels, and films. So far, superhero films have been the highest-grossing genre in the twenty-first century. The Marvel Cinematic Universe includes not only comic books and several blockbuster movies per year but also long-running television shows, video games, and merchandise. By 2017, Marvel Studios had produced fifteen films, with total box-office earnings of more than $11.6 billion, making it the highest-grossing film franchise of all time.

The 2016 blockbuster *Captain America: Civil War* took in close to $1 billion worldwide in its first two weeks. The film depicts the tension between respect for law and public institutions, on the one hand, and belief in vigilante virtue, on the other. Half of the vigilante Avengers, led by Iron Man, relinquish their autonomy to the United Nations. They believe that they need regulation and oversight to prevent them from inadvertently killing innocent civilians. The other half of the Avengers, led by Captain America, refuse to give up their freedom to fight crime wherever they please. They will not be constrained and regulated. In the end, Captain America is vindicated, and the United Nations representatives from member nations are shown to be corrupt. Echoing the plots of vigilante films from decades earlier, such as *Death Wish* and *Dirty Harry*, the lone vigilante triumphs over weak, ineffectual, and corrupt government officials.[24]

In recent decades, savvy political figures have tapped into the vigilante ethos in order to appeal to voters who were fed up with the status quo. In 1999, former professional wrestler and Navy SEAL Jesse Ventura, running as an independent, became governor of Minnesota. Like Eastwood, who became mayor of Carmel-by-the-Sea, California, Ventura was a celebrity who first won election for mayor, in Brooklyn Park, Minnesota. In addition to his persona as a tough-guy outsider, Ventura continually invoked his past as a SEAL to demonstrate that he was tough enough to deal with the threats facing Minnesota citizens. He suggested that his military experience made him particularly well suited to serve the state as governor in a time of danger.

In a notorious 2001 exchange with Dennis Anderson, the outdoors columnist for the *Minneapolis Star Tribune*, Ventura articulated the martial vigilante ethos. Ventura bragged about his military exploits in Vietnam and insinuated that naturalists and deer hunters like Anderson lacked courage and manly virtue. The governor boasted to Anderson, "I'll just tell you this: Until you hunted man, you haven't hunted yet. Because you need to hunt something that can shoot back at you to really classify yourself as a hunter. You need to understand the feeling of what it's like to go into the field and know that your opposition can take you out. Not just go out there and shoot Bambi. Or go out into the field and shoot pheasants and things like that."[25] Ventura was not "soft" like Anderson; he was tough enough to stand up to any man.

Ventura played up his tough-guy image. He was known for the outrageous statements he made, and many people understood them as showmanship. But his verbal strutting about "hunting man" linked his experience in wartime to the qualities required of the vigilante hero: the lone armed man in pursuit of dangerous enemies. After his election, fans sported T-shirts featuring a pugilistic Ventura and the words, "My Governor Can Beat Up Your Governor."

In other ways, too, the vigilante has become a very real figure on the American landscape. Today in many states, as a result of "stand-your-ground" laws, anyone who merely fears that another person might harm them can legally use deadly force against that person. In other words, fear is now a legitimate reason to kill another person, whether or not that fear is justified.

How did we get from the mythic gunslinger vigilante outlaw to the law-abiding vigilante citizen? The vigilante's weapon of choice—the gun—provides a starting point. Although the vast majority of gun owners are not vigilantes, Americans have become increasingly invested in their right to own firearms in order to protect themselves. It is not possible to construct a "typical" gun owner using psychological or demographic characteristics; there are many reasons why people purchase firearms. But guns offer more than simple utility to many of their owners. Owning a firearm contributes to the owner's identity and sense of self. The gun offers a feeling of self-mastery and protection against danger.

Whether or not they own guns, a majority of Americans favor having an armed citizenry.[26] This enthusiasm for personal firearms is a fairly recent phenomenon. According to one study, the "gun culture" in America does not date back to the drafting of the Second Amendment; nor is it an intrinsic feature of American national identity tied to the "wild west" and the frontier tradition. Rather, it is largely the result of business practices of the major gun manufacturers and their advertising strategies. First marketed as useful tools throughout most of the nineteenth century, guns were unexceptional commodities with little cultural baggage attached to them. Oliver Winchester, founder of the Winchester Repeating Arms Company, was more capitalist than gun enthusiast.

By the twentieth century, the usefulness of guns had declined, and it was up to companies like Winchester to stimulate demand for them. Winchester's early ads emphasized functionality. But the tone changed early in the 1900s. Gun sales soared, largely as a result of new advertising strategies that transformed the gun from a tool into an object of desire with emotional value. The gun, more than a mere weapon, came to have symbolic value that reflected the character traits of its owner.[27]

A century on, gun manufacturers continue to market their products to appeal to personal identity and self-presentation. A Bushmaster ad that was released in 2010, and that ran for more than two years, reflects the ideal spirit of the gun owner. The ad promised that after purchasing the weapon, the owner deserved to have his "man card" reissued. The ad promoted the Bushmaster Model XM15-E2S .223-caliber semiautomatic rifle. According to the company's 2010 press release, visitors to their website "will have to prove they're a man by answering a series of manhood questions." They included, "Do you eat tofu?" "Can you change a tire?" "Have you ever watched figure skating 'on purpose'?" The man card was valid for one year, unless it was revoked by friends who felt the holder had "betrayed [his] manhood" with "unmanly" traits such as being a "crybaby," a "coward," or a "cupcake." Though surely at least partially tongue-in-cheek, the ad reflected a theme that connected male prowess to guns. Bushmaster removed the ad from its website after Adam Lanza used the weapon advertised to kill twenty children and six adults at Sandy Hook Elementary School in 2012.[28]

In 2016, a reporter for National Public Radio wondered why so many Americans armed themselves. So he set off to interview handgun permit holders at the Texas Firearms Festival in Austin, Texas. He found that carrying a firearm affected how people perceived their environment, especially of how other people looked and acted. Sam Blackburn, a diesel mechanic, wore a National Rifle Association (NRA) cap to the festival and explained how he saw the world. He watched for people who looked like potential criminals, rather than any particular threatening or criminal behavior. "I pay attention to different people, weird people, maybe stereotype people. . . . Gangbanger-looking guys, maybe guys that look like they're up to no good or somebody that may think they're a Muslim extremist or something like that," he said. Doug Miller, owner of a small IT company who taught self-defense classes on the side, said, "It's exciting. I won't lie to you. There's some visceral response that you get from carrying a firearm."[29]

For some gun owners, especially men, owning a gun may offer compensation for perceived blows to their manhood. In 2015, sociologist Jennifer Carlson interviewed sixty male gun owners, most of them white, but including a small number of men of color. She found that gun ownership reflected a desire to reclaim a sense of dignity and security at a time of economic uncertainty. Some gun-owning men who no longer felt confident that they could provide for their families embraced the role of armed protector. The gun was a statement that the man could defend his family, even if he could not provide them with economic security. At a time of extreme income inequality and an unstable employment environment, the opportunity to "renew your man card" through gun ownership may have appealed to those who found the breadwinner role out of reach.[30]

As CITIZENS ASSERTED their rights to purchase and carry guns, measures to regulate and control gun sales and ownership withered. Gun control laws have a long history.[31] In the 1930s, in response to the wave of violence by notorious gangsters such as Al Capone and John Dillinger, President Franklin Roosevelt promoted a "New Deal for Crime," resulting in the nation's first gun control laws: the National Firearms Acts of 1934 and 1938. The first act levied hefty taxes on the manufacture or sale of sawed-off shotguns and machine guns and required the sales to be recorded in a national registry. The second required the licensing of all interstate gun dealers and a record of their sales. It also prohibited the sale of firearms to individuals indicted or convicted of violent crimes. For the next thirty years, gun violence declined, and no new federal laws were passed.

At the beginning of the 1960s, the murder rate in the United States was at its lowest point in the twentieth century. It then began to rise, along with gun violence. In 1966, 60 percent of all murders were committed with firearms, up 17 percent over the previous year. Gun violence rates varied by state and correlated with the presence of gun control laws. In 1967, the murder rate in the state of Washington, which had weak gun control laws, was nearly six times that of New York, a state with strict gun control laws. Southern states were consistently more likely to favor gun rights over gun control.[32]

Law enforcement officials long favored stricter gun laws. In the late 1960s, J. Edgar Hoover, FBI director, commented, "There are licenses for automobiles and dogs. Why not guns?"[33] After the assassinations of President John Kennedy, Robert Kennedy, and Martin Luther King Jr., President Lyndon Johnson called for new gun control laws. Along with the Omnibus Crime Control and Safe Streets Act of 1968, Congress passed a Gun Control Act that prohibited all felons, drug users, and those with mental illness from buying guns. The new law also raised the age for purchasing guns at federally licensed dealers to twenty-one and expanded licensing and recordkeeping regulations. But the disenchantment with law enforcement led to an increase in support for gun rights.

The rise in fear correlated with the decline in support for gun control. In 1959, 60 percent of Americans polled by Gallup believed that there should be a law prohibiting anyone from owning a handgun (with the exception of law enforcement). By 2015, 60 percent of those polled believed there would be fewer victims of gun violence if more law-abiding citizens carried firearms.[34] As with the crime rate, people hold views on gun violence that are at odds with the actual evidence.

Even when the murder rate declined in the 1980s to the lowest level since World War II, fear of crime increased, along with support for gun rights. John Hinckley's attempted assassination of Ronald Reagan in 1981, which wounded the president and three others, and permanently disabled Reagan's press secretary, James Brady, prompted calls for new federal regulations. The enthusiasm for gun control did not last. Subsequent firearm regulations were weak.[35] More than a decade after James Brady was wounded, Congress finally passed the Brady Handgun Violence Prevention Act of 1993. The law required background checks of gun buyers, although those records could not be preserved. The law also exempted private sellers.

Fueling the resistance to strong gun control legislation was the massive power of the gun lobby, particularly the NRA. In 1871, two Union Army veterans, Colonel William C. Church and General George Wingate, disturbed by the poor marksmanship of the troops they commanded during the Civil War, founded the organization. For the next century, the NRA remained an organization mostly for hunters and hobbyists who wished to learn about gun skills and safety. In the 1970s, however, the NRA became primarily political. It established a lobbying arm in 1975, the NRA Institute for Legislative Action (NRA-ILA).[36] Two years later, the NRA-ILA organized a grassroots revolt at an NRA meeting and took over the organization, changing its mission to a single-minded effort to prevent the passage of gun control laws.[37] With gun manufacturers providing significant funding, the NRA grew in numbers and power, tripling its membership in the 1980s and wielding massive influence in Washington. The organization fostered widespread support for the arming of civilians and won major legislative victories. By the turn of the century, public support for the NRA continued to grow, rising from 42 percent in 1995 to 56 percent in 2013.[38] During those same years, support for gun control dropped steadily, from 78 percent to 47 percent.[39] All of the gun laws passed at the federal level in the twenty-first century expanded gun rights rather than gun control.[40]

As IT BECAME easier to acquire firearms, new laws also expanded what gun owners could legally do with their weapons. Until the 1980s, in most states it was illegal to carry a concealed weapon in public except under special circumstances. That changed in the 1980s. Between 1987 and 2008, forty states passed laws allowing citizens to carry concealed weapons. Gun rights activists played on public fears. Bumper stickers stating "You can't rape a .38" encouraged women to arm themselves for protection.

Gun rights organizations began to appear on college campuses. Within a year after a mass shooting at Virginia Tech University in 2007, the newly formed Students for Concealed Carry claimed to have 30,000 members across the country.[41] In 2010, pro-gun groups made headlines by carrying firearms openly, showing off their guns on their hips in public places like Starbucks, a strategy they hoped would intimidate the public into supporting concealed weapons laws.[42]

Between 2007 and 2016, in spite of the continued dramatic decline in the rate of both violent and property crimes, the number of Americans with permits to carry concealed weapons more than tripled, to nearly 13 million people. That estimate is low, because not every state reported these statistics. Even people who did not have permits and did not carry firearms supported conceal and carry laws. In a 2015 Gallup poll, 56 percent of respondents said they'd feel safer if more Americans could get permits to carry concealed handguns.[43]

In states with conceal and carry laws, establishments that did not want guns on their premises were required to post notices on their entrances stating that firearms were banned. In 2014, Pete Matsko, a Clemson, South Carolina, restaurant owner (and owner of two handguns himself), posted such a sign in his eatery. His sign read, "If you are such a loser that you feel a need to carry a gun with you when you go out, I do not want your business," followed by a derogatory term that the newspaper did not print. Soon he was besieged with harassing phone calls and threats, prompting him to change his number and to ask the police to open his mail, in case it contained dangerous substances or devices. His website ratings plummeted and his business suffered. Other business owners faced a dilemma: whether to cater to those who supported gun rights or those who favored gun control. Sean Brock, another restaurant owner, kept a handgun beside his bed at night, but he did not want guns in his restaurant. He recognized that the stakes were high. Regardless of the quality of the food or service, he felt that his success depended on whether he would allow patrons to bring guns into his restaurant.[44]

Concealed carry laws do not contribute to public safety, according to the best available data. The Violence Policy Center reports that, between 2007 and 2015, there were at least 763 fatalities that resulted from 579 concealed carry shootings—the shooters were legally licensed to carry concealed weapons. In the vast majority of these cases, the shooters killed themselves or they killed someone else who was not a threat—they did not kill perpetrators of crimes. Only twenty-one concealed carry shootings were eventually ruled as lawful self-defense—less than 5 percent. And these statistics were gathered in only thirty-eight states and the District of Columbia; complete national statistics are not available, because Congress, responding to pressure from the gun lobby, opposed research and data collection on the effects of guns on public health.[45]

Concealed carry laws represented a step toward legalizing vigilante violence. The next step came with the stand-your-ground laws. These statutes are also known as "make-my-day" laws, in homage to the taunt Clint Eastwood's *Dirty Harry* character would offer before killing villains in the 1983 film *Sudden Impact*. The laws gave individuals the right to use deadly force against anyone who they believed might cause them physical harm, whether or not that person was armed, and whether or not that person actually intended harm.

Florida enacted the first such law in 2005. Backed by hard lobbying by the NRA, the bill in Florida passed the state legislature with a near-unanimous vote (94 to 20 in the House, 39 to 0 in the Senate). The bill's Republican sponsor, Representative Dennis K. Baxley of Ocala, said it would curb violent crime and make citizens feel safer, adding, "People want to know we stand on the side of victims of crime instead of the side of criminals." Governor Jeb Bush applauded the move, saying that in the face of a threat, "to have to retreat and put yourself in a very precarious position defies common sense."[46]

Miami's chief of police, however, opposed the bill and called it unnecessary and dangerous. He said that many innocent people, including children, could be harmed under the law, because it gave "total immunity" to any gun owner, including road-rage drivers and drunken sports fans. "Whether it's trick-or-treaters or kids playing in the yard of someone who doesn't want them there or some drunk guy stumbling into the wrong house," he said, "you're encouraging people to possibly use deadly physical force where it shouldn't be used."[47] Nevertheless, by 2015, thirty-three states had some form of stand-your-ground law. With these laws, vigilantes officially shed their outlaw status and became law-abiding citizens.

The spirit behind the Florida law found expression in a confrontation one evening in February 2012. A seventeen-year-old African American boy, Trayvon Martin, was walking to his father's fiancée's house in a gated community in Sanford, Florida, when he noticed he was being followed. He phoned a friend to say that he was afraid he was going to be attacked. Under Florida law, the teen could have turned and used deadly force against the person who he feared might cause him harm, with no legal consequences. His act of violence would have been legal under Florida's stand-your-ground law. Trayvon

Martin was not armed, however, and shortly after telling his friend he was afraid, he was dead.

The man following him was George Zimmerman, a white volunteer neighborhood-watch guard. In this case, the self-appointed guard did not work in cooperation with law enforcement; instead, he defied the police. He had called the police from his SUV to report a "suspicious person." They "always get away," he said, referring to the black youth. The police dispatcher told Zimmerman not to follow the boy. But Zimmerman, ignoring the police, got out of his SUV and followed Trayvon on foot. An altercation occurred, and Zimmerman shot the boy dead. At the trial, Zimmerman claimed self-defense, and the jury of six women—none of them African American—acquitted him.

As with so many fictional and real examples of vigilante violence, from our own era and this country's past, race was at the center of the Trayvon Martin case. After the verdict, President Barack Obama said, "Trayvon Martin could have been me 35 years ago. . . . I think it's important to recognize that the African American community is looking at this issue through a set of experiences and a history that doesn't go away."[48] Indeed, public opinion about the case split along racial lines. According to a poll by the Pew Research Center, 86 percent of African Americans were dissatisfied with the verdict, compared to just 30 percent of whites.[49]

As many pundits argued, it is highly unlikely that Zimmerman would have called the police about a "suspicious person" if he had seen a white teenager walking down the street that night. There was speculation that if Zimmerman had been black and Martin white, the black killer would have been convicted of murder and sent to prison.[50] Regardless, like Bernhard Goetz before him, Zimmerman became famous for his murderous act. Those who did not revile him admired him.[51]

Two years after Trayvon Martin's death at the hands of a self-styled vigilante, Curtis Reeves, a retired Tampa police captain, shot and killed Chad Oulson in a movie theater for texting during the film previews. The victim, apparently irked by the demand that he stop texting, had tossed popcorn at the armed man and paid with his life. The killer's attorney invoked Florida's stand-your-ground law in his defense, claiming that he feared that his life was in danger from the unarmed popcorn thrower. After three years of investigation, reviews of theater videos, and testimony of witnesses, Circuit Court Judge Susan Barthle dismissed the claim of self-defense under the stand-your-ground law. Nevertheless, the invocation of the law in a case of wanton violence indicates the extent to which the law has saturated the criminal justice system. Reeves pleaded not guilty to charges of second-degree murder and aggravated battery, and he was awaiting trial as of this writing in May 2017.[52] The Florida legislature passed Senate Bill 128 in May 2017 as well, which strengthened Florida's stand-your-ground law by shifting the burden of proof from the defendant to the prosecutor, and thus making it easier for defendants to claim self-defense on the basis of fear rather than on the basis of any real threat.[53]

Stand-your-ground laws have allowed many vigilante killers to argue that they are law-abiding citizens, especially if the killers are white and the victims are black. By 2015, in states with stand-your-ground laws, "justifiable homicides" had increased 85 percent. The shooting of a black person by a white person was deemed "justifiable" 17 percent of the time, while the shooting of a white person by an African American was found justifiable in only 1 percent of such cases. A 2012 study showed that in the vast majority of stand-your-ground cases in Florida, the victim was unarmed and the perpetrator had a gun.[54]

As laws changed to allow easier access to gun ownership and more lawful ways to commit violence with firearms, the numbers and profile of gun owners also changed. Most Americans do not own guns, and the percentage of Americans owning guns has steadily declined. In the 1970s, nearly half of all households had a gun. By 2014, only one-third did. One reason for the decline is that there were fewer hunters. As interest in hunting and other gun sports declined, so did gun ownership. But the number of guns in the country increased even as the number of individual gun owners declined.

In the early twenty-first century, there were 300 million civilian firearms in the United States—an all-time high of approximately one per capita. Per capita gun ownership in the United States is now far above that of all other nations, including those often described as lawless, such as Iraq, Mexico, and Colombia. The United States has 4.4 percent of the world's population, but more than 40 percent of its civilian-owned guns.[55]

So who owns all these guns? Men have remained more likely than women to own a gun, although that gap has shrunk. Fewer men now own guns, down from 50 percent in 1980 to 35 percent in 2014. The number of female gun owners has held steady, at 12 percent. Gun owners are more likely to be older than non-gun owners, and that gap has increased over time. Republicans are twice as likely as Democrats to own guns, and higher-income Americans are much more likely to own guns than those with lower incomes. Whites are twice as likely to own guns as African Americans and Hispanics, with 40 percent of white households owning guns, compared to fewer than 20 percent of African Americans and Hispanics. Still, African Americans are much more likely to be victims of gun violence than white Americans, which explains why they are, overall, much more supportive of gun control measures.[56]

Public opinion polls suggest a correlation among exaggerated fears, erroneous beliefs about violent crime, declining faith in government, and support for concealed carry and stand-your-ground laws. In 2004 and 2005, 65 percent of those polled said they would feel less safe in a public place knowing that concealed guns were allowed. But ten years later, a majority of those polled said that the nation would be safer if more people carried concealed weapons—a tacit endorsement of civilian use of violence for the protection of the public. During those same ten years, trust in government dropped from 39 percent to 19 percent. Although the rate of violent crime continued to decline, the majority of Americans believed that violent gun crimes had increased.[57] In 2014, for the first time in more than twenty years, more Americans favored gun rights than gun control.[58]

Do all the guns amassed in private hands, and the triumph of gun rights over gun control, actually improve public safety? The evidence suggests they do not. In spite of the declining rate of violent crime in the United States since the 1990s, it has remained high compared to that of other countries. At the end of the twentieth century, London and New York City had about the same number of robberies and burglaries each year, but for every victim killed by a robber or burglar in London, fifty-four victims died in New York. Harvard researchers collected data from twenty-six developed countries showing that where there are more guns, there are more murders. The US gun homicide rate is twenty-five times higher than that of the other advanced nations. Other developed countries with much lower rates of gun ownership and gun violence also have much stronger gun control laws. Within the United States, as we've seen, states with more guns have more gun deaths, and states with tighter gun control laws have fewer guns and gun deaths. More guns do not deter crime; clearly, they lead to more violence, or at least more lethal violence.[59]

Easier access to guns not only leads to more murders, but also dramatically increases the suicide rate. In fact, most gun deaths are suicides, and the numbers have increased. In 1999, for example, there were approximately 16,000 firearm suicides, compared to 11,000 gun murders. By 2013, those numbers had increased to 21,000 gun suicides and 12,500 gun murders. In 2015, about two-thirds of all gun deaths were suicides. Suicide attempts are much more successful with guns; fully 96.5 percent of people who shoot themselves die as a result, compared to fewer than 10 percent who attempt suicide by other means.[60]

Mass shootings are another example of how more guns do not make us safer. Defined as at least 4 people killed or injured by firearms in a single incident, mass shootings happen literally every day in America. In the single year of 2015, there were 372 mass shootings in the United States, more than one per day, resulting in 475 killed and 1,870 wounded.[61] Although large mass shootings attract substantial media coverage, only a small fraction of the total of firearm deaths result from horrific massacres. The statistics, and the possible comparison, are staggering. Between 1968 and 2015, more Americans within the nation's borders died from guns than on the battlefields of all the wars in American history. Murder and suicide by guns have taken more American lives every six months than all the terrorist attacks and the wars in Afghanistan and Iraq combined. In 2013 alone, guns killed more than 32,000 people within the United States.

The transformation of the vigilante outlaw into the upstanding, law-abiding citizen took place in conjunction with successful efforts by hate groups to achieve a measure of legitimacy. The Ku Klux Klan offers a case in point. In 2014, in the space of two months, Fairview Township in Pennsylvania experienced more than nine break-ins to vehicles and one attempted home burglary. This alleged crime wave prompted a Pennsylvania chapter of the KKK to establish a neighborhood watch in the town. Imperial Wizard Frank Ancona said that people in the town asked the Klan to address the crime problem, which they felt the police were not controlling properly. "It's just like any neighborhood watch program. It's not targeting any specific ethnicity. We would report anything we see to law enforcement," Ancona explained. "We don't hate people. We are an organization who looks out for our race. We believe in racial separation. God created each species after its kind and saw that it was good."

To promote their new initiative, Klan members distributed fliers in the town, assuring residents that they could sleep soundly knowing that the KKK was wide awake. Pennsylvania was among the states with a stand-your-ground law. A 2012 study by the Urban Institute, according to a summary by *Frontline*, found that "in non–Stand Your Ground states, whites are 250 percent more likely to be found justified in killing a black person than a white person who kills another white person; in Stand Your Ground states, that number jumps to 354 percent."[62]

With the Ku Klux Klan serving as neighborhood watch security guards, claiming legitimacy in the name of racial segregation, the meaning of vigilante virtue had come full circle. From the days of hooded outlaws lynching innocent black people to the twenty-first-century killings perpetrated under stand-your-ground laws, vigilantism has moved from lawless terrorism to lawful self-protection. Fear now provides a legitimate rationale for murder, whether or not there is any real threat. The legal use of lethal force in response to fear marks not only the acceptance of vigilante violence but also the acceptance of fear as a rational state of mind in almost any situation. From the Cold War onward, fear and its consequences have become commonplace.

Chapter 4

WOMEN: VICTIMS OR VILLAINS?

If babies had guns they wouldn't be aborted.

—*Campaign bumper sticker,*
Representative Steve Stockman (R-TX), 2013[1]

Representative Steve Stockman's incendiary 2013 bumper sticker was a bold statement intended to convey his support for gun rights, opposition to abortion, and pointed condemnation of feminism, a message that resonated with many of his constituents. Essentially, according to Stockman, women who aborted their fetuses deserved to be shot, because their "babies" were unable to protect themselves against their murderous mothers. The campaign slogan presented a grotesque but telling variation on the theme of vigilante violence. In this macabre scenario, the normally helpless infant is the vigilante, and the normally protective mother is the villain.

The strangely murderous "pro-life" message of Steve Stockman's bumper sticker reflects an extreme example of the backlash against feminism and the demonization of women who reject traditional gender roles. It also pointed to a change in the status of the fetus. Over the course of the twentieth century, the unborn gradually became defined legally as persons with their own rights, separate and sometimes in conflict with the rights of their mothers. In some jurisdictions, fetal personhood turned embryos into potential victims of crimes allegedly committed against them by their mothers and by abortion providers.[2]

Stockman's absurd slogan had a strange resonance with vigilante violence, but here, it was vigilante violence carried out in the name of protecting fetuses. If embryos could not protect themselves, somebody else had to. This allegedly "pro-life" message encouraged a wave of violence committed against abortion providers. Ever since the Supreme Court legalized abortion in the 1973 *Roe v. Wade* decision, abortion providers and clinics have been the targets of violence, with more than three hundred incidents, including arson, bombings, acid attacks, and murder, from 1973 to 2015. Between 1993 and 2015, eleven abortion providers were killed by antiabortion vigilantes.[3]

Organized vigilante violence in the name of protecting vulnerable "babies" symbolized a stark development in security culture. The womb, once the very symbol of security, was transformed from a place of safety, protection, and nurture to a site of vulnerability and danger. If the womb was not safe, no place was safe.

According to this fearful state of mind, in the years since World War II, safe spaces seemed to shrink until there were none left. Infiltration by communists and the threat of atomic attack, and then the possibility of criminal assault, all loomed large in the public imagination. The private single-family home could no longer keep its inhabitants safe. Sanctuaries of safety—public streets and spaces, neighborhoods and houses, nuclear families, and now even the womb—became sites of potential danger.

Abortion is an aspect of security culture that at first may appear to be distinct from fears of communist subversion, atomic attack, urban unrest, and physical assault by strangers. For instance, abortion may seem far afield from the fear of weapons of mass destruction, of strangers in public places, and of lack of faith in police and official institutions. But, in fact, when it comes to abortion and other "women's issues," we see not only the same dynamic at work—that is, the dynamic of exaggerated fears ultimately working against public safety—but also how anxiety both fueled and shaped fear of crime, physical assault, the breakdown of the nuclear family, and the ineffectiveness of government. And, in particular, this anxiety was over the vulnerability of women and children, as well as about potentially dangerous women and children.

As women gained rights, confidence, and empowerment, a backlash emerged that coalesced around three broad and intertwined narratives. One focused on women as dangerous—an idea that developed in the antiabortion movement. Another portrayed women themselves as vulnerable, especially as they left the home to enter jobs and public life. The third emerged around children, who, according to pundits, officials, and the media, were becoming much more vulnerable to harm as a result of neglect by mothers who abandoned their caretaking role. The common denominator in all of these narratives of danger was that women who resisted or abandoned their prescribed maternal role posed risks to themselves and their children.

Women responded to these narratives in various ways. At the same time that they asserted themselves as active participants in the world of work and public life, they also sought ways to protect themselves and their children from perceived dangers. Whether they carried weapons for self-defense, attended martial-arts classes, avoided going out alone at night, or hovered over their children to keep them safe, women heeded the warnings that they, and their children, were at risk.

The most extreme example of women as dangerous to their children came in the figure of the murderous pregnant mother. Considered vulnerable to their mothers' neglect or abuse from the moment of their conception, the unborn were unable to defend themselves, as Representative Stockman made graphically clear. The idea that the innocent fetus needed protection against the murderous mother began as early as the 1960s, but gained steam after the *Roe v. Wade* decision.[4]

This view of abortion, and the notion that fetuses were people under the law, was new. Throughout much of the nineteenth century, abortion was considered a form of birth control. Common understandings of the developing embryo marked the "beginning of life" at the time of "quickening," when a woman could feel the fetus move, usually around the fourth month of pregnancy. Abortion was not made illegal until the late nineteenth century, when physicians, who were almost all men, sought to take control of pregnancy and childbirth from midwives, who were almost all women. But well into the twentieth century, abortion laws were rarely enforced. The medical profession turned to enforcement in the middle decades of the twentieth century, making it increasingly difficult for women to obtain safe abortions.[5] In response, women began to demand safe, legal abortions, resulting, eventually, in the landmark *Roe v. Wade* decision.

Roe v. Wade enraged many who opposed abortion, giving rise to a powerful antiabortion movement that labeled women who sought abortions, as well as abortion providers, as "baby killers." Legal and medical journals put a professional veneer on these claims, running articles with titles such as "Fetal Versus Maternal Rights: Medical and Legal Perspectives," "Mother Versus Her Unborn Child," and "Keeping Baby Safe from Mom." The new medical specialty of fetology, along with new "fetal protection policies" in the workplace, court-ordered medical interventions, and the prosecution of women for crimes of fetal abuse, reinforced the notion that the mother and the fetus were two distinct individuals whose best interests were sometimes at odds.[6]

Although the majority of Americans have consistently supported abortion rights since the *Roe v. Wade* decision, the antiabortion movement has achieved many legal successes. States passed hundreds of laws restricting abortion in the years following the decision.[7] In addition, the criminalization of women for alleged crimes against their fetuses intensified. In cases when pregnant women refused recommended medical interventions, such as cesarean sections, hospital detentions, or intrauterine transfusions, courts often overrode the woman's preferences and forced her to undergo the unwanted procedure. Overall, the new laws took a particularly heavy toll on women of color, poor women, and immigrants. One 1987 study found that the vast majority of women subject to court-ordered medical interventions were members of racial minorities, and one-fourth were not native speakers of English.[8]

Mother-blaming took on an explicitly racialized cast in the alleged epidemic of "crack babies" in the 1980s. A flawed research study that was given undue emphasis on the major news networks falsely claimed that crack use during pregnancy resulted in a 500 percent increase in damaged babies. The study was based on just twenty-three infants whose symptoms were typical of premature babies, not particular to babies of mothers who used crack. As with sensationalized coverage of violent crimes, media reports spread misleading information and generated a false panic. In fact, even the author of the inaccurate study acknowledged that there was no epidemic of "crack babies." Alcohol abuse during pregnancy was a much more serious problem.[9]

Moreover, contrary to widespread myths, pregnant black women were not more likely to use illegal drugs than pregnant white women. A 1990 study published in the *New England Journal of Medicine* found that 15 percent of white women and 14 percent of black women used illegal drugs during pregnancy. But medical authorities reported ten times more African American women than white women to law enforcement officials for use of illegal substances during pregnancy. As a result, black mothers were arrested much more frequently on drug charges. The mainstream media continued to focus on black women. A 1991 cover story in *Time* magazine, for example, entitled "Crack Kids," focused exclusively on African American babies.[10]

The criminalization of pregnant women continued throughout the 1990s and into the twenty-first century as the war against drugs fueled increasing arrests and mass incarceration. Although the alleged epidemic of crack babies was exposed as false, the myth continued to shape and reflect public opinion and find its way into law. In 2014, Tennessee became the first state to authorize prosecutors to file assault charges against women whose fetuses or newborns were deemed to have been harmed by illegal drugs. These charges carried penalties of up to fifteen years in prison. The affected families had already suffered the effects of poverty, lack of available drug treatment, and meager Medicaid assistance as a result of state policies. The new law only increased the harm that women, children, and their families suffered from public policy.[11]

Mother-blaming, of course, was not new; nor did it end with a child's birth. Long before the modern feminist movement began, popular culture reflected prevailing ideas about the bad mother, especially the woman who refused to conform to the expected role of the submissive wife. Beginning in the 1950s, medical professionals and pundits expressed warnings about women who deviated from the proper role of wife and mother, implying that they put children at risk.[12]

An iconic film from 1955 illustrates this theme. *Rebel Without a Cause* is best remembered as a film about juvenile delinquents, troubled white middle-class youths rebelling against authority and committing crimes. But the film is actually a portrayal of the harms of bad parenting. The parents of the main character, Jim Stark, played by James Dean, violate expected gender roles, leading to confusion and lack of a male role model for Jim. His mother "wears the pants" in the family. She bosses her husband around, and the father—wearing an apron to do "women's work" in the kitchen—cannot stand up to her. Jim begs his father to "be a man," but he wilts in the face of his wife's tyranny. Natalie Wood plays Jim's romantic interest, Judy, whose hard-hearted father refuses to show her any affection. Sal Mineo's character, Plato, is a lonely boy whose wealthy parents are always traveling, leaving him with a good-hearted black maid who tries her best but cannot replace his mother. The film is not really about "rebels" against authority. The children want loving parents who behave according to proper gender roles: strong fathers and submissive mothers. Bad parenting, not youthful rebellion, leads to tragedy in the end.

Jim Stark's fictional, domineering mother was one stereotype of the dangerous woman; the neglectful working woman was another. Beginning in the 1960s, increasing numbers of women challenged and rejected the rigid domestic roles they were expected to fulfill. As more and more

In *Rebel Without a Cause*, the young "rebel" (James Dean) is confused and gets into trouble because his mother is too dominant and his father is too weak and feminized, as in this still where the father wears an apron and does "women's work" in the kitchen.

Source: Margaret Herrick Library, Academy of Motion Picture Arts and Sciences.

mothers of young children began entering the workforce, either by choice or by necessity, they came under fire for leaving their children unsupervised, or in the care of allegedly incompetent or even criminal caretakers. Women who held jobs outside the home faced guilt-inducing messages that they were neglecting their primary responsibility of caring for their children.

Increasingly, as fears of subversion, crime, and the breakdown of the family rose, news reports and articles geared to women asserted that children left unsupervised at home or in the care of others faced a number of possible fates, including physical and psychological harm or the development of criminal tendencies that rendered them dangerous to others. As more women entered the paid labor force, accusations of harm and neglect fell heavily on working mothers.[13]

These were largely postwar developments. Women's labor force participation increased throughout the twentieth century, accelerating in the postwar era. In 1900, only 19 percent of women held paid jobs outside the home, whereas in 1999, 60 percent did. Most of the increase came in the last third of the century, especially for married women with children. Until the 1930s, most wage-earning women were unmarried. Over the ensuing decades, more married women entered the workforce. By 1960, one-third of all married women with children under the age of six worked at paid jobs outside the home, and this proportion doubled over the next forty years: by 2000, two-thirds of all married women with children in this age group were in the workforce.

The feminist movement successfully expanded employment opportunities for women; it was less successful, however, in convincing federal, state, and local governments to help create family-friendly workplaces. Women's lives changed, but the structure of the paid labor force barely changed at all. Women had to adapt to the routine of work, but the workplace did not adapt to accommodate women's childbearing and family responsibilities. In the later decades of the twentieth century, most families could not survive on the wages of one earner, which prompted many women with children to take jobs. Whether or not they enjoyed their work, women often felt both anxious and guilty if they left their children in the care of others.

Married women still performed most of the household work, even if they held full-time jobs. This "double duty" was particularly stressful for mothers. In addition to the struggles of juggling work and family life, women generally earned less than men who held comparable jobs, and they faced greater economic and job insecurity.[14] These stresses made it particularly difficult for mothers—especially those with limited financial resources—to take care of their own children or pay others to care for them.

Rather than generating sympathy for struggling mothers, the great shift in women's workforce participation unleashed a flurry of warnings that mothers who left their children in the care of others put them in harm's way. Even the tolerant and liberal Dr. Benjamin Spock, the most widely read childcare expert, made it clear in the 1973 edition of his guidebook that if at all possible, mothers should stay home with their children: "Some mothers have to work to make a living. Usually their children turn out all right. . . . [B]ut . . . it doesn't make sense to let mothers go to work making dresses in a factory or tapping typewriters in an office, and have them pay other people to do a poorer job of bringing up their children." Fathers were, at best, helpers: "A man can be a warm father and a real man at the same time. . . . [O]f course, I don't mean that the father has to give just as many bottles or change just as many diapers as the mother. But it's fine for him to do these things occasionally. He might make the formula on Sunday."[15]

Dr. Spock was a more gentle critic than others: some warned that the mother who went to work instead of staying home with her children might indirectly cause crime because of the lawless acts of her neglected children. By allegedly endangering their children, women also allegedly endangered society. Women's increased participation in the paid labor force coincided with rising and exaggerated fears of crime, especially by youths. Pundits and professionals often implicated mothers if their children became criminals. Even the notorious murderer Charles Manson, who masterminded a horrific killing spree in Hollywood in 1969, deflected responsibility from himself to the parents of his young female followers. As he told the California court at his sentencing in 1970: "These children that came at you with knives, they are your children. You taught them. I didn't teach them. . . . It is not my responsibility. It is your responsibility. It is the responsibility you have toward your own children who you are neglecting, and then you want to put the blame on me again and again and again. . . . You make your children what they are. I am just a reflection of every one of you."[16]

Manson was hardly a credible commentator. For many, the mass murderer with hippie looks and young female disciples symbolized everything that was wrong with the counterculture. But some echoed Manson, casting blame on an entire cohort. In 1981, the Los Angeles police chief, Daryl Gates, remarked, "We've lost a whole generation. Totally lost. No self discipline. Total indulgence. Drugs. Lack of respect for the law. Lack of respect for values. A whole generation thumbed its nose at everything that was held sacred in this country. America has to take a look at its heart and soul."[17]

If an entire generation was lost, as Gates asserted, mothers were to blame. A 1981 article in *Time* magazine reporting on the increase in crime in the suburbs blamed parents for not adequately protecting their homes, and also for turning their children into criminals: "As more and more husbands and wives hold down jobs, their unoccupied homes make tempting daytime targets for burglars. . . . The thieves are often the unattended sons of working couples who, say police, steal to keep up with the rising cost of marijuana." In this scenario, working parents were potential victims of burglaries, and at the same time indirect facilitators of crime, because they had abandoned their domestic responsibilities. If they were victimized, it was their own fault, just as it was their fault if their children turned to drugs and became petty thieves. Although both fathers and mothers were implicated in the article, *Time* did not suggest that the men should be the ones to give up their jobs and tend to their homes and children. The clear implication was that the women should.[18]

Home security manuals from this period warned that the dangerous criminal stalking your street might be your neighbor's child. Keep windows secure, wrote Thomas Dale Cowan, in a 1982 *Popular Mechanics* guide, because children can climb through small openings and burglarize your home. Be aware, cautioned another, of the parents in the neighborhood who resist crime-fighting initiatives. They might be trying to protect their own children from being caught red-handed.[19]

In addition to potentially turning their children into criminals by venturing into the workforce, mothers allegedly increased the possibility of becoming crime victims simply by leaving their homes. Authorities blamed women for creating criminals, and then warned them that dangerous youths were roaming the city streets, looking for opportunities to attack them.

In fact, women were more likely to be assaulted by someone they knew than by strangers. They were not necessarily safe in their homes, where considerable violence against women occurred.[20] In the 1970s, feminists began to call attention to the issue of widespread domestic violence, which had long been hidden from public view. Feminist activists launched initiatives such as Take Back the Night marches and rallies to call attention to sexual violence and domestic abuse. Those efforts eventually helped to achieve the passage of the 1994 Violence Against Women Act (VAWA), which improved the criminal justice system's response to domestic violence and rape.

Nevertheless, the media continued to focus on assaults on women by strangers in public places, although those crimes were extremely rare. Not surprisingly, by the 1980s public opinion polls showed that women were more likely than men to fear becoming victims of crime, even though they were least likely to actually be victimized.[21]

Men were consistently more likely than women to be victims of violent crime, especially by strangers. Women's chances of becoming victims at home, however, were another story. In 1985, the American Bar Association reported that on average one woman was assaulted by her male partner in the United States every eighteen seconds. Those attacks accounted for 20 percent of all emergency calls to police and 40 percent of serious injuries treated in hospital emergency rooms. The report noted, "More women are injured by their husbands than by muggings, automobile accidents and rapes combined."[22] Throughout the late twentieth century, fewer than one-third of female victims were assaulted by strangers, compared to nearly half of male victims of violence. For both men and women, most violent crimes occurred between people who knew each other.[23]

In striking contrast to the reality, women were presumed to be more vulnerable to assault by strangers and more in need of self-protection than men. This complex story involves a number of interwoven developments, including exaggerated fears of crime, the liberalization of weapons laws, and feminist self-empowerment. In the 1970s and 1980s, feminists achieved a number of major successes: access to professional schools and previously male-dominated occupations; reproductive rights, including the right to safe and legal abortion; and the identification of domestic violence and rape as violent crimes, a category that was previously underreported and protected by both personal and official silence. Feminist activism called attention to the common practices of shaming and blaming that prevented many victims from filing charges against their attackers, most of whom were known to them.

One response to feminist efforts to expose domestic violence and highlight rape as a violent crime was the rise of a cottage industry selling self-defense methods for women. Books, articles, manuals, and self-defense classes advising women to be wary began to appear in the 1960s. Guidebooks with titles such as *Self Defense for Women: A Simple Method* offered suggestions for protection against "the types of attacks which are commonly made against women," even though such attacks were not "common." The authors explained why women needed self-defense training: "Most women will do almost anything rather than engage in a physical fight with a man . . . [because] the concept of fighting is so tied with the concept of masculinity." Women needed to resist the idea that fighting "is not feminine."[24]

Although men were three times as likely as women to be assaulted by a stranger, and most acts of violence against women were committed by men they knew, the authors nevertheless geared their defense strategies toward women's vulnerability to attacks by strangers out in public. They suggested walking near curbs rather than buildings, carrying a whistle, and avoiding driving "in a place and time in which there could be danger. Keep windows closed and doors locked—do not park in the dark."[25]

The drumbeat continued into the 1970s. In 1972, *Good Housekeeping* warned, "Women, either on the street or in their cars, are often subject to criminal attacks." In other words, the magazine, like the *Self Defense for Women* guidebook, vastly distorted the likelihood of attacks on women. The article offered twenty-one tips for women on how to protect themselves, including "Dress with discretion so as not to stimulate interest," and "*Always* check the back of the car for intruders."[26]

Warnings that danger lurked on every street corner prompted many nervous women to arm themselves. Liberalized weapons laws made it easy and inexpensive to carry tear gas, which had originally been developed for use by the military and police.[27] In California, applications for licenses and sales of tear gas increased dramatically in the 1970s. Milo Speriglio, head of the Nick Harris Detective Academy in Los Angeles, reported in 1981 that the Academy received 3,000 inquiries a day from people seeking advice on self-protection. The California Tear Gas School taught a course in the use of tear gas at a makeshift practice range at a Holiday Inn in Santa Monica. In one session, after spraying one of the silhouetted targets, one woman said, "Killed that sucker flat," according to a *Newsweek* reporter. Another exclaimed, "Got him." Upon completing the class participants received permits to carry and use tear gas for self-defense. As they left the session, most were armed with tear gas canisters. One woman remarked, "I feel better already."[28]

By then, mace had long been another option. Physicist Alan Litman had developed chemical mace in 1962, describing it as a weapon specifically for women to use for their own protection. He claimed that mace would not cause permanent injury, although physicians said it could cause burns and eye damage. Police officials in San Francisco, Ann Arbor, Michigan, and Madison, Wisconsin, banned the use of mace, but it remained popular. In 1968, a sociologist asked a class of one hundred students at the University of Texas at Austin if any of them carried a chemical weapon such as mace. More than half the women in the class raised their hands.[29]

As the feminist movement gained momentum, women resisted the idea that they were weak and dependent and in need of male protection. If the world was as dangerous for women as the media suggested (which it was not), they would learn how to protect themselves. Women began to develop their own versions of do-it-yourself defense. Feminist historian Roxanne Dunbar-Ortiz recalled, "We decided to make self-defense a priority for organizing, because it seemed really important in Boston. . . . And the headlines were 'More Slain Girls' in the newspapers, on all the newsstands. So we started street patrols for the factories down by the river, where women were constantly being mugged, assaulted and raped. We formed a whole project around rape."[30]

In 1973, a group of Boston-area women concerned about violence against women distributed an "Information Sheet for Members of the Press" about "Self-Defense for Women." The statement read, "It's time to fight back! Women have a right to self-defense. We refuse to become prisoners in our own homes, or to go out only during daylight. We refuse to succumb to the violence perpetrated against us, by 'friends' and strangers, in our homes, on the streets, at our jobs. Women must defend ourselves and each other. Only when we make it dangerous for men to attack women, will the violence end."[31] Feminist self-defense classes appeared throughout the country in the 1970s and 1980s, with varying formats and fees.

Feminist efforts to empower women through building physical strength and confidence unintentionally helped to expand the market for self-defense advice books that exaggerated women's vulnerability and heightened women's fears of strangers. For example, in 1979, the first woman to teach physical education at the US Military Academy wrote a book for civilian women titled *Self-Defense for Women: The West Point Way*. The author warned that women should "read and learn the techniques presented in the book's fifteen chapters. Your life may depend on it!" The author described rare and heinous crimes as if they happened every day; she offered a "stark reminder that survival in the urban jungles of today's society is becoming an around-the-clock aspect of life for women of all ages. No woman is immune from the actions of the criminal elements of society. . . . [E]very woman is forced to assume a greater degree of responsibility for her own safety." The frequent use of the term "urban jungle" carried not-so-subtle racial connotations. "Don't delay! The urban jungle is becoming more dangerous *everyday*!"[32]

Horrific crimes gained huge coverage in the media, prompting women to change their behavior in order to avoid attack. The case of the "Hillside Strangler" in the late 1970s demonstrates the widespread panic that massive coverage of violent crime could generate. Ten young women were murdered over the course of four months; the perpetrators turned out to be two men who were cousins. A year after the murders, *Newsweek* observed that in the wake of the Hillside Strangler murders, fearful Los Angeles women flocked to self-defense classes and rushed to purchase weapons.[33]

By the 1980s, many people accepted the assertion that women were particularly vulnerable in public, and women embraced a variety of self-defense strategies. One study reported that 54 percent of women made sure they had a companion with them when going out at night, compared to 15 percent of men. By 1988, two-thirds of women polled said they had become "especially alert and cautious" in order to avoid becoming victims of crime. A study by two sociologists compared what they defined as "feminist" approaches to self-defense to "traditional" approaches. Traditional approaches, they argued, involved limiting mobility and relying on male protection, large dogs, and devices such as chemical sprays and whistles. Feminists, by contrast, promoted both psychological and physical defense strategies—"practical, self-defense skills, sometimes called 'street fighting' techniques"—to provide self-protection and independence. Reflecting the women's empowerment movement, which stressed autonomy, the authors encouraged women "to learn dirty street fighting, to kick and yell and gouge."[34]

Even recreational activities that promoted women's health, fitness, independence, and enjoyment became fraught with danger, according to exaggerated media reports. *U.S. News and World Report* asserted, in 1980, that "women who enjoy such outdoor activities as jogging or hiking should be aware of a chilling fact. . . . Female sports enthusiasts are being assaulted, raped and even murdered with growing frequency in some parts of the country." The article suggested taking along a dog, a can of tear gas, a whistle, or a stick, or mastering some form of self-defense. "Above all, say experts, never go to isolated locations alone or in small groups, especially at night, no matter how tempting the solitude seems."[35]

On April 19, 1989, when a female jogger was actually attacked and raped in New York City's Central Park—a very rare occurrence—it seemed to confirm everything people believed about the vulnerability of women, especially women out at night in urban areas heavily populated by minorities. In an effort to respond to the immense public pressure to find and arrest the perpetrators, five innocent minority youths were quickly rounded up. They were intimidated by police interrogators into making confessions, wrongfully convicted of the crime, and sentenced to long imprisonments. On May 1, Donald Trump spent $85,000 on full-page ads in New York City's four daily papers calling for the execution of the young men. Decades later, as the result of DNA tests and the detailed confession of the actual perpetrator, the men were exonerated and released. But in October 2016, shortly before his election to the presidency, Donald Trump continued to insist that the falsely accused young men were guilty of the crime.[36]

As we've seen, the 1990s witnessed a dramatic decline in violent crime but a steady rise in fear. The mainstream media continued to insist that women were vulnerable in public and safe at home. In 1990, the *Washington Post* featured a story about two black-belt martial arts experts who moonlighted after their day jobs teaching women how to defend themselves in the event of an attack. The men wore suits that made them look like spacemen in order to endure the blows they encouraged their female students to inflict on their bodies: kicks to the groin, jabs to their eyes, and blows to the rest of their bodies.

Their course was called "D.C. Model Mugging," and the two men took turns playing the role of "ordinary" attackers, as if muggers and rapists were "ordinary" men. "We try to simulate your ordinary attacker. . . . The ordinary rapist isn't looking for a fight, so we try to play someone who is not looking for a fight, is surprised to find himself in one and tries as best he can to defend himself with normal male skills." One of the instructors said, "It really breaks my heart" that he had to provide this training, but "if I don't fill her with both fear and anger, then she won't learn to fight in that adrenaline state."[37] The course cost $650 for five sessions of five hours each (the equivalent of $1,200 in 2016), and involved subjecting paying customers to the kind of verbal harassment and threats that, the instructors claimed, usually accompanied assaults. While Model Mugging courses could increase women's strength, confidence, and ability to protect themselves, they also fostered and exploited fear. The cost of the course made it available only to affluent women.[38]

A 1998 guidebook articulated the prevailing assumptions of the time. Personal safety should be a woman's top priority, above "family, career, home, job, and so on." "Nothing else matters if you aren't safe," the author wrote. "With every decision you make, always consider the safety factor. If you approach personal safety as a *lifestyle*, setting priorities will become second nature."[39] By the end of the century, nearly one in five women had obtained self-defense training or education to protect themselves from crime.[40]

The feminist movement achieved important gains in terms of increasing women's confidence, physical strength, and self-empowerment—and self-defense strategies, products, and classes contributed to those gains. At the same time, a focus on self-defense reflected an acceptance of pervasive danger and did nothing to resist the exaggerated claims of women's potential victimization. Although it was true that women were vulnerable, and needed to be able to defend themselves, the widely held belief that strangers were particularly dangerous encouraged them to be distrustful and fearful when out in public places.

At a time of rising crime and the liberalization of weapons laws, women's self-empowerment also gave rise to a female version of the vigilante spirit, and this spirit, like the male version of vigilantism, appeared in the popular culture. Typically, Hollywood films celebrated the male vigilante who rescued vulnerable women.[41] But there were some exceptions, especially in the wake of the feminist movement. In these films, female protagonists took the law into their own hands, often in revenge against men who attacked them or a loved one. As in the male vigilante genre, these films often depicted law enforcement as ineffectual and unable to bring villains to justice, forcing the women to take on the task themselves. Sometimes there is a sympathetic male cop who tries to help, but ultimately the women are on their own.[42]

Probably the best-known film of this genre is *Thelma and Louise* (1991), an extremely popular film that offered a women's version of the vigilante scenario. But unlike the lone male vigilante, it featured two women who not only take the law into their own hands, but protect each other. A combination of girlfriend buddy movie and thriller, *Thelma and Louise* centers on two ordinary women. Restless and dissatisfied with their men, they plan a getaway. The trip takes a deadly turn when one of them, Louise, shoots and kills a man who tried to rape Thelma after an encounter at a bar. The women flee, and during their flight they rob a convenience store for money, blow up a truck to punish its lewd, harassing driver, and force a policeman at gunpoint into his patrol car's trunk.

Eventually they are trapped and surrounded by an armada of local and federal law enforcement. Rather than surrender, they drive off a cliff together in a bond of friendship and suicide. The heroines have some of the marks of male vigilante heroes as they take the law into their own hands to protect themselves and each other. But, unlike the triumphant male movie vigilantes, who are vindicated in the end and celebrated as heroes, Thelma and Louise have to die. The female vigilantes could not have come home to a hero's welcome. They have abandoned their men and violated every legal and cultural code in their ill-fated adventure, so they take the only way out. Male vigilante heroes almost never suffer such a fate.[43] In spite of the no-way-out-but-death ending, the protagonists in *Thelma and Louise* came to represent women's assertiveness in the face of men who tried to control, rape, harass, betray, or even rescue them.

The film also glorified the female gunslinger. Guns, like tear gas, mace, and self-defense, provided a source of self-protection for women.

In *Thelma and Louise*, the two women protagonists take the law into their own hands, vigilante-style.

Source: Margaret Herrick Library, Academy of Motion Picture Arts and Sciences.

Although accurate statistics on gun ownership by gender are difficult to obtain, women have probably always been less likely to purchase guns than men. In the mid-1990s, approximately 42 percent of men said they owned a gun, compared to only about 10 percent of women.[44] But for many of the women who did own guns, the gun became an extension of their identity.

Owning a gun was not only a means of self-defense but also a political act and an ideological statement. Gun-toting women did not see themselves as victims. Just as owning a firearm enhanced men's sense of their masculinity, some female gun owners considered their firearms to be central to their womanhood. These women may not have identified themselves as feminists, but they did insist on female empowerment. Many connected gun ownership to motherhood and saw their need for a gun as an extension of their role as protectors of their children.[45]

For some women, owning a gun admitted them into a gendered community with special female training, clubs, and fashions. Women formed exclusive gun clubs, such as A Girl and A Gun Women's Shooting League; The Well Armed Woman, "a club for women who share an aim"; She Can Shoot; Mothers Arms; Armed Females of America; and Babes with Bullets. The National Rifle Association (NRA) boasted separate programs for women, including shooting clinics, women-only hunts, and the "Refuse to Be a Victim" safety program.[46]

The NRA catered specifically to women via a journal, *Women and Guns*, "the only magazine written for women gunowners, by women gunowners." Guns advertised and reviewed in the magazine were presented as both menacing and feminine. A perusal of the January 1992 issue suggests the ways in which women constituted themselves as a gun-owning community that embraced femininity and motherhood along with firearms. An article on Colts and Cobras pointed out that "the intimidation value of these guns is high. Physically on the large side, with a heavy barrel, both the snub-nose and the 4-incher exude considerable presence!" The photo of a Colt .357 accompanying the article shows it on a flowered tablecloth with reading glasses next to a book about herbs. Advertisements in the magazine often placed guns in female spaces. An ad for a Beretta Model 86m .380 pistol pictured the gun on a bedstand, with a clock radio and a framed photo of a mother with her two daughters. Another ad suggested a gun—rather than a man—for "When You Need a Bodyguard. . . . What with all the crime in the streets these days, a woman needs a bodyguard more than ever."[47]

Alongside the advertisements for firearms, *Women and Guns* promoted gun accessories that appealed to feminine fashions and tastes. A photo showed a woman tucking a gun into the back waistline of her skirt. Another featured a handbag with a side compartment to hold a gun, demonstrating how a woman could be "safe but feminine and stylish." One woman modeled "the Bianchi Hip Hugger holding a Glock 19," which enabled her to "conceal a sizeable handgun well, even bending over, as shown." The advertised holsters included the Flash Bang, or the "Concealed Midriff Holster," worn underneath the bra, with the gun's handle nestled between the woman's breasts. The ad noted that the Midriff Holster was "Ideal for small and medium frame guns. Straps included for use with heavier guns. One-size—adjustable. Beige with lace."[48] An advertisement for the "Waller Soft Safe gun holding purse" featured a photo of the purse displayed on a flowered doily with a lamp, a stuffed animal, a compact, a perfume bottle sprayer, a framed photo of children, car keys, and a jeweled ring, and on top of the purse is a handgun and a string of pearls.[49] As *Women and Guns* made clear, within the NRA, women, by the 1990s, were a distinct gun-owning community with their own concerns, motivations, and fashions.

Women writing in the magazine insisted that guns signaled female empowerment rather than fear. The associate editor of *Women and Guns*, Peggy Tartaro, explained, "They ask, 'Just who are you afraid of?' You explain that 'you have translated your fear into empowerment.'" The writer expressed the widespread view shared by many, if not most, gun owners that government and law enforcement would not protect them, so they needed to arm themselves. "What the antigunners refuse to understand is that gun ownership doesn't make you less afraid of crime. . . . Instead, what women and men who own guns are less afraid of is that they will be forced to rely on outside forces (police, politicians, Good Samaritans) to save us," Tartaro wrote.[50]

NRA women resented the notion that they were unable to protect themselves, a view they ascribed to their ideological opponents. According to Tartaro, "those in the gun control movement, generally thought to be liberal, seem to have some sexist notions about the abilities of women," because they continued to see women as victims. Tracey Martin, the NRA's special events manager, urged women to oppose pending legislation calling for a seven-day waiting period for purchasing a firearm. She assailed the male-dominated media for failing to promote "gun rights as a women's rights issue," adding, "The American media must be made to understand that waiting periods kill women. Plain and simple. And that's not okay."[51]

Twenty years later, the *New York Times* proclaimed that the "Rising Voice of Gun Ownership Is Female." The article pointed to the proliferation of women's shooting clubs and to the ways in which firearm manufacturers increasingly marketed guns to women. Some advertisements appealed to women's protective impulses, such as the one by Colt in the 1990s depicting a mother tucking her child into bed, with the caption "Self-protection is more than your right. . . . [I]t is your responsibility." As in earlier decades, companies still focused on taste and fashion with smaller guns, custom colors (especially pink), handbags with hidden gun compartments, and fashion accessories. Companies like Cobra Firearms and Sweet Shot cultivated a new market with products like the "salmon kiss" leather handbag for concealed carry, leopard-print shooting gloves, and bullet rosette jewelry. Sweet Shot's company motto was "Look cute while you shoot!"[52]

Reflecting a feminist resentment of stereotypes of women, even if they would not describe themselves as feminists, some pro-gun women chafed at pitches to their feminine tastes. Gun advocate Celia Bigelow asserted, "I didn't buy my AR-15 for a certain color or because of 'direct marketing.' I bought it because it will protect me from violent intruders. Any ladies out there without guns, you should too." One female gun enthusiast described feminine firearms products as "infantilizing"; another said it was "a slap in the face" to assume women would prefer pink guns.[53]

Indeed, women gun enthusiasts often expressed a sense of feminist empowerment. One forty-two-year-old businesswoman who called herself a "virgin gun shooter" described her first experience at a firing range. After emptying a ten-round magazine, she felt exhilarated, saying, "It was awesome. . . . The sense of control, of being in charge of me." The *New York Times* reported that women and men learned to shoot for different reasons. For women, it was not just a hobby or for self-defense, but "a statement of independence and personal power." Gun clubs for women cropped up on college campuses. At Mount Holyoke in 2002, about fifty women students belonged to a campus chapter of the Second Amendment Sisters. One member boasted, "One of my guy friends said, 'You're a chick with a gun—I'm scared.'"[54]

A portrait photographer, Lindsay McCrum, published a book vividly illustrating women's personal attachment to their guns in 2011. *Chicks with Guns* includes photos of seventy-eight women and girls, ranging in age from eight to eighty-five and representing a wide range of backgrounds, cultures, classes, and parts of the country, posing with their guns. The photographer herself poses with her Sears semiautomatic long rifle caliber. McCrum, who became interested in guns at the age of eight, said she "hated it when the girls in the movies would hold their ears and scream when the hero would drop his gun. I'd yell at the TV for the girl to pick up the gun. . . . I'd be damned if I was going to be a helpless girl waiting for a man to save me. . . . Now I am certain that I will be no one's damsel in distress."

One woman pictured in the book, Lake, a white single mom with an eight-year-old daughter, sleeps with her gun next to her. In the photograph, the mother and daughter pose together on bed with a floral bedspread. Lake holds a Smith & Wesson .357 Magnum; her daughter holds one of her vintage cap guns. Another, Alice, a young African American woman, is pictured holding a Smith & Wesson 12-gauge riot gun in a wilderness scene at a lake. She is the mother of three girls, "all of whom," she vows, "will be well versed in the art of shooting, while having the heart to shoot if necessary." Other portraits in the book include a woman in a wheelchair wearing vintage clothes surrounded by antiques in a study, gun in hand. These portraits suggest that for many gun-owning women, firearms are an extension and reflection of who they are—a part of their identity.[55]

Although the portraits in *Chicks with Guns* highlighted the interests and personalities of the featured women, the prominence of weapons in the photos suggested self-protection. The book reflected the motivations of many gun-owning women. Fear for their own safety, and for the safety of their children, prompted many women to purchase guns. High school counselor Janna Delany said she worried about crime. "It's more just for me personally to give myself a little bit of peace of mind, [if] somebody [was] trying to carjack me or hold me up at a gas station or stopped at a red light or something," she said. Robyn Sandoval, executive director of the national women's shooting league A Girl and A Gun, said carrying a handgun had become an extension of motherhood, a way to protect her children. She also wanted to make her children aware of anyone in their surroundings who looked dangerous, whether or not those individuals were doing anything wrong. "Family situational awareness is a big deal," she said. "When we go to a restaurant, my 9-year-old [is thinking] who looks suspicious? What are people doing? What's an anomaly. Let's point out people in their cars. We make a game of it, of who can find somebody in their car just sitting there."

In keeping with the maternal theme, some women described their firearms as if they were children or pets. "We name our guns," Sandoval said. "I have Francesca, Dolly, Gracie. And we talk about 'em like, 'I'm takin' Gracie to the mall with us.'" A schoolteacher, Bettylane Chambliss, said, "My small one is my Baby. And my dad will say, 'Do you have your gun with you?' And I went, 'Oh, yeah, I got Baby with me. I'm fine.'"[56]

WHETHER OR NOT they purchased firearms for protection, large numbers of parents feared that their children were at great risk of harm at the hands of strangers. Just as officials and the media exaggerated dangers to women, they also vastly distorted dangers to children. Like women, children, in reality, were at greater risk of harm in their homes or their cars than in public places. Nevertheless, newspapers and television news drew attention to rare but heinous crimes, giving the impression that the greatest threat to children was strangers.

Widespread anxieties about children's vulnerability emerged in the early years of the Cold War, as large numbers of women entered the paid labor force, leaving their children in the care of others. In the 1950s, along with the "lavender scare," which targeted homosexuals as risks to national security, a "sexual psychopath" panic began to permeate the daily news. Parents worried that sexual predators were on the loose, and on the prowl for children. Shocking crimes gained extensive media coverage, serving as cautionary tales.[57]

A particularly horrific crime became the basis for *The Child Molester*, a twenty-minute educational film based on the case of two girls who were abducted and murdered in North Park Lake, Pennsylvania. Produced in 1964 by the Highway Safety Foundation, best known for its driver's education films, *The Child Molester* recreated the crime using actors and was shown in schools well into the 1970s.[58]

The film begins with two eight- or nine-year-old girls playing in a park who are lured into a car by a man who offers them candy. The next scene takes place at the police station, where the parents wait. Echoing the ominous fear-inducing aura of Cold War civil defense films, such as *Duck and Cover*, the narrator says that most child molestations can be prevented if children are taught "to know their enemy." "What does a child molester look like? Do they have sinister faces?" The screen shows a frowning man at a bus stop. "Or do they look like people you see every day?" The narrator warns that any stranger could be a sexual predator. The scene then shifts to show the man dragging the screaming girls into a secluded area. The film ends with actual police photographs of the real-life grisly crime scene, showing close-ups of the murdered girls lying in pools of blood. The narrator explains that the girls were murdered, and that this is a true story. The final scene shows a girl's shoe floating downstream near the murder site. Although the film was eventually pulled from public viewing, it terrified the children who saw it. Decades later, many remembered having nightmares and fears that lasted weeks, months, or even years.[59]

The media attention devoted to this and other horrifying crimes gave the impression that public places such as parks, theaters, and city streets were crawling with "perverts" and rapists waiting for an opportunity to pounce. Self-defense manuals from the time often included advice on child protection. A typical guidebook from 1967 offered a chapter on "Protecting Your Children." Instead of noting the common dangers children face in the home, however, such as injuries suffered from unsafe environments, the chapter begins by alerting parents to the danger of sex criminals, particularly "perverts" who might stalk them in public. The guidelines focus on helping children avoid being kidnapped. They should walk in groups while out of the home, and in the home parents should lock all doors to the outside but keep the door open to a child's room so they can hear any unusual noises.[60]

By the 1970s and 1980s, when increasing numbers of mothers held jobs that made it impossible for them to supervise their children all day, kidnapping had become a major national preoccupation. If Bernhard Goetz became the byword of vigilantism in this period, the 1979 disappearance of six-year-old Etan Patz in New York became the same for kidnapping. The crime prompted President Ronald Reagan to proclaim May 25 as National Missing Children's Day; it was first observed in 1983 on the anniversary of Etan's disappearance. The panic over missing and abducted children reached a high point in the 1980s. The panic fueled the Reagan administration's efforts to shift public policy away from providing for the material needs of children toward protecting them from alleged threats from dangerous strangers.[61]

Another kind of law passed in response to fears of child abduction was "memorial" legislation named for child victims, such as the 1996 America's Missing Broadcast Emergency Response Alert system (AMBER), named for nine-year-old Amber Hagerman, who was abducted and murdered in Arlington, Texas. Although the AMBER Alert system has had a negligible effect on child safety, it holds considerable symbolic value. Responses such as this were mainly "crime control theater," similar to the symbolic value of civil defense drills.[62]

Kidnappings received enormous media coverage, far out of proportion to their frequency, from the 1970s onward. In 1984, the nonprofit National Child Safety Council began the Missing Children Milk Carton Program "to address the nationwide tragedy of missing and abducted children." The program was launched after two Iowa boys disappeared. More than seven hundred independent dairies across the nation cooperated with the program by printing the photographs of missing children on milk cartons. In total, more than 3 billion milk cartons have carried photographs of missing and abducted children to the homes and schools where parents and children began their days over breakfast. The program lasted only a few years, because it did not result in the recovery of significant numbers of missing children, and it frightened youngsters and their parents, giving the impression that innocent children were frequently snatched by strangers.[63]

These programs and the publicity about kidnappings did little to help children in distress, but they did create considerable fear. In 1987, 76 percent of the children surveyed by the Roper Center said they feared being kidnapped; in fact, it was the most common fear reported in the poll. In a 1991 Mayo Clinic survey, 72 percent of the parents questioned said they feared that their children might be abducted. More than a third said that stranger kidnapping was a "frequent" worry, and greater than other prominent fears, such as auto accidents, choking, or sexual abuse. In 1997, a survey found that child abduction and murder were the principal fears of parents.[64]

But, like the more general fears of crime, these specific fears were misguided. In the 1990s, only 3 percent of the cases handled by the National Center for Missing and Exploited Children were abductions by strangers. In 1999, for example, there were 117,200 child abductions by family members and 33,000 non-family abductions. Nearly all of the non-family abductions were abductions by acquaintances—only 115 were stranger abductions. The overwhelming majority of missing youths—approximately 628,900—were runaway or "thrown-away" children. That same year, 2,931 children under the age of fifteen died as passengers in car accidents. One study pointed out that a child "is vastly more likely to have a heart attack, and child heart attacks are so rare that most parents (correctly) never even consider the risk. Moreover, children abducted by strangers were harmed less frequently than those taken by people they knew."[65]

By the early twenty-first century, children taken by strangers represented about 0.01 percent (one-hundredth of one percent, or 1 in 10,000) of all missing children in the United States. These rare crimes, like all crimes, had been declining for decades. Children, like women, were more at risk among family and friends. According to David Finkelhor, director of the Crimes Against Children Research Center at the University of New Hampshire and a researcher for the National Incidence Studies of Missing, Abducted, Runaway, and Thrownaway Children, one of the problems with the kidnapping panic was the assumption that children were always better off with their families.

Professionals and police who dealt with missing children were trained to find the children and bring them back home. "Sadly, the majority of missing children are suffering from severe and protracted conflict in their families," Finkelhor explained. "They run away or are pushed out because they are at odds with their parents and siblings or because they are victims of abuse and neglect. They are taken or held by parents battling fruitlessly over custody rights. Bringing these children home generally does nothing about the conflict and abuse that eat away at their mental health and well-being."[66]

Nevertheless, fears of dangerous strangers abducting children from the safety of their homes found expression in the popular culture. One recent film trilogy fused the stranger abduction narrative to the tropes of the vigilante genre. *Taken* (2008) stars Liam Neeson as Bryan Mills, an ex-CIA operative. His sixteen-year-old daughter lives with his former wife and her wealthy, ineffectual stepfather. Mills reluctantly agrees to allow his virginal daughter to spend the summer in Paris with a friend, even though he feels that the mother and her new husband are too sheltered in their daily lives to recognize the possible dangers involved. On arrival in Paris, the daughter and her friend are abducted by Albanian immigrant sex traffickers. Mills pursues the kidnappers and kills dozens of low-level criminals in the process. After a violent kidnappers spree and massive destruction of property, he finds the girls and brings them home—never facing arrest or any consequences for his violent acts. The next two films in the series, *Taken 2* (2012) and *Taken 3* (2014), follow similar plots. These films played to public fears of vulnerable women and children, the incompetence of official law enforcement, and the need for heroic vigilante men to use massive violence in order to find and kill the villains. By 2017, the *Taken* series had grossed more than $932 million worldwide.

While these films fed fears, they did not offer realistic solutions: most parents were not equipped to be vigilante heroes. But many companies offered more practical, everyday solutions. Products intended to help parents keep their children safe included leashes, harnesses, alarms, electronic monitors, and do-it-yourself "child protection safety kits" containing such items as fingerprinting tools and ID cards. Insurance companies offered kidnapping insurance policies. Continental Insurance offered a "Missing Children" plan. For $288 per year, parents could secure assistance in the event their child was abducted, in the form of a private investigator, counseling services, up to $10,000 in travel funds—and up to $50,000 for a reward or ransom. More recently, GPS child tracking devices have become more popular. Although these need to be worn (implants are not yet feasible), some models are unobtrusive and can be sewn into clothing.[67]

As MORE AND more women entered the workforce, parents did their best to keep their children safe when they were not able to be with them. The percentage of stay-at-home mothers declined from 49 percent in 1967 to 23 percent in 1999.[68] If a friend or family member was not able to care for their children, mothers generally took them to day-care centers during their working hours. In 1965, approximately 10 percent of preschool children of employed mothers went to day-care centers; by 1993, 40 percent did so.[69]

From the very start, day care for young children was controversial, giving rise to studies and debates over whether it was good or bad for them.[70] Women encountered warnings that they put their children at risk if they went to work and left them in the care of others. In fact, women and their children were more likely to be harmed at home than anywhere else, as a result of domestic violence, accidents, the presence of guns, or unsafe domestic spaces filled with lead in the paint or asbestos in the ceilings.

In the midst of questions surrounding the value of day care for children's development, another issue emerged that turned into a national panic: child-care providers who allegedly abused and sexually assaulted the children in their care. The child-care panic occurred throughout the same period that child abduction was an issue, from the 1970s through the 1990s. Perhaps the most notorious episode was the 1984 McMartin case. The McMartin family had operated a well-respected preschool in Manhattan Beach, California, for nearly thirty years when the school was accused of molesting children in satanic rituals. Over the next several years, every member of the McMartin family, as well as three teachers, were indicted on hundreds of charges of sexual assault and human sacrifice. The preschool closed and all the members of the family spent time in prison. After the long and costly case, based on circumstantial evidence and problematic interviews with preschool children, in which no physical evidence was ever found, all members of the family were acquitted. Although the McMartins were exonerated of all wrongdoing, the damage was done, leaving the McMartin family and many other families destroyed in the process.

The McMartin preschool was among more than fifty child-care centers across the country that faced criminal charges of satanic sex abuse. As with violence against women, although child abuse was a problem, and the increasing recognition and attention was needed, the way it was portrayed was misleading. Most child abuse cases involved relatives or friends of the victims. The child-care panic resulted in imprisonment and financial ruin for many innocent individuals, and put all day-care providers under suspicion. The media attention surrounding the issue also placed blame on working mothers for leaving the care of their children to others.[71]

Of course, there were child-care facilities that did not properly care for children. The lack of government funding and adequate regulation left working parents with few options. But the panic over ritualized abuse of children in day-care centers exposed the widespread fear that children—like women—were particularly vulnerable when outside the presumed safety of their homes.[72] By the end of the twentieth century, the panic over satanic sexual abuse in child-care centers had diminished, but the fear that children outside their homes were at high risk of harm when they were not being watched by their parents did not.

The typical response to these fears by the early twenty-first century was for parents to become overprotective of their children, imagining all kinds of potential harm. Ironically, children had generally roamed more freely—without supervision—during the era when most mothers were full-time homemakers rather than participants in the paid labor force.

Between 1969 and 2001, the percentage of children who walked or biked to school decreased from 42 percent to 16 percent. Between 1997 and 2003, children's participation in sports and outdoor activities in general declined. In 2012, American children spent 90 percent of their leisure time at home, and they were closely supervised.[73]

Mothers interviewed for a 2012 study in Minnesota by Solveig Moen Brown recognized that they had experienced more freedom when they were children than their own children experienced, and claimed that the world felt much more dangerous for children than it had a generation earlier. The assumption that the world had become a more dangerous place, however, simply was not true. One mother acknowledged the disconnect between fear and reality, noting that "our perception of it is what is so heightened, from stranger danger type of stuff to getting hit by cars, and dying of accidents and illnesses. Kids' safety is at an all-time high, and yet we think of it as at an all-time low, and that's a curious cultural shift that I can't account for." Another mother reported that she wouldn't take her eyes off her daughter when the daughter walked to a neighbor's house until she was inside, and made her daughter call when she was coming home, for fear that she would be abducted. Many mothers interviewed feared sexual predators and abuse.[74]

In interviews with one hundred parents, researchers at the University of Virginia came to similar conclusions, finding that "nearly all respondents remember childhoods of nearly unlimited freedom, when they could ride bicycles and wander through woods, streets, parks, unmonitored by their parents." But they were terrified of allowing their own children similar freedom. Many said they feared their children would be abducted, in spite of the fact that crime rates were lower than when they themselves had been children.[75]

Every mother in the 2012 study by Brown believed that raising children had been easier for their parents' generation than it was for them. Although the numbers of women working outside the home had increased, public policies and institutional support for childrearing had not. The cultural expectation for individual responsibility left parents—especially mothers—with the burden of "doing it all." Several mothers in the study reported that they took antianxiety medications to help manage their stress and worry.[76]

In place of government assistance, parents could turn to various consumer products to help them manage and surveil their children, and even surveil their babysitters. Capitalizing on fear and distrust, savvy entrepreneurs developed and marketed "nanny cams," hidden cameras that parents could place in their homes to monitor babysitters. As one of many companies asserted, "It's always nerve-wracking leaving your child in the hands of another person; even if that person is a close friend or relative. When it's a stranger, or someone watching your child for the first time, it can be even more distressing." With the advertised nanny cam, "you never have to worry again about leaving your child in someone else's care."[77]

The 2012 study reported that parents from other countries often found America's obsession with child safety and fears of abduction perplexing. A newcomer from Berlin, who had recently moved with his family to a suburb of Washington, DC, found that his eight-year-old daughter had wandered out alone to explore the neighborhood shortly after they arrived. She returned home and eagerly reported what she had discovered: a park and some neighbors walking their dogs. But she saw no children out playing. "When this story comes up in conversations with American friends, we are usually met with polite disbelief. Most are horrified by the idea that their children might roam around without adult supervision. In Berlin, where we lived in the center of town, our girls would ride the Metro on their own—a no-no in Washington. Or they'd go alone to the playground, or walk a mile to a piano lesson. Here in quiet and traffic-safe suburban Washington, they don't even find other kids on the street to play with."[78]

The expectation of constant supervision had become so pervasive that parents were sometimes arrested for taking their eyes off their children. In one case in April 2013, a ten-year-old and his six-year-old sister were picked up by police because they had been allowed to walk home alone from a park near their home in Maryland. For the crime of encouraging their children's independence, their parents were found guilty of child neglect by the state's Child Protective Services.[79] In another case, in March 2008, a Chicago mother was arrested for leaving her child alone in her car for five minutes when she dashed into a shop. Another woman was arrested in August 2014 for stepping a few yards away from her car with her daughter for a few minutes while her toddler slept in his car seat.[80]

Yet children are unquestionably far safer today than at almost any time in the past. At a time when debates rage over whether or not "helicopter parents" should hover over their children, or "free-range" kids are better off, studies show that even "free-range" children are safer than the children of previous generations. A reviewer of these studies confessed that he, too, overprotects his children: "Like most parents today I enjoyed far more independence as a child than my children do. I biked to school at eight and roamed the gritty streets of New Haven while not much older. By those standards, my kids live under a kind of house arrest, rarely alone at home, and they're escorted to and from school, sports practice, and pre-arranged, adult-supervised 'play dates.' All of which is highly irrational and counterproductive: kids are far safer—even without lock-down parenting—than we think."[81]

From 1970 to 2013, all crimes against children—including physical and sexual abuse, assault, robbery, larceny, and stranger abduction—declined by more than half. By 2013, the chance of a child being kidnapped and murdered was about 1.5 million to 1. Children were three times more likely to be struck by lightning. Protective measures have actually created more danger. Children were safer walking or biking to school than in cars. And parents' fears of children playing outdoors have contributed to declining physical activity, rising childhood obesity, and a growing lack of independence, which carries far greater risks.[82]

What accounts for the rising panic about children's safety when they are out of their parents' sight? Part of it is the ongoing anxiety surrounding women's participation in the paid labor force, leaving their children unsupervised or in the care of others. But that does not explain the pervasive fear that children roaming freely outside their homes are subject to attacks by strangers. The assumption that public spaces are dangerous—for women as well as children—reflects the decades-long trend identifying public spaces as dangerous, and the family home as safe. Yet the actual risks are just the opposite: public spaces tend to be safer than private homes for both women and children, and strangers are far less likely than family members and acquaintances to cause harm. Fears of rising crime at a time when crime was decreasing, distrust of police and other official institutions, and misplaced assumptions about the safety of the home fueled anxieties about women's and children's vulnerability.

These fears have informed and sanctioned a public policy turn to the right. The dismantling of welfare policies, the vastly increasing gap between the wealthy and the poor, the struggle of middle-class families to achieve a decent standard of living, the lack of family-friendly workplaces—all of these developments led to worries about family security. But as the nation's politics moved to the right, the conservative emphasis on individual responsibility and a faith in the marketplace left many families to fend for themselves.

In this environment, the media, experts, pundits, and officials increasingly portrayed women and children as uniquely vulnerable to harm from strangers. But strangers are rarely the problem. Women are definitely at risk: one in four American women become victims of domestic violence at some point in their lives. Children are indeed vulnerable, too: in the United States, more than 16 million children, or one in five, do not get enough to eat. The abortion rate has declined steadily since 1990, but the infant mortality rate remains among the worst in the developed world. More than 6 infants die for every 1,000 live births in the United States, mostly as a result of poverty.[83] These are real threats and dangers, but guns and self-defense measures will not address these harms.

Self-defense and martial arts training for women may have provided some women with a measure of strength and confidence, and some women, like some men, found their identity shaped or reinforced by owning guns. But the emphasis on danger and the need for physical safety may have created more problems than it solved. Children's well-being, health, and self-confidence likely have suffered, and working mothers probably often worry unnecessarily. Security and self-defense measures have fostered an atmosphere of fear that has led to guilt and anxiety for working women, distrust of child-care providers, and the targeting of particular groups—such as young black men—as particularly threatening. Many people have been harmed by those unfounded fears. And nobody is any safer.

Chapter 5

LOCKED-UP AMERICA: SELF-INCARCERATION AND THE ILLUSION OF SECURITY

> The issue is the extent to which Americans are becoming a country of separate communities walled off inside their fortresses. . . . It's too bad we need gates to protect ourselves from each other, but on the other hand, it's really nice to know that you can go for a walk at night and not get hurt.
>
> —*Jeff Butzlaff, city manager of Canyon Lake, an incorporated gated community, 1995*[1]

By the late twentieth century, the notion of the home as both a safe haven and a fortress had come full circle. In the early years of the Cold War, the home was the place where parents, especially mothers, would instill the values of self-sufficiency and independence in their children. Privacy would enable them to nurture citizens who would take those values into the wider world. The home and the family would contain the dangers of the age, through the embrace of proper gender roles and discipline. But over time, the idealized middle-class suburban family began to unravel. In the face of new potential dangers, including social upheaval, crime, and unrest, people came to think that the socializing influence of the private home, with its wholesome environment for nurturing self-reliance, might not suffice. Without the internally fortified nuclear family, with a male breadwinner and a female homemaker, the home would now require external fortification.

Gradually the home shifted from the place that *provided* protection to the place that *needed* protection. Unlike in 1945, when *House Beautiful* featured a welcoming image of a suburban home on its cover, as described in Chapter 1, in 1964 the magazine commented on the shift from the ideal of a private paradise to a barricaded fortress. The July issue that year included a full-page illustration of a fortified house, with cannons, boarded-up doors and windows, alarms, guard dogs, locks, loudspeakers, and a large sign announcing "Burglars Go Home."[2] *Ladies' Home Journal* followed suit in 1968 with an article featuring several gadgets that could be purchased to make the home more secure against intruders.[3] These magazines—aimed at women—pointed to the need for a new kind of domestic security.

A siege mentality began to transform the urban landscape. Not only private homes but also new public buildings reflected the impact of fear, embodying an architectural trend known as "fortress urbanism," characterized by protected interiors and a look of outward aggressiveness suggesting that public space is fraught with danger. Reminiscent of Cold War–era bunkers, this style of architecture warned not only of the possibility of a nuclear attack, but also of urban disruption, crime, and protest, not to mention the lively but chaotic dynamic of life on the city streets.

Many structures built in the 1960s, including schools, corporate offices, and government buildings, subtly reflected a turn toward social control, segregation, and an increasingly martial society. Numerous urban schools built during the decade looked like large concrete bunkers, sometimes with few or no windows. The idea was to keep children,

MAKING YOUR HOME SAFE AGAINST INTRUDERS

Crime in the United States is increasing five times faster than the population; burglaries have risen more than 40 percent since 1960; every 27 seconds a burglary takes place somewhere, yielding cash and property valued at $142 million a year and incalculable anguish to residents of homes and apartments. As a result, insurance rates are climbing and families are becoming increasingly fearful for their safety and their property (see The Journal "Voice of Women" Poll on pg. 26).

What can be done to make the home safe from intruders?

To find the best answers, the *Journal* talked to law-enforcement officers, locksmiths, electronics engineers and other experts in the field of burglary prevention. All agree on three basic rules:

1. You must have good locks, properly installed, on *all* vulnerable doors and windows—to keep intruders out.

2. You should have some sort of alarm device at the *most* vulnerable entrances to your home—to frighten an invader away if he does get in.

3. You have to *remember* to secure all locks, set the alarm and take certain other precautions to avoid making your home inviting to criminals.

If you live in an apartment, take a look at the lock on your front door. Chances are that it is a simple spring latch; you slam the door behind you and it "locks" automatically. But does it really? A burglar can slip a celluloid strip in front of that sort of lock—into the crack between the door and the wall—and the door will swing open at once.

"In New York's best apartment houses," says Detective Robert McDermott of the New York City Police Department's Burglary Squad, "sixty percent of the burglaries are carried out with these little celluloid strips. Most take place in the early afternoon or midafternoon when the kids are out playing, the husband is out working and the lady of the house is out shopping."

It is simple and inexpensive to replace such a latch with a "deadlatch," which employs a little metal catch that renders the celluloid strip useless. The Kwikset Deadlatch (about $1.50) is obtainable from locksmiths and hardware stores, and is easily installed by a handyman or the building superintendent.

In a high crime area further security may be necessary. Bob Rognon, 73, has been a locksmith as long as he can remember, as was his father before him, and his grandfather—and as is his wife. Still active in his locksmith shop on East 59th Street in New York City, Rognon is familiar with all locks.

"It is very important to add an auxiliary lock in addition to the regular lock on your door," Rognon says. "This should be a deadbolt—a sliding bolt that locks with a key and holds the door firm. The best are hard to pick open and take a lot of time, which the average burglar doesn't have. Remember, burglars like to get in and out of a home in less than an hour. If they can't open your lock, they'll generally go elsewhere."

The auxiliary deadbolt lock is mounted above your regular *(continued)*

One hundred percent safety from burglars and other intruders is impossible in this day of soaring crime. But, by equipping your home with these and other crime-fighting devices, you can often discourage prowlers or scare them away. By ARTHUR HENLEY

The Magic Eye Door Viewer (left) has a helpful wide-angle peephole. The Loxem cylinder lock with deadbolt (below) opens only from inside.

Experts recommend using keys that can't be duplicated easily—such as this Ace Tubular Key.

The police are automatically notified when this Modularm electronic device detects an intruder in your home.

Kwikset Deadlatch can't be opened with the simple celluloid strip many apartment-house burglars use.

Jewels and other valuables are safer in this Lift Alarm Security Box. When the box is picked up, or the knob is turned, an alarm bell clamors noisily.

For doors and windows, a Burglar Lockalarm can be a handy sentry.

This Pinkerton Radar-Eye Minuteman Alarm emits a radio-wave beam that penetrates walls and can detect the slightest movement.

66

The *Ladies' Home Journal* in 1968 featured these early security gadgets for its female readers to help them keep their homes and families safe from intruders.

Source: Courtesy of the Meredith Corporation.

especially teenagers, from breaking windows or using them to enter or exit the school. Windows might also distract students from their schoolwork. But the result was a prison-like aura, which was not lost upon the students who were effectively trapped inside. Security and social control also informed the design of many new government buildings, such as the concrete block that is Boston's City Hall. Like many other Cold War–era buildings, they were examples of a "brutalist architecture" that emphasized security and separation from the city streets outside.[4]

In the suburbs, the security mentality was evident not only in architecture but also in the locks and other gadgets described by *House Beautiful* and *Ladies' Home Journal* in the 1960s, which became a major new segment of the consumer product market. Advertisements for all sorts of home security devices, safe rooms, locks, bars, and bolts became ubiquitous. Guidebooks exhorted consumers to purchase the latest products, warning them of the threat to their families if their homes were not secure. One 1967 advice book falsely claimed that the crime rate had increased five times faster than the population over the previous five years. The population had actually increased at a greater rate than crime during those years.[5]

Companies that stood to profit from fear of crime did their best to whip up terror. In 1970, for example, General Telephone and Electronics took out a two-page ad in *Time* magazine promoting their new home intercom system. An intercom might provide useful and convenient communication. But the ad evoked fears of a notorious serial killer who had raped and murdered eleven women in the early 1960s. One side of the ad was a full-page photo of a man wearing a trench coat, face obscured by a hat. The facing page said, in large bold letters, "Who's downstairs ringing your bell? A friend? Or the Boston Strangler?"[6]

A 1983 study described a "growing fortress mentality that will eventually see all of us behind triple-locked doors, sound- and light-sensing devices on every window, two Dobermans at the ready, and a loaded shotgun in every room." Indeed, sales of burglar alarms that could "convert a home into an electronically fortified castle" were increasing by 20 percent a year. A 1972 guide advocated alarms and other electronic

This advertisement for a home intercom raised fears that dangerous strangers might appear at your door hoping to get into your home.

Source: Courtesy of Verizon Communications, Inc.

devices to provide peace of mind, but warned that anyone purchasing a security system should do a thorough background check on the technician who installed it, to be sure he wasn't a robber or a con man.[7]

Overall, the private security business in the United States exploded between 1970 and 1991, increasing from $3.3 billion in revenue to $52 billion—or from $17 in revenue per capita to $208.[8] Security products—for inside and outside the home—became more elaborate. Recommendations for secured and locked "safe rooms" now came with instructions as specific and detailed as the guidelines for fallout shelters decades earlier. A 1982 home security handbook suggested fireproofing the safe room, sealing it with a solid door with several heavy locks, and including a smoke detector, lights, sensors, emergency equipment, a fire extinguisher, a first aid kit, a flashlight, a telephone, and a radio. This interior room could store valuables, but its main purpose was to serve as a safe haven during a break-in, which the authors described as nearly inevitable. They also suggested homemade hiding places for valuables, such as fake floorboards or desk drawer bottoms, along with professionally made safes bolted to the floor.[9]

In 1981, *Newsweek* described sophisticated security products at the high end of the market, such as a $15,000 bulletproof "bionic" briefcase, complete with a bomb detector, a telephone bug detector, a tape recorder detector, a voice-stress analyzer, and a high-intensity bulb that could blind an attacker for fourteen hours. More common were the less costly audio sensors, motion detectors, pressure-sensitive mats, and "panic buttons" that gave homeowners a sense of security. These products had their downsides. Some did not work as promised. Others generated so many false alarms that some police departments, including New York City's, refused to respond to addresses that had previous false alarms. Homeowners or their pets were the ones most likely to set off the alarms. In some cases, security systems and devices may have increased rather than lowered the risk of harm; police officers responding to false alarms might not be available to deal with a real emergency. Nevertheless, new gadgets and alarm systems continued to flood the market. By the early twenty-first century, consumers could contemplate a custom-built "quantum sleeper," a bulletproof cocoon with CD and DVD players, a microwave oven, and a refrigerator.[10]

The gadget frenzy reflected the erroneous assumption that the best way to avoid crime was to retreat to the home and seal it tightly against all possible intrusions. Never mind that the home was probably the least safe place to be, given the relative frequency of accidents and domestic violence. Yet the fortified home became a symbolic sanctuary against the imagined threats that loomed outside.

FEAR OF CRIME generated mass incarceration, coerced as well as voluntary. Millions of Americans were locked up in prisons, surrounded by guards, gates, walls, towers, and fences. At the same time, millions of other Americans locked themselves up in prisons of their own making, also surrounded by guards, gates, walls, towers, and fences. In many ways, mass incarceration and self-incarceration were related. Both stemmed from the growing fear of crime and distrust of outsiders across the nation and from the pernicious racial attitudes that still prevailed. Both trends were overreactions to the risk of becoming a crime victim, and both achieved little or nothing in the way of improved safety and security. Both trends harmed Americans as individuals and also harmed society.[11]

Nowhere is self-incarceration more obvious than in the rapid proliferation of gated communities across the nation's residential landscape. Gated communities have existed since the nineteenth century, when they were few in number and reserved for the rich. The recent trend toward gated communities began in the late 1960s, a time of tremendous social and political turmoil. The trend grew in the 1970s and skyrocketed during the 1980s and 1990s, when crime rates dramatically declined. By the turn of the twenty-first century, gated communities were the fastest-growing form of housing in the United States. In 2001, walls enclosed more than 7 million households. If walled neighborhoods and privately guarded apartments are included, 28 million Americans, approximately 10 percent of the population, lived in such places.[12]

Gated communities are the ultimate expression of postwar suburban design and intention. The suburbs offered and promoted privacy, a retreat from public life, a celebration of private property, leisure amenities, and nuclear families. Suburbs were largely homogeneous and used legal as well as other means to keep out "undesirable" residents. Zoning divided commercial areas from residential ones. Lack of public transportation further isolated the city from the suburb, and suburban planners designed cul-de-sacs in order to prevent through-traffic and keep "strangers" out of neighborhoods. Gated communities are "extreme" suburbs, in many ways an almost predictable culmination of suburban development. They represent the most recent manifestation of a long trend toward increasing control and privatization of residential areas.[13]

In an effort to achieve security and independence, residents of gated communities isolate themselves from public life, from government infrastructure, from commercial businesses, and from people who are different from themselves. They work to restrict access to streets, parks, playgrounds, beaches, and swimming pools, and even to utilities and schools in or near their neighborhoods. Residents self-select in order to ensure that their neighbors share their background, socioeconomic level, and values.[14]

In the late twentieth century, many people who moved into gated communities sought safety and security along with a nice place to live. They often expressed a wish to live near people like themselves because of a fear of "others." In one survey from 1999, 70 percent of gated community residents said that security was a major reason for moving into the development—only 1 percent said it was not important. The vast majority of residents believed there was less crime in their compounds. And although they believed they were safer, in fact they were not. There was no significant difference in crime rates between gated and non-gated communities with residents of similar income levels. Unfriendly warnings and physical barriers did little to keep out crime, in part because some of the residents who lived inside the gates committed crimes against their neighbors.[15]

For the residents of these communities, the gates are markers of separation. The homogeneity and isolation from the rest of the society contributed to stereotyping and lack of understanding of people who were different from those who lived inside the gates, especially racial minorities. Although there were no longer laws restricting who could live behind the gates, developers marketed gated communities as secure residential environments that offered both safety and a sense of belonging. Using words like "your new home town" or a "totally new way of life," they suggested that residents would find that their neighbors were very much like themselves in terms of wealth, race, and values.[16]

For some, the gates represented an escape from the dangerous city. According to one resident of the elite gated community of Blackhawk in San Ramon, California, security "comes from knowing that if you see someone on the street, you know they're ok." Another resident compared that feeling of safety with her fear of city streets: "Contrast that with San Francisco. I wouldn't talk to anyone on the street there during the day." A neighbor echoed those sentiments: "I don't like going to San

Francisco. I don't feel comfortable in San Francisco. I don't leave my building when I get there, except to come home." Her husband agreed: "It's almost a release and relief to come back here. You're dealing with elements that are sometimes very undesirable. It's like the old moat and castle. You get back to your spot and you feel secure."[17]

But the sense of security has often been a false one. One resident of the tony Yacht Haven in Newport Beach, California, said that the gates "give an illusion of safety, but they are really not safe at all." She did not let her kids out on the street alone because of the lack of security. Her husband agreed. But he still liked having the gate there, "let's face it, for the status symbol."[18]

Similar issues plagued Canyon Lake, a development in the Southern California desert. Hostile to local governments making policies and zoning restrictions, the residents incorporated their compound in 1991 and became a full-fledged independent city run by a property owners association (POA). Jeff Butzlaff, the city manager of Canyon Lake, said there was some truth to the claim that his city's residents had withdrawn from the community at large. "The issue is the extent to which Americans are becoming a country of separate communities walled off inside their fortresses," he said. "It's too bad we need gates to protect ourselves from each other, but on the other hand, it's really nice to know that you can go for a walk at night and not get hurt."[19]

Gates promised security, safety, community, and freedom—but they rarely delivered on any of these. According to a 1995 study, an illusion of safety made the wide streets more dangerous, because cars sped and children played without the wariness they gain when living on public streets. In some cases, police and fire emergency vehicles had trouble entering these communities because of restricted access. Researchers reported that children living in these communities became especially fearful of strangers who looked different from themselves.[20]

Whether inhabited by the wealthy or by those of modest means, gated communities sometimes actually heightened feelings of vulnerability. Residents often complained that security was lax and that outsiders could enter too easily. Some residents said they experienced a "false sense of security" because they worried about the handymen, gardeners, domestics, and even the private guards who came to work on their property and at their neighbors' homes every day.[21]

Residents of these compounds often willingly gave up their independence in exchange for feelings of safety and belonging, often at the cost of conformity. Homeowner associations developed policies that restricted the freedom of residents to construct and decorate their homes as they wished, sometimes enforcing rigid behavioral codes. They devised standards for exterior home maintenance, paint colors, and design as well as for landscaping, and sometimes even regulated the interior furnishings that could be seen from the outside and the hours that residents could socialize in their own yards.

Some associations limited the size of pets or enforced a minimum age for children. They often specified which plants, trees, and shrubs were allowed, and determined strict designs for fences and decks. Associations banned certain personal items, such as window air conditioners, swing sets, and satellite dishes. Some activities were typically forbidden, such as hanging laundry outside, leaving garage doors open, or parking trucks or other large vehicles in driveways.[22]

Calling these gated residential compounds "communities" is a misnomer, in reality. Although residents hoped for neighborhoods that were cohesive, friendly, and open, the gates did not always foster those characteristics. Even inside the gates and walls, as survey data demonstrate, there was little sense of community or concern for the common good. According to researchers Edward J. Blakely and Mary Gail Snyder, who studied gated compounds, a community is more than simply a shared residential neighborhood. It requires mutual responsibility, significant interaction, and a cooperative spirit. But these qualities rarely existed in gated communities.[23]

In fact, the values that homeowners brought to gated communities were often antithetical to the creation of true communities. As one disappointed resident complained, "I found that people weren't so friendly, they just stayed in their houses. We had different expectations. There was a community pool, and you'd think that with all the people in such a tight area that people would be more bonded together. I don't find that that's been the case." Blakely and Snyder learned that residents did not feel strong commitments to one another. They described gated compounds as "artificial creations, faux communities."[24]

Clearly, that's what many residents desired. One resident of Blackhawk remarked, "It's a really independent group here, and it's a setting where you can get into your own thing, and you don't have to be really a participant in any community activity, even inside Blackhawk." Another admitted, "I don't know if we have many real friends here." In one survey, most respondents said their gated communities were "friendly," but only 8 percent said they were "neighborly and tight knit," compared to 28 percent who said they were "distant or private."

Very few residents were active in the governance of their communities. In theory, gates were expected to promote more interaction and cooperation among residents, but research demonstrated very little difference between gated communities and other places in terms of collective citizenship. Nor did the residents express any strong connection to the world outside the gates. Homeowner associations minimized residents' investments in public services. Gated compounds often owned and paid for their own streets, services, and utilities and provided their own private security guards. Residents paid significant fees for their infrastructure and security, which were independent of public funding and oversight.

Gated compounds that became incorporated as autonomous cities empowered their homeowner associations to function as city councils and levy taxes. Some built their own schools. In some of these gated cities, private patrols issued parking and speeding tickets within the compound. Not surprisingly, residents resented paying local taxes that supported the public at large, since they were already paying for their own private infrastructure.[25]

In the early twenty-first century, with the rich getting richer, high-end gated communities for the super-rich featured larger, more elaborate, and more fortified homes. In North Beverly Park, a gated community of palatial homes in Los Angeles, Hollywood producers, business tycoons, movie and sports stars, and other billionaires lived in homes as large as 20,000 to 30,000 square feet; a few were more than 40,000 square feet. These homes were certainly secure; however, residents paid for their privacy not only with their millions but with their freedom.

According to the *Los Angeles Times*, by 2006 the "intensely private, security-obsessed" culture of one such community, Beverly Park, was "secretive, even paranoid." Residents who gave interviews "urged caution and begged anonymity, so as not to arouse the wrath of the homeowners' association." In addition to the massive homes, there were shared spaces inside the gates, including an expansive four-acre children's park. But it was usually empty. Children did not play there, and in fact there were few people visible outside in Beverly Park at all except for domestic workers, gardeners, and construction workers, who were under surveillance by ubiquitous hidden security cameras. Nevertheless, the wealthy residents were glad to be there. As one remarked, "There is nothing that compares to this in the world. It would be like the Hamptons, gated."[26]

On the opposite coast, in New York City, where gates around communities are impractical, mansions for the wealthy are sometimes fortified inside as well as outside. "Safe rooms" became nearly standard in townhomes for the super-rich. Alan Wilzig, for example, the former chief executive of the Trust Company of New Jersey, spent $150,000 to fortify his $38.5 million townhouse in Lower Manhattan, according to an article from 2015 in the *New York Times*. The forty-foot-wide, two-story property, with video cameras and motion detectors in every corner, has a secret "safe room" that doubles as the master bedroom. In that room, his family can retreat behind a door that weighs 1,488 pounds. Although the room looks like a normal bedroom, it is equipped with a peephole that offers a 180-degree view of the hallway outside, because, as Wilzig explained, "it can be just as important to know when it's safe outside to be safe inside." The bedroom windows are covered with a transparent bulletproof polymer, and the drywall is reinforced by Kevlar and steel. Wilzig noted that in spite of its sophisticated fortifications, it is not "a level three secured space, because you could get through there with an R.P.G. [rocket-propelled grenade]." He added, "But if you bring an R.P.G. into New York, you're pretty determined."[27]

A residence once owned by actress Gwyneth Paltrow, and later occupied by former US senator Bob Kerrey (D-NE), who before his Senate terms had been governor of Nebraska, and later became president of the New School in New York City, had an eight-by-twelve-foot bulletproof safe room inside the master bedroom that looked like an "old walk-in closet," according to Kerrey, in the same *New York Times* article discussing Wilzig. "There was nothing about it that gave it away as anything but a place to hang your clothes." According to the *Times*, "when an alarm or a doorman is not enough, advances in designs and materials have made it possible to enjoy the safety of Fort Knox amid the comfort of a Four Seasons suite." But the comfort level was tempered by fear, even for the very rich. The president of a company that installed safe rooms noted, "The world is a very scary place right now, especially for people of means; they feel cornered and threatened. . . . When you have so much to lose, and you can afford to, you put a premium on your safety." Although city officials and police did not know how many safe rooms had been built, or if they were ever used, the company's business more than doubled between 2005 and 2015.[28]

Gated communities and safe rooms promised safety but often trapped their occupants in isolated and potentially dangerous spaces. For those who wanted safety as well as freedom on the open roads, large vehicles seemed attractive. Perhaps the perfect symbol of the trend toward privatized protection was the sport utility vehicle (SUV), a "gated community on wheels," in the words of environmental scholar, Randel Hanson. They served as "mobile security units" that reflected individualism and privatization over concern for others on the road or in public spaces.[29]

The first SUV, the Jeep Cherokee, was introduced after World War II as a civilian version of a military vehicle. In the 1980s, automakers developed new versions of the SUV and captured a large segment of the automobile market. SUVs quickly became the fastest-growing segment of the auto industry during the last two decades of the twentieth century, outpacing minivans, which were similar in size and had similar features. By 2004, light trucks, a category that is based on weight and therefore includes pickups, minivans, and SUVs, constituted the majority of the new vehicle market. These gas-guzzling vehicles were exempt from stringent fuel efficiency requirements because they were often used for freight or other commercial purposes. But two-thirds of these vehicles were not used for such purposes; instead, they were purchased for family transportation, or even for individual commuters.[30]

Families often chose these large vehicles because they appeared to offer safety; as with guns and other manifestations of the security culture, however, the opposite was often the case. During the last two decades of the twentieth century, rollovers accounted for one-third of all road fatalities in the United States, and SUVs were more prone to rollovers than automobiles, even at speeds as low as twenty-five miles per hour. As a result, SUV rollovers resulted in three times the death rate of automobile rollovers. SUVs were also more likely than cars to have braking failures. Overall, the National Highway Traffic Safety Administration reported in 2005 that SUV occupants were 11 percent more likely than the occupants of cars to die in a traffic accident. SUVs were also dangerous to other cars. In the event of a side impact collision with an SUV, car occupants were sixteen times more likely to die than in these types of accidents with other cars.[31]

But for SUV owners, *feeling* safe was actually more important than *being* safe. David Bostwick, Daimler Chrysler's director of market research, said that SUV buyers were not really interested in safety. "It's not safety as the issue, it's aggressiveness, it's the ability to go off the road," he said.[32] Automakers hired market researchers and psychologists to study the deepest yearnings of potential consumers and used the findings to determine the design and advertising campaigns for their vehicles. They learned that SUV owners wanted a rugged vehicle, even though 80 percent of SUV owners lived in cities and only 13 percent ever drove them off-road. Psychological needs, more than pragmatism, motivated SUV buyers.

Market researchers tried to determine what to highlight in SUV design and marketing from the 1990s onward. At Ford, for example, marketing specialists tried to assess the values of potential buyers by watching movies that were popular at the time, such as *Rambo*, *Rocky*, and *Top Gun*. Most SUV owners were men, but women owned one-third of all SUVs early on in the period; their numbers increased to 40 percent by the early twenty-first century.[33]

SUVs carried a different appeal than the family-oriented minivan. A market research study that compared 4,500 SUV and minivan purchasers showed little demographic difference between them on the surface: owners of both vehicles were typically affluent married couples in their forties with children. Yet consultants for the auto industry found that the buyers tended to be somewhat different psychologically. According to the survey research, SUV buyers tended to be more restless, less social people with strong fears of crime. Minivan buyers appeared to be more self-confident and social, more involved with family and friends, and more active in their communities. Minivan owners expressed a greater degree of sexual satisfaction compared to SUV drivers, who tended to be more sexually insecure.[34]

SUVs were marketed specifically to respond to potential buyers' fears of crime. One study concluded that the popularity of the SUV reflected American attitudes toward random violence and "the importance of defended personal space." One promotional blurb described the SUV as "a rolling urban command center . . . a mobile techno sanctuary sculpted in urban armor" with an "intimidating" style. The vehicle had protective shutters when parked, and bullet-resistant windows, to make "any mission possible." The large, intimidating vehicles fit the vigilante ethos and offered the fantasy of escape, aggression, and conquest, serving as "weapons" on the road and "armored cars for the battlefield." Designed to evoke masculinity and aggressiveness, SUVs resembled semitrucks, with the look of ferocious lions with bulging muscles.[35]

SUV owners reflected these views when expressing the fears and insecurities that had prompted them to purchase the vehicles. One owner called his SUV an "urban assault vehicle," adding, "The world is becoming a harder and more violent place to live, so we wrap ourselves with the big vehicles." Another said, "It gives you a barrier, makes you feel less threatened." Women often described the security features: "It's easier to see if someone is hiding underneath or lurking behind it," said one.[36] Dr. Clotaire Rapaille, a French-born medical anthropologist, served as a consultant to several major automakers. He concluded that SUVs were designed to be masculine and assertive, and that they appealed to Americans' deepest fears of crime and violence. "The big, powerful SUVs with a message of 'don't mess with me' are going to be around for some time, because American culture is not going to change," he said.[37]

In 1992, the Hummer appeared, a civilian version of the Humvee, which the US armed forces used in the First Gulf War. The actor and former professional bodybuilder Arnold Schwarzenegger, who would later go on to serve as governor of California (2003–2011), had urged automakers to develop such a vehicle, insisting that it would bring the aura of the military to the streets of US cities. The Humvee had to undergo a redesign at AM General, the contractor that made the military version, before it could be declared street legal, but once the Hummer became available, at 6,400 pounds, it weighed twice as much as a regular SUV, cost over $50,000, emitted more than five times the pollution of a regular car, and got less than ten miles per gallon of gas. According to one news article, "Schwarzenegger flew to Indiana to buy the first two off the assembly line." General Motors purchased the brand in 1999 and developed smaller models: the H1 for "rugged individualists," the H2 for "successful achievers," and the H3 for the under-twenty-five-year-old set.[38]

In 2001, Schwarzenegger promoted the new Hummer H2 at its unveiling in Times Square. Proud owners included the governor of Minnesota and ex-wrestler Jesse Ventura. The Hummer was the automotive version of the masculine vigilante—H2 owners said the vehicle embodied "testosterone," and a Sierra Club official called it "the equivalent of a tank." By 2005, it had become the best-selling large luxury SUV in the United States.[39] Although the gas-guzzling Hummer models did not survive the economic collapse of 2008, their presence on American streets at the turn of the twenty-first century was a symbol of the times.

SUV sales plummeted in the recession that followed, but as soon as the economy rebounded, so did the demand for SUVs. In the single year of 2014, one-third of all new vehicles being purchased were SUVs, and sales rose 12 percent—double the rate of increase for the auto industry as a whole—to more than 5.5 million vehicles.[40] For those who could afford them—such as the residents of gated communities and residential fortresses—the illusion of security mattered more than safety itself.

In 2008, Larry Hall built the ultimate walled community: a twenty-first-century version of the early Cold War fallout shelter, created for the super-rich. CEO of the Survival Condo Project, Hall paid $300,000 for a decommissioned underground Atlas missile silo in a rural area north of Wichita, Kansas, which had housed a nuclear warhead from 1961 to 1965. Hall then invested nearly $20 million to create twelve underground luxury condos at the site. He completed the project in 2012 and advertised the units at $3 million for a full-floor condo and half that for a half-floor condo. He kept one for himself and sold the rest. The silo had been built to withstand a nuclear strike. Today, the structure can support seventy-five humans, with renewable sources of food and fuel that can last at least five years, and potentially indefinitely. In the event of a crisis, SWAT-team-style armored trucks ("the Pit-Bull VX") will fetch owners within a 400-mile radius and deliver them to their luxury bunkers, where a guard in military camouflage holds a semiautomatic rifle. As Hall explained, "It's true relaxation for the ultra-wealthy. They can come out here, they know there are armed guards outside. The kids can run around." Inside there is a swimming pool, a clinic, a gym, a movie theater, a library, an armory filled with guns, and a shooting range for target practice (in case nonmembers attack the compound).

The bunker offers protection, but not freedom. As in other gated communities, the condo association sets the rules, and in this compound residents can face incarceration for breaking them: "We can lock people up and give them an adult time-out," said Hall. "There's controlled access in and out, and it's governed by the board." It's a price the owners are willing to pay for the security they crave. Asked what would

An armed guard provides security at the high-end Survival Condo Project, constructed in a decommissioned underground missile silo near Wichita, Kansas. The silo housed a nuclear warhead from 1961 to 1965.

Source: Photo by Dan Winters; permission granted by the photographer.

happen if there was an effort to seize his bunker in a crisis, Hall replied, "You can send all the bullets you want into this place. . . . We've got a sniper post."[41]

The wealthy owners of the bunker condos were not the only one-percenters who were afraid. Ironically, those with so much money they presumably had nothing to worry about were worried. After making their fortunes, many feared that the struggling 99 percent would unleash their resentments and come after them. Robert H. Dugger, a former financial industry lobbyist and partner at a hedge fund, remarked, "Anyone who's in this community knows people who are worried that America is heading toward something like the Russian Revolution."[42]

In the spring of 2016, Antonio Garcia Martinez, a forty-year-old Silicon Valley entrepreneur and San Francisco resident, bought a five-acre plot on an island in the Pacific Northwest to escape from "the roving mob." Equipped with generators, solar panels, and thousands of rounds of ammunition, he hoped he would be safe. But he confessed that in the event of a crisis, "one guy alone" would not be able to survive. "You're going to need to form a local militia," he admitted. The government would be useless. "Preppers," as survivalists like Martinez are known, consider the acronym for the Federal Emergency Management Agency, FEMA, to mean "Foolishly Expecting Meaningful Aid."[43]

Super-wealthy survivalists represent the extreme edge of the trend toward self-incarceration in gated communities as well as of the aggressive bunker mentality that prompts many people to drive menacing SUVs. The fear that motivates their retreat to allegedly safe spaces echoes the terrors of the early Atomic Age. Instead of subversives, they fear criminals. Instead of atomic attack, they fear the "roving mob" that might unleash an American version of "the Russian Revolution."

Survivalism, once considered a fringe movement, has taken hold, and not only among some of the nation's wealthiest individuals, but also among the mainstream. In 2012, the National Geographic Channel launched the reality TV show *Doomsday Preppers*. Each episode featured Americans preparing for S.H.T.F. (when the "shit hits the fan"). More than 4 million viewers watched the premiere; by the end of the first season it was the most popular series in the channel's history.[44]

In some ways, the prepper phenomenon suggests that fear in America has come full circle. From backyard fallout shelters to luxury condos in missile silos; from fenced-in postwar single-family homes to gated communities; from *Duck and Cover* civil defense films to *Doomsday Preppers*, Americans have redesigned their responses to perceived danger. In the process, they have imprisoned themselves, distrusted each other, and turned their backs on the common good. No one is any better off, and certainly no one is safer.

Epilogue

BACK TO THE FUTURE: THE TWENTY-FIRST CENTURY

Make America Great Again

—*Ronald Reagan, campaign slogan, 1980*
—*Donald Trump, campaign slogan, 2016*

Security culture unfolded at the beginning of the twenty-first century much as it had in the last half of the twentieth. The first major crisis of the new century, the terrorist attacks of September 11, 2001, revived fears of external threat that had been dormant since the early years of the Cold War. Although commentators asserted that the attacks were unprecedented, the responses to the attacks were not. Americans were already so steeped in security culture that it did not take much for them to redirect their fears once again. As one resident of a gated community explained a year after the attacks, "Would I move into another gated community? The short, wimpy answer is yes. I'm getting old, and in this post-9/11 world it's not such a bad thing having someone—even a rent-a-cop—to watch over you."[1] Yet neither a gated community nor a rent-a-cop would provide any protection in a terrorist attack like the one that took place on September 11, 2001. The security strategies of the twentieth century were as useless after September 11 as they had been before.[2]

As President George W. Bush declared a "War on Terror," officials put into place rules, regulations, and strategies geared toward reassuring citizens, if not actually protecting them. Security expert Bruce Schneier termed many of these efforts "security theater." The most obvious of the ritualized performances were the attempts to achieve airport security. Most Americans and foreign visitors patiently accepted the long waits in security lines at airports, the frequent checking of documents, the random baggage checks, and the routine pat-down searches. Although it certainly makes good sense to prohibit passengers from taking weapons onto flights, many of the other security measures did little to make anyone safer. Limiting liquids to three-ounce containers, taking off shoes in security lines, and similar procedures were unlikely to thwart anyone who was seriously planning to create mayhem on an airplane. The government spent billions of dollars on such rituals. They might make travelers *feel* safer—but they are not likely to actually make anyone safer.[3] These measures give the illusion of security, as did the home bomb shelters and the "duck and cover" campaigns of the early Cold War years. But just as the civil defense campaigns did nothing to minimize the danger of death from an atomic attack amid an escalating arms race, these highly visible but feeble efforts at airport security offered little actual protection.[4]

Airport security measures were among several official strategies to address the threat of terrorism, whether or not citizens felt those measures were necessary. In spite of the astonishing attacks on September 11, 2001, which were widely televised, individual citizens did not suddenly become more fearful for their personal safety.[5] Immediately after the attacks, a Roper Center poll found that, when asked if their confidence in terms of their own personal safety from terrorist attack had gone up or down, nearly half of those polled (47 percent) said "no change." Only 38 percent said their confidence had gone down. Two-thirds said they had "a great deal" or "quite a bit" of confidence in their own personal safety from terrorist attack. When asked a month later about their emotions concerning the attacks, most respondents (82 percent) said they felt sorrow for the victims and their families. One-third wanted retribution against the attackers or feared more attacks to come. But only 6 percent were concerned about their own personal safety. In November 2001, fully 78 percent of those polled said they thought it was "unlikely" that they or their family members would be hurt or killed in an attack similar to that of 9/11, and that percentage remained roughly the same a year later.[6]

The government's reaction, however, was quite different. Plans drawn up in an earlier era of constant preparedness for atomic attack immediately went into effect. Taking cues from Cold War–era emergency procedures, defense establishment officials quickly retreated into fallout shelters constructed during the early years of the Cold War. After they emerged, with no clear enemy state against which to retaliate, the president declared the War on Terror, and the military mobilized for battle against non-state foes who threatened Americans at home and abroad.[7]

Americans tend to assume that terrorists are Islamic extremists from the Middle East, just as they associate crime with black men. The media contributes to this perception by focusing disproportionate attention on violence committed by Muslims. But with a few notable exceptions, domestic terrorists tend to be American-born white men. In fact, in the years since September 11, 2001, more Americans inside the United States have been murdered by white supremacists, antiabortion fanatics, antigovernment extremists, and other white terrorists than by radical Muslims.[8]

The president declared the War on Terror nonetheless. It is easier to declare a War on Terror than to actually wage one when the enemy is a collection of non-state actors who operate in many places around the world. Although the Bush administration unleashed military conflicts in Afghanistan and Iraq, much of the waging of the War on Terror was political and symbolic, largely focused on domestic concerns. The president utilized the wartime powers accorded the executive branch, which allowed the administration to compromise and constrict the normal workings of a democratic society in the name of national security.

This approach was not new. By the beginning of the twenty-first century, war talk was familiar to Americans. War metaphors as well as militarization had shaped American life ever since World War II. Presidents had declared a War on Poverty, a War on Crime, and a War on Drugs. The Cold War was in effect a war on communism. In the years since World War II, the language of wartime had become a permanent feature of American life.[9]

Thus, even though the attacks of 9/11 were unpredictable, the national response was remarkably predictable, both on the part of leaders and on the part of citizens. When the president declared a War on Terror immediately after the attacks, few Americans objected. The war he launched was in many ways modeled on older wars—not on World War II, but on the various military actions of the Cold War, as well as on the nuclear arms race. The Bush administration increased the defense budget by $48 billion (a sum larger than the entire defense budget of any other nation) and developed new nuclear weapons, according to the details of a secret Pentagon report made public by the *New York Times* in March 2002.[10]

In its domestic ramifications, the War on Terror drew on the strategies of the anticommunist crusade of the 1950s, but focusing on Muslims. Vigilantism against Muslims took the form of hostility, threats, racist slurs, assaults, and even murder. President Bush called for tolerance toward Muslims, noting, "We welcome legal immigrants but we don't welcome people who come to hurt Americans."[11] Yet post-9/11 anti-terror policies allowed people of Arab descent to be rounded up for questioning and incarceration without due process. Colleges cooperated with federal investigators, who questioned students from Middle Eastern countries at more than two hundred campuses in the United States.[12]

Government officials encouraged citizens to help identify potential terrorists inside the country, echoing civil defense measures from the early Cold War era as well as crime-fighting strategies from the late twentieth century. Bush and the Office of Homeland Security called upon citizens to create a "national neighborhood watch" to spot terrorist threats.[13] In July 2002, the Bush administration called for the establishment of

Operation TIPS (for Terrorism Information and Prevention System), a program using volunteers whose jobs frequently brought them into people's homes (delivery people, utility workers, and so on) to report suspicious activity. Essentially, the volunteers were being authorized and encouraged to spy on their fellow citizens. Although the TIPS program was canceled because of its violations of civil liberties, the proposal illustrates the Bush administration's eagerness to round up anyone who appeared suspicious.[14]

Security mania after 9/11 took remarkably familiar form. As we have seen, during the Cold War, perceived danger gave rise to calls for women to retreat to the home and for men to provide them with protection. Those tropes came first in response to the Atomic Age, and reappeared in the face of exaggerated fears of criminal attacks on women from the 1960s onward. After 9/11, traditional gender roles resurfaced.[15] Suddenly, "manly" men were again the nation's heroes, and they were charged with protecting vulnerable women. Bush took every opportunity to show himself in military gear, roughing it on the ranch, or boasting about his gun collection.[16]

The media became saturated with images and stories of strong men rescuing vulnerable, weak women. Perhaps the most egregious fiction regarding women's alleged vulnerability that emerged in the post-9/11 era was the story of Jessica Lynch, a nineteen-year-old soldier who was injured in the Iraq War. A media frenzy recounted her alleged capture and rescue after an ambush by Iraqi forces. Contrary to the fabricated story of her heroic rescue by male soldiers, who allegedly freed her from brutal treatment, Lynch apparently was not treated poorly in the Iraqi hospital. She later told a different story, of the concern, care, and kindness that she received from the Iraqi health-care providers. Lynch was bewildered and annoyed that her experience had been exploited and twisted into a story of helplessness and rescue in order to uphold the myth of male heroes protecting and rescuing a young, helpless, and victimized woman soldier.[17]

Back home, the role of women as domestic protectors made a comeback. On June 2, 2003, *Time* magazine proclaimed, "Goodbye, Soccer

Mom. Hello, Security Mom." *Time* asserted that in the wake of 9/11, the latter had become the new norm: "She's worried, she wants answers and she likes toughness in a President." She thinks "her civil liberties seem less important than they used to, especially compared with keeping her children safe." This, too, was a myth. A year later, *Time*'s pollster confessed, "We honestly could not find much empirical evidence to support it." Nevertheless the idea took hold. In 2016, Juliette Kayyem published *Security Mom*, a guidebook offering women advice, according to its subtitle, on *Protecting Our Homeland and Your Home*.[18]

After September 11, 2001, nothing at home really changed. The security culture Americans had previously accepted remained in place long after the attacks. The government established new security measures that met no major resistance. The nation went to war, but aside from those who volunteered for service and their families, most Americans stood on the sidelines. All of the responses to 9/11 grew out of developments that predated the attacks. By the end of the twentieth century, Americans had already altered how they lived in order to manage their fear. Personal responses to fear had mirrored the national response as far back as the beginning of the Atomic Age, when there had been a heightening of alarm, a proliferation of arms, and a bunker mentality, rather than investment in the common good. The principles of individualism, unfettered capitalism, the sanctity of the home, and a suspicion of outsiders that gained salience in the early Cold War era outlived the Cold War itself and continued after the 9/11 attacks.

Fifteen years after the attacks of September 11, 2001, Donald Trump won the presidency by promising, essentially, to turn the entire country into a gated community. He would build a wall to keep out Mexicans, he said—charging, "They're bringing drugs. They're bringing crime. They're rapists"—although there was no evidence that immigrants from Mexico committed more crimes than native-born Americans.[19] Moreover, Trump's insistence that violent crime was increasing—an assertion he repeated frequently during the campaign—was incorrect. Violent crime had been declining for decades.[20] Trump's wall, like the walls around gated communities, was unlikely to make the nation or its citizens any safer.

Yet Trump's message resonated with millions of mostly white Americans whose fears had generated anger and resentment against strangers, minorities, and outsiders who, they wrongly assumed, threatened their security. Trump tapped into perceptions that had taken root over the previous half-century, perceptions that had been firmly implanted in American consciousness by the end of the twentieth century. And his message drew an avid following that ultimately landed him in the White House.

It was not a new message. In 1997, twenty years before Donald Trump became president of the United States, literary scholar Nicolaus Mills wrote *The Triumph of Meanness*. "What has really been lost," he observed, "is the idea of nationhood. We simply write off . . . whole segments of the population. . . . More prisons. More police. Less welfare. Decaying public schools. . . . It is fortress America with gated suburbs and guarded apartment houses and private schools and private security forces." Well before the dawn of the twenty-first century, fearful Americans had retreated from a commitment to the public good.[21]

Trump promised security. During the campaign, he vowed that he had a secret plan to bring a quick victory in the Middle East that would destroy the Islamic State of Iraq and Syria, known as ISIS: "I have a simple message for [ISIS]: Their days are numbered. I won't tell them where and I won't tell them how. . . . But they're going to be gone. ISIS will be gone if I'm elected president. And they'll be gone quickly."[22] Trump's confident assertions appealed to fearful and war-weary Americans, but his plan for victory was murky, at best.

Like his anti-immigrant stance, and his vague promise of triumph in the Middle East, Trump's proposals for keeping the nation and its citizens safe from nuclear attack were ill considered. Regardless of the diplomatic efforts of the United States and the Soviet Union, and then Russia, that had reduced the combined stockpile of nuclear weapons from more than 60,000 in 1985 to fewer than 15,000 today, Trump asserted that the United States "must greatly strengthen and expand its nuclear capability until such time as the world comes to its senses regarding nukes." He told a reporter, "Let it be an arms race. We will outmatch them at every pass and outlast them all."[23]

Amassing nuclear weapons, like building a wall at the nation's border and banning immigrants, would do little to address the real insecurities plaguing the nation, many of which were caused by a massive and growing income gap.[24] But Trump managed to convince millions of Americans that their woes were caused by minorities and immigrants—"rapists" and "criminals"—who had allegedly gained undeserved privileges from an incompetent liberal government, a government that did not even deserve his tax dollars. Trump won, in part, not in spite of his lack of government experience or public service, but because of it. When three pages of his 1995 federal tax return were leaked to the *New York Times*, they showed he had not paid federal taxes that year, because of his ability to claim a $1 billion loss. (Trump had refused to make his tax returns public, a practice that is common, but not required, of presidential candidates.) When the Democratic candidate, Hillary Clinton, confronted him about the return in a televised presidential debate, he did not deny that the returns were his, or that he had not paid 1995 taxes. Instead, he bragged about it: "That makes me smart," he said.[25] The fact that Trump's supporters were not troubled by his decision to avoid paying taxes demonstrates how deeply antigovernment sentiment had taken hold.

The media also helped elect Trump. Every outrageous statement he made during the campaign provided headlines in the news—the best free publicity a candidate could have wanted. Although the mainstream media appeared to disapprove of his outbursts and antics, the publicity helped Trump stay in the public eye. Much as the news media had long devoted exaggerated coverage of rare, violent crimes, they gave unwarranted visibility to Trump's unorthodox campaign.

Meanwhile, popular cable news networks such as Fox and right-wing websites like Breitbart News actively promoted Trump's candidacy. After the election, the time-honored distance between the press and the presidency collapsed the moment that Trump appointed Stephen Bannon as his chief strategist. Bannon was the driving force behind Breitbart, which notoriously ran headlines that degraded racial minorities and women while whipping up fear of crime. In 2010, Bannon enthused, "Fear is a good thing. Fear is going to lead you to take action."[26] That perspective fed the security culture and helped Trump win the election.

Trump persuaded only about 25 percent of eligible voters to vote for him—but that was enough to take the electoral college, even though Hillary Clinton won the popular vote by nearly 3 million votes. The ones who really determined the outcome of the election were the 42 percent of eligible voters who stayed home—and the 6 million more who were disqualified from voting as a result of felony convictions.[27] The vast majority of Americans did not vote for Donald Trump—they either voted for his opponent or they did not vote at all. More citizens did not vote for anyone than voted for either candidate, reflecting a massive disengagement from the most basic privilege and responsibility of citizenship.

The factors that propelled Trump to the White House, including voter apathy, did not emerge suddenly during the campaign. They had been brewing for half a century. Trump's election in many ways marked the triumph of fortress America, with its pro-gun policies, legal vigilantism, mass incarceration, anti-immigrant sentiments, antipathy to women's and minority rights, fortified homes and vehicles, and deep-seated hostility to government. Shortly after taking office, Trump spoke at a meeting of the National Rifle Association. His attorney general, Jeff Sessions, initiated efforts to reinstate harsh and punitive criminal justice sentencing guidelines, breathing new life into calls for "law and order." Trump called for a return to notorious "stop and frisk" practices, enabling police to use racial profiling. The most damaging aspects of the security culture received a major boost from the Trump administration.

As the twenty-first century unfolds, there is little evidence that Americans are safer, or more empowered, as a result of their weapons, the number of their fellow citizens who are imprisoned, their gated communities, their protective gadgets, and their SUVs. But fear has created an armed and bunkered citizenry. There are more guns on the streets, locks on the doors, and walls around neighborhoods, and soon there are likely to be more walls along the nation's borders.

Hostility toward government and lack of concern for the common good may have made the nation considerably *less* secure. While citizens were distracted by street crime that harmed relatively few people, unregulated private enterprise and a rapidly widening gap between the very wealthy and everyone else were at work, producing profound insecurity for millions of Americans. Locks on the doors did not protect families against losing their homes through mortgage foreclosure. Guns in their pants did not prevent citizens from losing their shirts to corrupt financiers. Americans looked over their shoulders to see if strangers were approaching, but they failed to notice that right in front of them, the super-rich, the one percent, were sucking up the nation's wealth at the expense of everyone else. They feared and locked up the wrong culprits; those causing the most harm to American security continued to live the good life.

This misplaced fear led to the electoral victory of Donald Trump. Democracy depends on citizens accepting their differences and trusting one another, at least to the extent that they understand themselves as belonging to a civic sphere as well as a private sphere. It requires investing in the well-being of the people, and holding the government accountable as the institution that represents, and acts on behalf of, the citizens. If Americans distrust and even fear one another as well as the government, and have no commitment to the public good, then the basic social and political practices that ensure a healthy democracy cannot survive.

ALL IS NOT lost. The twenty-first century has witnessed some glimmers of hope that the necessary cultural and political transformations required to revive American democracy may be gaining momentum. The massive organizing effort that resulted in the election of Barack Obama to the presidency in 2008 illustrates what can happen when citizens are energized. The election of the first African American president, in the midst of a powerfully racialized security culture, demonstrates the possibility that fortress America could eventually be dismantled. Yet the race-based hostility that dogged his presidency persisted throughout both of his terms in office and helped to elect Donald Trump in 2016. Race was undeniably a major factor in that election. In 2012, researchers found that 79 percent of Republicans held antiblack views, along with 32 percent of Democrats—one-third of voters from Obama's own party. In 2011 and 2012, nineteen states enacted voting restrictions aimed at suppressing the black vote. The challenge of reviving a robust democracy under these circumstances is daunting, but not hopeless.[28]

Along with Obama's election, the movement for LGBT rights, culminating in marriage equality, demonstrates that Americans can transcend deep-rooted prejudices. Even the criminal justice system can be reformed. Polls taken in 2016 showed that large majorities of Americans of both political parties had come to realize that mass incarceration did not serve any useful purpose. Eighty percent of respondents opposed mandatory minimum sentences and said judges should have discretion in setting prison terms. Many who had little compassion for those enmeshed in the carceral system nevertheless thought that too much public money was spent housing criminals.[29] In spite of the Trump administration's efforts to reinstate punitive sentencing, public opinion no longer supports those policies.

Perhaps the most significant and powerful organized opposition to Trump's America is the Black Lives Matter movement. Momentum for the movement came about in response to the murder of the black teenager Trayvon Martin by the white vigilante George Zimmerman in 2012. The movement itself took shape in response to the killing of a young black man, Michael Brown, by a police officer in Ferguson, Missouri, in the summer of 2014, and the many police killings of black people that followed. Black Lives Matter focused attention on the reality and prevalence of police violence against African Americans. Cellphone videos brought to light brutal practices that had long been hidden from public view. The movement has helped change public attitudes, and possibly spurred government action: the US Department of Justice's report on policing in Ferguson was a damning indictment of the police department's practices.

These recent developments suggest that while deep problems persist, some of the harshest aspects of the security culture might ease in the future.

The Black Lives Matter movement is perhaps the most well-organized challenge to the law-and-order worldview, but there are other signs of opposition as well. The most promising sign may be the massive expression of dissent that has emerged in the wake of the 2016 election, beginning with millions of protesters all over the country marching in defiance the day after Trump's inauguration. Resistance to Trump has ignited a level of political activism on the part of ordinary citizens that has not been seen since the social movements of the 1960s and 1970s. Perhaps Americans are finally ready to dismantle fortress America and revive our ailing democracy.

If American democracy is to survive and thrive, the stirrings we see in the wake of Trump's election will need to be sustained and strengthened. The outpouring of support for immigrants, Muslims, and other minorities has demonstrated a massive pushback against the fear-mongering that has targeted those groups. Signs on streets, storefronts, and colleges and other schools asserting that "Everyone is welcome here" represent an embrace of strangers who have long been feared.

Hundreds of groups in localities across the country have confronted their elected representatives and demanded that they be held accountable to the people they serve. By showing up at town hall meetings and asserting their concerns, by phoning their elected representatives to express their opinions, and by organizing at the grassroots level to energize voters, citizens have begun to breathe new life into the civic sphere. Scores of new political organizations, national and local, are mounting massive resistance to the policies of the Trump administration.

In the wake of the election, the news media has also found a new mission. After decades of exaggerating the dangers of crime by focusing on heinous but rare acts of violence, the mainstream news outlets now face the problem of "fake news" coming from right-wing media outlets that supported both the candidacy and the presidency of Donald Trump. "Fake news" has led to outrage, with calls for honesty and accountability in the media. With Trump consistently fabricating "alternative facts" and attacking journalists who are critical of him, journalism has become another avenue for efforts to set the record straight. Mainstream news organizations, including the *New York Times* and the *Washington Post*, are hiring reporters and gaining subscribers.[30] Diligent journalists are uncovering important stories that the Trump administration has endeavored to hide, such as the possible connections between Trump's advisers and Russian officials. Trump's attacks on the media have motivated an army of journalists to find out and report on what goes on behind closed doors.

At the same time, activists are marshaling their forces to create coalitions to promote peace, the environment, and social justice. Ahmad Abuznaid, cofounder of the Dream Defenders, a Miami-based racial-justice organization, noted, "We know the same companies that are building our prisons are the ones building our bases."[31] Although a viable peace movement has not yet coalesced, these sparks of activism portend possibilities ahead.

There are symbolic gestures as well. As a result of Trump's comments about the need to escalate the arms race, within days of his inauguration the Science and Security Board of the *Bulletin of the Atomic Scientists* moved the Doomsday Clock thirty seconds closer to midnight, to two and a half minutes, reflecting the board's sense of urgency regarding the possible destruction of the planet. Composed of scientists, including nuclear physicists and climate experts, the board meets twice each year to discuss where the clock's hands should fall in light of world events. The Doomsday Clock made its debut on the cover of the bulletin's June 1947 edition, showing the clock at seven minutes to midnight. Since that time, the clock has moved both closer and farther away, depending on the board's assessment of the risk of global disaster.

With the end of the Cold War in 1990, the minute hand slowly moved backward, to a full seventeen minutes away from midnight. It has slowly moved up again in the years since. "Unchecked climate change, global nuclear weapons modernizations, and outsized nuclear weapons arsenals pose extraordinary and undeniable threats to the continued existence of humanity," the bulletin's editors said in January 2015.

"World leaders have failed to act with the speed or on the scale required to protect citizens from potential catastrophe." The half-minute move in 2017 brings the clock the closest to midnight that it has been since 1953, the year after the United States and the Soviet Union both conducted tests of the hydrogen bomb. When the scientists moved the clock in 2017, they declared, "Never before has the Bulletin decided to advance the clock largely because of the statements of a single person. But when that person is the new president of the United States, his words matter."[32] The Doomsday Clock brings scientists' concerns about nuclear and environmental dangers to public attention.

Despite the hopeful signs, it is not yet clear what lies ahead. Whether or not symbolic gestures like the Doomsday Clock, the organizing momentum of Black Lives Matter, the energy of those who took to the streets to march in protest against Trump's election, the grassroots activists who jam town hall meetings, and the energized journalists who are exposing corruption can coalesce into an effective and powerful opposition remains to be seen. The challenge of reviving democracy requires an energized nationwide organizing effort.

It is not clear whether the forces supporting fortress America will prevail, or whether the newly energized opposition will triumph. When Americans fear and distrust each other, we become weaker and less secure. Perhaps the misguided fears that have harmed our democracy will give way to an embrace of energized citizenship. There are signs that this might be happening. If the momentum continues, we might see a new commitment to the common good. That is the only way that Americans will be able to build a truly safe and secure society. After all, citizens need to remember that beyond all the guns, gates, and screaming headlines, the vast majority of people in this country have no desire to harm anyone. If, rather than retreating from each other, Americans could come together in mutual trust and support, democracy might yet flourish. Perhaps Americans are finally ready to abandon fear and embrace democracy.

ACKNOWLEDGMENTS

Many people and institutions made this book possible, and I am humbled by their generosity. I am enormously grateful for sabbatical supplemental funding from the University of Minnesota, as well as the generous resources from the Regents Professorship that funded research assistants and travel to archives. I was extremely fortunate to receive fellowships from the John Simon Guggenheim Memorial Foundation, the National Endowment for the Humanities, the Huntington Library—where I spent a wonderfully productive year—and the Rockefeller Foundation, which gave me the opportunity to spend a month writing at the Bellagio Study and Conference Center in Bellagio, Italy. Thanks to Jennifer Frost at the University of Auckland and to Mary Dudziak at Emory University for the opportunity to share this work in progress and gain constructive feedback at symposia at their respective universities.

Thanks to my colleagues at the University of Minnesota, especially the faculty and staff in the History Department, whose patience and support made it possible for me to finish this book during my first year as department chair. Amanda Nelson saved my life more than once as I climbed my way up the steep learning curve of a big and complex department.

I benefited immensely from the help of undergraduate and graduate research assistants at the University of Minnesota: Daniel Kilgore, Emma Nelson, Sharon Park, Andrew Paul, Robert Smith, and Patrick Wilz. Special thanks to Matt Becker, Caley Horan, Daniel LaChance,

Scott Laderman, Sharon Leon, Julia Mickenberg, and Jason Stahl, not only for their help when they were graduate students but also for their intellectual generosity and friendship in the years since they have gone on to their own distinguished scholarly careers.

Thanks also to the staffs at the University of Minnesota Libraries, the Schlesinger Library at Harvard University, the Margaret Herrick Library of the Academy of Motion Picture Arts and Sciences, and the Huntington Library—especially Jennifer Watts, curator of photography and visual culture, and Susi Krasnoo, who helped with everything. During research trips to Cambridge, Nancy Cott and Judy Smith provided housing, meals, friendship, and consultation as I worked through the ideas for this book.

Lara Heimert and Dan Gerstle at Basic Books are the best editors anyone could hope for. My agent Sandy Dijkstra is a whirlwind of enthusiasm whose help at every stage spurred me onward. I want to thank everyone at Basic Books, especially Stephanie Summerhays and Alia Massoud, as well as Elise Capron and the staff at the Dijkstra Agency, for all the help and support they provided. A special shout-out goes to Katherine Streckfus, copyeditor extraordinaire.

I could not have completed this project without my friends. Thanks to Amy Kaminsky for long talks and walks along the Mississippi River. Her son, the late Jonathan Kaminsky, was a wealth of knowledge, wisdom, and wit. Lynn Dumenil, Sara Evans, Estelle Freedman, and Riv-Ellen Prell read drafts and gave me valuable criticism and suggestions. I thank them all for their encouragement, support, and especially for their precious friendship.

My children, Michael, Daniel, and Sarah, inspire me to write with the clarity and passion they bring to their own elegant prose. Each of them took time from their busy lives to read drafts, provide me with helpful criticisms and suggestions, and discuss the project with me. My remarkable daughter-in-law, Rachel Proctor May, always gave me new ideas to think about. Grandkids Ezrah Josephine May and Isaiah Nelson May lifted my spirits with their impish fun.

Lary May read drafts, shared ideas, offered encouragement, and kept me going through this project from beginning to end. His intellectual curiosity, playfulness, and love have sustained me throughout the many years of our life together.

NOTES

Introduction: The Bunker Mentality

1. See Paul Boyer, *By the Bomb's Early Light* (Chapel Hill: University of North Carolina Press, 1994).

2. See Elaine Tyler May, *Homeward Bound: American Families in the Cold War Era*, 4th ed. (New York: Basic Books, 2017).

3. See Carol A. Stabile, *White Victims, Black Villains: Gender, Race, and Crime News in US Culture* (New York: Routledge, 2006).

4. Michael Sherry demonstrated how the concept of "war" has permeated every major national initiative since World War II. Andrew Bacevich documented the many ways in which the country became militarized in its institutions, popular culture, values, and daily life. Mary Dudziak pointed out that the nation has been in a perpetual state of wartime, even during times generally considered to be "peacetime." Joseph Masco explored the psychological and emotional legacy of the Cold War that continues into the post-9/11 era. Many others have analyzed the culture of fear, the punitive criminal justice system, mass incarceration, gun violence, and other manifestations of the security culture. See Michael Sherry, *In The Shadow of War: The United States Since the 1930s* (New Haven, CT: Yale University Press, 1997); Andrew Bacevich, *The New American Militarism: How Americans Are Seduced by War*, 2nd ed. (New York: Oxford University Press, 2013); Mary Dudziak, *War Time: An Idea, Its History, Its Consequences* (New York: Oxford University Press, 2013); Joseph Masco, *Theater of Operations: National Security Affect from the Cold War to the War on Terror* (Durham: University of North Carolina Press, 2014). Additional relevant works are cited throughout the notes.

5. By the early 1990s, the percentage of American households with guns was far above that of other industrialized countries. For comparative data on gun

ownership, see "International Homicide Comparisons," GunCite, last updated May 19, 2006, www.guncite.com/gun_control_gcgvinco.html.

6. See Edward J. Blakely and Mary Gail Snyder, *Fortress America: Gated Communities in the United States* (Washington, DC: Brookings Institution Press, 1997); Keith Bradsher, *High and Mighty: SUVs—The World's Most Dangerous Vehicles and How They Got That Way* (New York: PublicAffairs, 2002).

Chapter 1: Gimme Shelter: Security in the Atomic Age

1. Quoted in Kenneth D. Rose, *One Nation Underground: The Fallout Shelter in American Culture* (New York: New York University Press, 2001), 34.

2. Cover photo, *House Beautiful*, January 1945. Quotations from Irene Moore, "A Proper Dream House for Any Veteran," 34–37. For a fuller discussion, see Elaine Tyler May, "Shelter Me: The Suburban Dream in Cold War America," in Jennifer A. Watts, ed., *Maynard L. Parker: Modern Photography and the American Dream* (New Haven, CT: Yale University Press, in association with the Huntington Library, 2012); Jennifer Watts, curator of photographs at the Huntington Library, called *House Beautiful* the "ultimate tastemaker in this period." Jennifer A. Watts, "Swimming Alone: The Backyard Pool in Cold War California," in Daniell Cornell, ed., *Backyard Oasis: The Swimming Pool in Southern California Photography, 1945–1982* (New York: Palm Springs Art Museum and Delmonico Books, 2012), 52.

3. Box Office Mojo, "The Best Years of Our Lives," n.d., www.boxofficemojo.com/movies/?id=bestyearsofourlives.htm&adjust_yr=1&p=.htm.

4. *The Best Years of Our Lives*, William Wyler, director (Samuel Goldwyn, 1946).

5. Martin Sherwin, *A World Destroyed: Hiroshima and Its Legacies* (Palo Alto, CA: Stanford University Press, 1975).

6. For more on the militarization of "peacetime" and ongoing war, see Mary Dudziak, *War Time: An Idea, Its History, Its Consequences* (New York: Oxford University Press, 2012); Michael S. Sherry, *In the Shadow of War: The United States Since the 1930s* (New Haven, CT: Yale University Press, 1995); Andrew Bacevich, *The New American Militarism: How Americans Are Seduced by War* (New York: Oxford University Press, 2005).

7. Laura McEnaney, *Civil Defense Begins at Home: Militarization Meets Everyday Life in the Fifties* (Princeton, NJ: Princeton University Press, 2000), 13–14; see also Daniel Yergin, *Shattered Peace: The Origins of the Cold War*, 2nd ed. (New York: Penguin, 1990), 5, 193–220.

8. For poll data on attitudes toward communists and communism used in this chapter, see John Kenneth White, "Seeing Red: The Cold War and American Public Opinion," Conference on the Power of Free Inquiry and Cold War International History, Session VI, National Archives, www.archives.gov

/research/foreign-policy/cold-war/conference/white.html. For more polling data throughout the twentieth century see this site and also Roper Center for Public Opinion Research, Cornell University, iPoll, at https://ropercenter.cornell.edu/ipoll-database.

9. Susan L. Carruthers, *Cold War Captives: Imprisonment, Escape, and Brainwashing* (Berkeley: University of California Press, 2009), 3.

10. Quoted in E. J. Dionne, "Inevitably, the Politics of Terror," *Washington Post*, May 25, 2003, https://www.washingtonpost.com/archive/opinions/2003/05/25/inevitably-the-politics-of-terror/c4fdf19a-8d88-4109-9c2f-06602221928f/?utm_term=.1e417d790f9e.

11. Ellen Schrecker, *The Age of McCarthyism: A Brief History with Documents* (Boston: St. Martin's Press, 1994).

12. See Elaine Tyler May, *Homeward Bound: American Families in the Cold War Era*, 4th ed. (New York: Basic Books, 2017); David K. Johnson, *The Lavender Scare: The Cold War Persecution of Gays and Lesbians in the Federal Government* (Chicago: University of Chicago Press, 2006).

13. For data examined from online opinion polls, see "Self Defense, Personal Safety—Public Opinion Polls," Roper Center for Public Opinion Research, Cornell University, https://ropercenter.cornell.edu. One June 1948 poll asked: "Some people say we should now take certain steps in order to make an agreement with Russia more likely. Would you favor the U.S. . . . announcing to the world that we will not use the atom bomb except in self-defense?" Seventy-one percent of respondents favored the statement.

14. National Security Council Paper NSC-68, "United States Objectives and Programs for National Security," was a Top Secret report completed by the US Department of State's Policy Planning Staff on April 7, 1950. The fifty-eight-page memorandum, among the most influential documents composed by the US government during the Cold War, was not declassified until 1975. Its authors argued that one of the most pressing threats confronting the United States was the "hostile design" of the Soviet Union. The authors concluded that the Soviet threat would soon be greatly augmented by the addition of more weapons, including nuclear weapons, to the Soviet arsenal. They argued that the best course of action was to respond in kind with a massive buildup of the US military and its weaponry. From the US Department of State, Office of the Historian, https://history.state.gov/milestones/1945-1952/NSC68; see also "United States Objectives of National Security," in McEnaney, *Civil Defense Begins at Home*, 29.

15. See public opinion polls cited above.

16. McEnaney, *Civil Defense Begins at Home*, 13–15.

17. Dwight D. Eisenhower, First Inaugural Address, January 20, 1953, Washington, DC, available at Eisenhower Presidential Library, www.eisenhower.archives.gov/all_about_ike/speeches/1953_inaugural_address.pdf. For the text of

Eisenhower's commencement address at University Park, Pennsylvania, on June 11, 1955, see "President's Penn State Talk Text," *Los Angeles Times*, June 12, 1955, 28.

18. See public opinion polls cited above.

19. See Julia Mickenberg, *Learning from the Left: Children's Literature, the Cold War, and Radical Politics in the United States* (New York: Oxford University Press, 2015).

20. For the numbers and history of the CPUSA, see Harvey Klehr, *The Heyday of American Communism: The Depression Decade* (New York: Basic Books, 1984), 3–5; Victor G. Devinatz, "Communist Party of the United States of America (CPUSA)," Encyclopedia Britannica, www.britannica.com/topic/Communist-Party-of-the-United-States-of-America; Anthony Summers, *Official and Confidential: The Secret Life of J. Edgar Hoover* (New York: G. P. Putnam, 1993, 191); Fraser Ottanelli, *The Communist Party of the United States: From the Depression to World War II* (New Brunswick, NJ: Rutgers University Press, 1991), 43.

21. See May, *Homeward Bound.*

22. Frank Hobbs and Nicole Stoop, *US Census Bureau Demographic Trends in the 20th Century*, Census 2000 Special Reports, US Department of Commerce, Economics and Statistics Administration, US Census Bureau, CENSR-4, November 2002.

23. Elizabeth Gordon, "The Responsibility of an Editor," manuscript for speech delivered to the Press Club Luncheon of the American Furniture Mart, Chicago, June 22, 1953, 14, 15, 21, quoted in Dianne Harris, "Making Your Private World: Modern Landscape Architecture and *House Beautiful*, 1945–1965," in Marc Treib, ed., *The Architecture of Landscape, 1940–1960* (Philadelphia: University of Pennsylvania Press, 2002), 182.

24. Joseph Howland, "Good Living is NOT Public Living," *House Beautiful*, January 1950, quoted in Harris, "Making Your Private World," in Treib, ed., *The Architecture of Landscape*, 193.

25. Thomas D. Church, *Gardens Are for People: How to Plan for Outdoor Living* (New York: Reinhold, 1955), 189–190;Wooster Bard Field, *House Planning* (New York: McGraw Hill, 1940), 176. Wooster Bard Field was an architect and professor of engineering drawing at Ohio State University. See also Dianne Harris, *Little White Houses: How the Postwar Home Constructed Race in America* (Minneapolis: University of Minnesota Press, 2012), chap. 4.

26. Jeff Wiltse, *Contested Waters: A Social History of Swimming Pools in America* (Chapel Hill: University of North Carolina Press, 2007), 205.

27. Gary R. Edgerton, "Television in America," Oxford Research Encyclopedia, Oxford University Press, May 2016, http://americanhistory.oxfordre.com/view/10.1093/acrefore/9780199329175.001.0001/acrefore-9780199329175-e-291.

28. See Kenneth Jackson, *Crabgrass Frontier: The Suburbanization of the United States* (New York: Oxford University Press, 1985); Thomas J. Sugrue, *The Origins*

of the Urban Crisis: Race and Inequality in Postwar Detroit (Princeton, NJ: Princeton University Press, 2014).

29. For government data on housing values, see "Historic Census of Housing Tables: Home Values," US Department of Commerce, US Census Bureau, n.d., https://www.census.gov/hhes/www/housing/census/historic/values.html; for income data, see "Indicator 16: Median Family Income," National Center for Education Statistics, Institute of Education Sciences, n.d., https://nces.ed.gov/pubs98/yi/yi16.pdf.

30. See Jeffrey M. Hornstein, *A Nation of Realtors: A Cultural History of the Twentieth-Century American Middle Class* (Durham, NC: Duke University Press, 2005), especially chapters 6 and 7; Mike Davis, *City of Quartz: Excavating the Future in Los Angeles* (New York: Verso, 1990), 63.

31. On urban renewal, see Samuel Zipp, *Manhattan Projects: The Rise and Fall of Urban Renewal in Cold War New York* (New York: Oxford University Press, 2010).

32. Rick Lyman, "Wilkinson, Defiant Figure of Red Scare, Dies at 91," *New York Times*, January 4, 2006 (from www.nytimes.com-obituaries).

33. "Bowron Warns of Peril from Reds Living in L.A.," editorial, *Los Angeles Times*, February 7, 1951. Unless otherwise noted, emphasis is reproduced from the original.

34. Patricia Hampl, *A Romantic Education* (New York: Houghton Mifflin, 1981), 37–39.

35. Quoted in Carruthers, *Cold War Captives*, 5.

36. Advertisement, Norfolk and Western Railway, *Newsweek* 42, no. 10 (September 7, 1953), 13; Becky M. Nicolaides, *My Blue Heaven: Life and Politics in the Working-Class Suburbs of Los Angeles, 1920–1965* (Chicago: University of Chicago Press, 2002), 25; advertisement for the Freedoms Foundation, Valley Forge, Pennsylvania.

37. See Lynn Dumenil, "'The Insatiable Maw of Bureaucracy': Antistatism and Education Reform in the 1920s," *Journal of American History* 77, no. 2 (1990): 499–524; advertisement, Electric Light and Power Companies, *U.S. News and World Report* 28 (May 28, 1950): 25.

38. Caley Horan, "Actuarial Age: Insurance and the Emergence of Neoliberalism in the Postwar United States" (PhD diss., University of Minnesota, 2011). These quotations appeared on a number of insurance industry posters that have been collected by Caley Horan. I am grateful to her for allowing me to use these materials. Her book is forthcoming from the University of Chicago Press.

39. *In Our Hands*, 1950, is the third film in a four-part anticommunist series. See https://archive.org/details/0837_In_Our_Hands_Part_3_How_To_Lose_What_We_Have_18_47_04_00.

40. David Monteyne, *Fallout Shelter: Designing for Civil Defense in the Cold War* (Minneapolis: University of Minnesota Press, 2011), 14.

41. McEnaney, *Civil Defense Begins at Home*, 19–20.

42. Ibid., 51; "Defense Booklet Distribution Begins as Berry Takes Office," *Los Angeles Times*, February 6, 1951; Benny Perez, "San Pedro Naps in Face of Possible 'A-Bomb' Disaster," *San Pedro News Pilot*, February 24, 1951.

43. "L.A. Will Lack Bomb Shelters, Says Allen," *Los Angeles Examiner*, January 19, 1951. The article quotes County Manager Wayne Allen as saying, at a meeting of the Los Angeles Junior Chamber of Commerce on January 18, 1951, "Our economy will not permit widespread construction of public bomb shelters." See also "Steps Taken to Locate Adequate Bomb Shelter," *Los Angeles Times*, September 16, 1951, F11; "City Adopts Backyard Shelter Law," *Los Angeles Daily News*, February 19, 1951.

44. McEnaney, *Civil Defense Begins at Home*, 149; Monteyne, *Fallout Shelter*, xiii–xxi, 46, and chap. 4; see also Tom Vanderbilt, *Survival City: Adventures Among the Ruins of Atomic America* (New York: Princeton Architectural Press, 2002), esp. chap. 3, which explains how architecture designed for civil defense heightened fears; Sherry, *In the Shadow of War*; Andrew Bacevich, *New American Militarism*; and Dudziak, *War Time*.

45. Carl Ritter, "Hjelte Urges Defense Thinking," *San Pedro News Pilot*, February 23, 1951, in Fletcher Bowron Papers, Huntington Library, San Marino, California; "Valley Defense Told by Hjelte," *[San Fernando] Valley Times*, February 22, 1951; "Defense Director Warns of Split-Second Disaster," *Los Angeles Times*, February 22, 1951; Rose, *One Nation Underground*, 11, 24, 32–34.

46. "Foreign Affairs Survey," September 1946, Roper Center for Public Opinion Research, Cornell University, iPoll, https://ropercenter.cornell.edu/ipoll-database.

47. Jean Jacobsen, "Berry Outlines Defense Plan for Soroptimists," *Los Angeles Mirror*, "Her Mirror" section, February 21, 1951; Dorothy Dietz (woman's editor), "Civil Defense Begins in the Home, Soroptimists Told by Director," *Los Angeles Daily News*, February 21, 1951; Norma H. Good Hue, "'Look-Think' Slogan Told for Defense," *Los Angeles Times*, February 21, 1951, quoting Berry; "Problems of Defense Setup Told at Meet," *Los Angeles Daily News*, February 16, 1951 (explaining that the "magnitude of the civil defense problem, its current state of confusion and the supreme necessity for bringing order out of chaos were discussed today by a county-state defense coordinator"); "Institute of Govt. Warned L.A. Prime A-Bomb Target," *Los Angeles Herald*, February 2, 1951; "Bomb Defense Group Steps Up Recruiting," *San Pedro News Pilot*, January 19, 1951.

48. "Civil Defense Apathy Hit by Warren," *Santa Cruz Sentinel*, January 7, 1951, 13; "Robertson Expects Five A-Bombs May Hit Cal.," *Los Angeles Herald*, January 12, 1951; "Attack Perils Outlined: 260,000 Deaths by A-Bomb Seen," *Los Angeles Times*, April 18, 1951; "Civil Defense Chief Fears Deadly Peril of Germ War," *Los Angeles Mirror*, April 19, 1951; "A-Bomb on L.A.—75,000 Would Die; Berry Hits Apathy," *[Hollywood] Citizen News*, April 18, 1951. On the eve of the

anniversary of the Pearl Harbor attack, December 6, 1951, the *Los Angeles Mirror* issued an edition labeled "EXTRA—Operation Wake Up," with a full front-page photo of a mushroom cloud and, over the photo in large type, "L.A. MOCK BOMBED."

49. "Call Sounded for 1,500,000 Defense Aides," *Los Angeles Times*, February 20, 1951, in Bowron Papers; Staff, "The Pilot's Log," *San Pedro News Pilot*, February 27, 1951; Tige Clinton, column in *Wilmington (CA) Press Journal*, February 28, 1951; "Recruiting of Block Wardens to Start," *[San Fernando] Valley Times*, February 23, 1951; "Civil Defense Czar Taps the 'Pork Barrel,'" *Daily People's World*, February 16, 1951. The reporter continued, "Civilian defense apparently is going to kill more people with higher taxes than it can possible save in the event of an improbable enemy attack." At a two-day meeting of the California State Senate's Civilian Defense Committee, "politicians vying for a chance at the new 'pork barrel' outnumbered spectators by five to one. [Los Angeles] County Supervisor Roger Jessup licked his chops at the prospect of the county squandering $6 million on civil defense and then got into a wrangle with Sen. George H. Hatfield, committee chairman, as to whether the bite should be put on county or state taxpayers. As the tragi-comedy ended, Fire Chief John H. Alderson stood out like a sane man in bedlam when he blasted the proposed expenditure of $110 million for bomb shelters as a 'tragic waste.'" "State 'Defense' Chiefs Squabble over the Spoils," *Daily People's World*, February 20, 1951, in Bowron Papers.

50. Matthew Farish, "The Ordinary Cold War: The Ground Observer Corps and Midcentury Militarization in the United States," *Journal of American History* 103, no. 3 (December 2016): 629–655; Bruce D. Callander, "The Ground Observer Force," *Air Force Magazine*, February 2006, www.airforcemag.com/MagazineArchive/Pages/2006/February%202006/0206goc.aspx. Callander states, "Over the years of the Cold War, more than 800,000 volunteers stood alternating shifts at 16,000 observation posts and 73 filter centers."

51. "Civil Defense Declared Local Responsibility," *Los Angeles Times*, January 17, 1951. The article explained, "Civil Defense is a program of 'help yourself.' The military will move in only as a last resort. It is a program of local community and individual responsibility." See also "We're Not Ready for Disaster, State's Defense Chief Warns, Civil Corps Enlistment Held Urgent," *Los Angeles Times*, January 23, 1951; Rose, *One Nation Underground*, 27n33; "Urges Rush on A-Shelter," *Los Angeles Mirror*, January 11, 1951; "Defense Chief Suggests Home Bomb Shelters," *Eastside Journal*, January 10, 1951; "On Civilian Defense," editorial, *[San Fernando] Valley Times*, January 29, 1951.

52. "Citizens Warned Against 'A-Bomb Shelter Fever,'" *Los Angeles Examiner*, January 25, 1951; "Bomb-Shelter Building Not for Novices," *Los Angeles Daily News*, January 11, 1951; "Defense Director Warns of Split-Second Disaster," *Los Angeles Times*, February 22, 1951; "Civil Defense Chief," editorial, *Los Angeles Times*, January 30, 1951. The *San Pedro News Pilot* reported, sarcastically, "Port

residents can rest assured that City Fathers are on the alert these days for any possible costly effects from an atom bomb or other type air-raid which may strike Los Angeles. Just to make sure they were protecting the citizen's [*sic*] money adequately they had a special stamp prepared to stamp on plans for bomb shelters. It reads as follows: 'Approval of these plans by the Department of Building and Safety does not insure obsolute [*sic*] protection against heat, blast or radioactive effects that may occur as a result of a bomb explosion.' What a load off the taxpayers mind . . . except for the building fee of course, which local authorities are not advised of at this time." Staff, "The Pilot's Log," *San Pedro News Pilot*, February 26, 1951; "Civil Defense Chiefs Outline Plans to Southern California Chapter of A.I.A.," *Southwest Builder and Contractor*, February 23, 1951; "Backyard Shelters Termed 'Waste,'" *San Pedro News Pilot*, February 27, 1951; "Back-Yard A-Bomb Shelter Peril Told," *Los Angeles Mirror*, January 26, 1951; Dan W. Green, "Comment Upon Men and Issues," *Independent Review*, February 23, 1951, in Bowron Papers; Alderson quote from "Shelters May Prove to Be Death Traps," *Wilmington (CA) Press Journal*, February 16, 1951, in Bowron Papers. For the advertisement for the "all-concrete blast resistant house," see Figure 5, and advertisement, Portland Cement Association, *Better Homes and Gardens* 33, no. 6 (June 1955): 3.

53. McEnaney, *Civil Defense Begins at Home*, 52–53; Monteyne, *Fallout Shelter*, 12, 35.

54. Monteyne, *Fallout Shelter*, 19; William S. Barton, "Experts Weighing A-Bomb Peril Here," *Los Angeles Times*, July 26, 1950, 1A.

55. "Meaning of U.S. 'Emergency' Shown—Official Sources Supply Replies to Questions Asked on Crisis," *Los Angeles Times*, December 15, 1950, 11.

56. "Mayor Bowron to Be Guest of S.C.A.I.A.," *Building News*, February 15, 1951. The article tells of plans for Bowron's appearance at an upcoming architects meeting. Before his talk a short documentary film would be shown, *You Can Beat the A Bomb*. See also "Civil Defense Seminar to Start at SC Feb. 15," *Los Angeles Times*, January 14, 1951; "Lecture to Take Public Behind Atomic Scenes: Daily Discussions at May Co. Will Explain Uses of Fission Energy in War and Peace," *Los Angeles Times*, April 12, 1951, 13.

57. *Duck and Cover*, Federal Civil Defense Administration, 1951, available at Internet Archive, https://archive.org/details/gov.ntis.ava11109vnb1.

58. "Tell L.A. Germ War Menace," *Los Angeles Herald*, February 16, 1951; "L.A. Warned on Use by Enemy of Smallpox," *Los Angeles Times*, January 2, 1951; "Urge L.A. Families to Learn First Aid," *[San Fernando] Valley Times*, February 7, 1951; *What You Should Know About Biological Warfare*, Ray (Reid H.) Film Industries and US Civil Defense Administration, 1952, available at Internet Archive, https://archive.org/details/WhatYouS1952.

59. Paul Jordan-Smith, "Books and Authors: Religious Writers in Pulpit Digest Give Sermons and Essays on Bombs," *Los Angeles Times*, July 4, 1954, D6;

Dwight D. Eisenhower's acceptance speech at the Republican National Convention, August 23, 1956, in Gregory Bush, ed., *Campaign Speeches of American Presidential Candidates, 1948–1984* (New York: Frederick Ungar, 1985), 62–71.

60. "Mansfield Sees Danger in 'Limited' Atomic War-Doctrine Expounded by Dulles, Might Lead to National Suicide, Democrat Says," *Los Angeles Times*, April 18, 1955, 25.

61. Marvin Miles, "Times Man 3100 Yards from Blast," *Los Angeles Times*, May 6, 1955, 1.

62. Graham Berry, "Nevadans Charge Fall-out Danger," *Los Angeles Times*, June 27, 1957, 1.

63. Alton L. Blakeslee, "Scientists Explain H-Bomb 'Fallout,'" *Los Angeles Times*, April 18, 1955, 24.

64. "Short Vision Memories," in "A Short Vision, Legacy Project," Conelrad Adjacent, June 26, 2011, http://conelrad.blogspot.com/2011/06/short-vision-legacy-project.html.

65. "Sputnik and the Dawn of the Space Age," NASA, https://history.nasa.gov/sputnik.

66. *Sputnik Mania*, David Hoffman, director (Varied Directions International, 2007).

67. See Paul Boyer, *By the Bomb's Early Light: American Thought and Culture at the Dawn of the Atomic Age* (Chapel Hill: University of North Carolina Press, 1994).

68. See Vincent Intondi, *African Americans Against the Bomb: Nuclear Weapons, Colonialism, and the Black Freedom Movement* (Palo Alto, CA: Stanford University Press, 2015); SANE, "We Are Facing a Danger Unlike Any Danger That Has Ever Existed," *New York Times*, November 15, 1957. For more on liberalism and civil rights during the Cold War era, see Steve Fraser and Gary Gerstle, *The Rise and Fall of the New Deal Order, 1930–1980* (Princeton, NJ: Princeton University Press, 1989); James Patterson, *Grand Expectations: The United States, 1945–1974* (Oxford: Oxford University Press, 1996); Mary Dudziak, *Cold War Civil Rights: Race and the Image of American Democracy* (Princeton, NJ: Princeton University Press, 2000); Thomas Borstelmann, *The Cold War and the Color Line: American Race Relations in the Global Arena* (Cambridge, MA: Harvard University Press, 2001); William P. Jones, *The March on Washington: Jobs, Freedom, and the Forgotten History of Civil Rights* (New York: Norton, 2013).

69. See Boyer, *By the Bomb's Early Light*; Robert J. Lifton, *The Broken Connection* (New York: Simon and Schuster, 1979).

70. Rose, *One Nation Underground*, 1–4.

71. Ibid., 8–9.

72. John F. Kennedy, Cuban Missile Crisis Address to the Nation, October 22, 1962, available at American Rhetoric, www.americanrhetoric.com/speeches/jfkcubanmissilecrisis.html.

73. Rose, *One Nation Underground*, 37, 79–84, 191–202.

74. Ibid., 10, 31; Susan Roy, *Bomboozled: How the U.S. Government Misled Itself and Its People into Believing They Could Survive a Nuclear Attack* (New York: Pointed Leaf Press, 2011).

75. Amy Swerdlow, *Women Strike for Peace: Traditional Motherhood and Radical Politics in the 1960s* (Chicago: University of Chicago Press, 1993).

76. Ibid.

77. Rose, *One Nation Underground*, 70, 108–109.

78. Ibid., 70, 98–111.

79. For a discussion of this episode, see ibid., 110–111.

80. See *The Atomic Cafe*, Jayne Loader, Kevin Rafferty, and Pierce Rafferty, directors (Archives Project, 1982); *Dr. Strangelove: Or How I Learned to Stop Worrying and Love the Bomb*, Stanley Kubrick, director (Columbia Pictures, 1964).

81. Boyer, *By the Bomb's Early Light*; Spencer R. Weart, *Nuclear Fear: A History of Images* (Cambridge, MA: Harvard University Press, 1988); Paul Shambroom and Laura Westlund, *Paul Shambroom: Picturing Power* (Minneapolis: Weisman Art Museum, University of Minnesota, 2008); Paul Shambroom, *Shrines: Public Weapons in America*, work in progress, September 2010. See also Vanderbilt, *Survival City*, and *The Atomic Cafe*.

82. Edwin Bacon and Mark Sandle, eds., *Brezhnev Reconsidered: Studies in Russian and East European History and Society* (New York: Palgrave Macmillan, 2003).

83. Pew Research Center, "Public Trust in Government: 1958–2015," November 23, 2015, www.people-press.org/2015/11/23/public-trust-in-government-1958-2015.

84. For comparative data on gun ownership, see *International Journal of Epidemiology* 27, no. 216 (1998), and GunCite.com, www.guncite.com/gun_control_gcgvinco.html.

Chapter 2: The Color of Danger: From Red to Black

1. Quoted in Mike Davis, *City of Quartz: Excavating the Future in Los Angeles*, with photographs by Robert Morrow (New York: Verso, 1990), 213; quotation from *Los Angeles Examiner*, October 15, 1961.

2. Paul K. Saint-Amour, "Bombing and the Symptom: Traumatic Earliness and the Nuclear Uncanny," *Diacritics* (Winter 2000): 59–82; Paul K. Saint-Amour, *Tense Future: Modernism, Total War, Encyclopedic Form* (Oxford: Oxford University Press, 2015); Paul K. Saint-Amour, "Air War Prophecy and Interwar Modernism," *Comparative Literary Studies* 42, no. 2 (2005): 158–159. See also Paul Boyer, *By the Bomb's Early Light: American Thought and Culture at the Dawn of the Atomic Age* (Chapel Hill: University of North Carolina Press, 1994); Robert J. Lifton, *The Broken Connection* (New York: Touchstone, 1980).

3. New York epitomized urban danger in much of the media and popular culture. See Brian L. Tochterman, *The Dying City: Postwar New York and the Ideology of Fear* (Chapel Hill: University of North Carolina Press, 2017).

4. Katherine Beckett, *Making Crime Pay: Law and Order in Contemporary American Politics* (New York: Oxford University Press, 1999), 25.

5. See Isabel Wilkerson, *The Warmth of Other Suns: The Epic Story of America's Great Migration* (New York: Random House, 2010); Michael Flamm, *Law and Order: Street Crime, Civil Unrest, and the Crisis of Liberalism in the 1960s* (New York: Columbia University Press, 2005), 5.

6. Beckett, *Making Crime Pay*, 17–18, quotation on p. 31.

7. Michael Carlson, "Obituary: Tony Schwartz: His Daisy Girl TV Ad Was a First, and Helped Put Lyndon Johnson in the White House," *Guardian* (London), June 28, 2008, and Martin Mittelstaedt, "An Unholy Alliance: Politics and the Boob Tube," *Globe and Mail* (Canada), both from LexisNexis.

8. Flamm, *Law and Order*, 36. All quotes and descriptions of television ads are from the website www.livingroomcandidate.org, which includes the ads themselves, the transcripts, and the voting outcomes of each election.

9. The film, called *Choice*, was not shown on mainstream TV but was shown on news stations. See YouTube, https://www.youtube.com/watch?v=xniUoMiHm8g. See also Flamm, *Law and Order*, 44.

10. "Choice (1964): The Scrapbook," Conelrad Adjacent, October 13, 2010, http://conelrad.blogspot.com/2010/10/choice-1964-scrapbook.html.

11. On the film, see Samuel G. Freedman, "The First Days of the Loaded Political Image," *New York Times*, September 1, 1996, www.nytimes.com/1996/09/01/arts/the-first-days-of-the-loaded-political-image.html. For more on conservative women and momentum in California, see Lisa McGirr, *Suburban Warriors: The Origins of the New American Right* (Princeton, NJ: Princeton University Press, 2001). See also Flamm, *Law and Order*, 44.

12. Samuel Walker, *Popular Justice: A History of American Criminal Justice*, 2nd ed. (New York: Oxford University Press, 1997), 180. For the quotations by George Wallace, see Fred P. Graham, *The Self-Inflicted Wound* (New York: Macmillan, 1970), 10. See also Flamm, *Law and Order*, 35.

13. Flamm, *Law and Order*, 83–84.

14. Michelle Alexander, *The New Jim Crow: Mass Incarceration in the Age of Colorblindness* (New York: New Press, 2012), 40.

15. Khalil Gibran Muhammad, *The Condemnation of Blackness: Race, Crime, and the Making of Modern Urban America* (Cambridge, MA: Harvard University Press, 2011).

16. Rick Perlstein, *Nixonland: The Rise of a President and the Fracturing of America* (New York: Scribner, 2008), 146–152. For handbill text, see p. 150. For original handbill, see Paul Douglas Papers, Chicago History Museum, Box 1117, Percy Materials.

17. Flamm, *Law and Order*, 74–75.

18. For quotations and poll data, see Flamm, *Law and Order*, 37, 97, 101; *U.S. Riot Commission Report: What Happened? Why Did It Happen? What Can Be Done? Report of the National Advisory Commission on Civil Disorders*, with a Special Introduction by Tom Wicker of the *New York Times* (New York: Bantam Books, 1968), 1–2.

19. Franklin Zimring, *The Great American Crime Decline* (New York: Oxford University Press, 2007), 29–30. See also Beckett, *Making Crime Pay*.

20. Jonathan Simon, *Governing Through Crime: How the War on Crime Transformed American Democracy and Created a Culture of Fear* (New York: Oxford University Press, 2007), 78, 90–99.

21. Beckett, *Making Crime Pay*, 32.

22. University of Michigan, Office of Research Administration, *University of Michigan Bibliography*, 1955.

23. For quotations and poll data, see Flamm, *Law and Order*, 37, 97, 101.

24. Flamm, *Law and Order*, 4.

25. For quotation, see Alexander, *New Jim Crow*, 47.

26. Gregory Bush, ed., *Campaign Speeches of American Presidential Candidates, 1948–1984* (New York: Frederick Ungar, 1985), 159.

27. Flamm, *Law and Order*, 1–2.

28. For quotation, see www.livingroomcandidate.org.

29. See Richard Nixon, "Remarks to Newsmen in Denver, Colorado," August 3, 1970, American Presidency Project, University of California at Santa Barbara, www.presidency.ucsb.edu/ws/print.php?pid=2608. See also David Garland, *The Culture of Control: Crime and Social Order in Contemporary Society* (Chicago: University of Chicago Press, 2001); Marie Gottschalk, *Caught: The Prison State and the Lockdown of American Politics* (Princeton, NJ: Princeton University Press, 2014), 7.

30. Nixon's domestic policy chief, John Ehrlichman, quoted in Dan Baum, "Legalize It All: How to Win the War on Drugs," *Harper's*, April 2016, http://harpers.org/archive/2016/04/legalize-it-all.

31. Quoted in Flamm, *Law and Order*, 127.

32. From the FBI's official website, The Vault, at https://vault.fbi.gov/cointel-pro: "The FBI began COINTELPRO—short for Counterintelligence Program—in 1956 to disrupt the activities of the Communist Party of the United States. In the 1960s, it was expanded to include a number of other domestic groups, such as the Ku Klux Klan, the Socialist Workers Party, and the Black Panther Party. All COINTELPRO operations were ended in 1971. Although limited in scope (about two-tenths of one percent of the FBI's workload over a 15-year period), COINTELPRO was later rightfully criticized by Congress and the American people for abridging first amendment rights and for other reasons." See also *The*

Black Panthers: Vanguard of the Revolution, Stanley Nelson, director (Public Broadcasting System, 2015).

33. *Los Angeles Examiner*, October 15, 1961; *Los Angeles Examiner*, September 5, 1961; *U.S. News and World Report*, September 18, 1961, all quoted in Davis, *City of Quartz*, 213, 217, 220.

34. George Sokolosky, "Communists Aiming at US Youth as Target," *San Diego Union*, August 24, 1960, quoted in Davis, *City of Quartz*, 212.

35. Alisa Sarah Kramer, "William H. Parker and the Thin Blue Line: Politics, Public Relations and Policing in Postwar Los Angeles" (PhD diss., American University, 2007); quotations from Davis, *City of Quartz*, 294–295.

36. Sophia Spalding, "The Constable Blunders: Police Abuse in Los Angeles's Black and Latino Communities, 1945–1965," University of California at Los Angeles, Department of Urban Planning, 1989, unpublished, 7, cited in Davis, *City of Quartz*, 295.

37. Yorty used a similar tactic against students at UCLA. Both mayors gained political support as a result of their law-and-order tactics and harsh treatment of student protests.

38. Jeffrey T. Manuel and Andrew Urban, "'You Can't Legislate the Heart': Minneapolis Mayor Charles Stenvig and the Politics of Law and Order," *American Studies* 49, no. 3/4 (Fall/Winter 2008): 195–219.

39. Research and Forecasts, Inc., with Ardy Friedbert, *America Afraid: How Fear of Crime Changes the Way We Live. Based on the Widely Publicized Figgie Report* (New York: New American Library, 1983), 141; Robert Suro, "Driven by Fear: Crime and Its Amplified Echoes are Rearranging People's Lives," *New York Times*, February 9, 1992, www.nytimes.com/1992/02/09/weekinreview/driven-by-fear-crime-and-its-amplified-echoes-are-rearranging-people-s-lives.html; Linda Heath, Jack Kavanagh, and Rae S. Thompson, "Perceived Vulnerability and Fear of Crime: Why Fear Stays High When Crime Rates Drop," *Journal of Offender Rehabilitation* 33, no. 2 (2001): 1–14.

40. Corey Robin, *Fear: The History of a Political Idea* (New York: Oxford University Press, 2006); James Brooks, "The Fear of Crime in the United States," *Crime and Delinquency* 20, no. 3 (1974): 241–244.

41. Poll data from Roper Center for Public Opinion Research, Cornell University, iPoll, https://ropercenter.cornell.edu/ipoll-database.

42. US Department of Justice, Federal Bureau of Investigation, Uniform Crime Reporting Statistics, Uniform Crime Reports, 1940–1960, https://www.ucrdatatool.gov; "Table Ec190–198. Reported Homicides and Homicide Rates, by Sex and Mode of Death: 1900–1997," in Susan B. Carter, et al., eds., *Historical Statistics of the United States: Millennial Edition Online* (New York: Cambridge University Press, 2006), http://hsus.cambridge.org/HSUSWeb/HSUSEntryServlet. For population, see "Population and Housing Unit Estimates," US

Department of Commerce, US Census Bureau, https://www.census.gov/programs-surveys/popest.html; "Table Aa6–8. Population: 1790–2000 [Annual estimates]," in Carter et al., eds., *Historical Statistics of the United States.*

43. "A Response to Fear," *Time* 96 no. 5 (August 3, 1970): 10.

44. See Estelle Freedman, *Redefining Rape: Sexual Violence in the Era of Suffrage and Segregation* (Cambridge, MA: Harvard University Press, 2013).

45. "First Scream, Then Scram," *U.S. News and World Report*, April 1963, p. 1, which included excerpts from the *Washington Post* of March 17, 1963.

46. "History of Battered Women's Movement," Indiana Coalition Against Domestic Violence, www.icadvinc.org/what-is-domestic-violence/history-of-battered-womens-movement.

47. "A Response to Fear," 10.

48. Ibid.

49. Ibid.

50. Walker, *Popular Justice*, 212; Research and Forecasts, *America Afraid*, 12; poll data from Roper Center for Public Opinion Research, Cornell University, iPoll, https://ropercenter.cornell.edu/ipoll-database.

51. Research and Forecasts, *America Afraid*, 69; "Crime: The Shape of Fear," *The Economist*, November 29, 1980, 36. For crime and population, see US Department of Justice, Federal Bureau of Investigation, Uniform Crime Reporting Statistics, https://www.ucrdatatool.gov; "Table Aa6–8. Population: 1790–2000 [Annual estimates]," in Susan B. Carter et al., eds., *Historical Statistics of the United States.*

52. Research and Forecasts, *America Afraid*, xi, 6, 11, 13.

53. Ed Magnuson, "The Curse of Violent Crime," *Time*, March 23, 1981, http://content.time.com/time/magazine/article/0,9171,952929,00.html.

54. Christian Parenti, *Lockdown America: Police and Prisons in the Age of Crisis* (New York: Verso, 2008), chap. 2.

55. Walker, *Popular Justice*, 217–218; see also Alexander, *New Jim Crow*, 17, 87, 112.

56. Walker, *Popular Justice*, 214–216.

57. White men constituted 78 percent of arrests for drunk driving in 1990. See Alexander, *New Jim Crow*, 206–207. See also Eduardo Romano, Robert B. Voas, and John C. Lacey, *Alcohol and Highway Safety: Special Report on Race/Ethnicity and Impaired Driving*, National Highway Traffic Safety Administration, December 2010.

58. Jennifer Light, *From Warfare to Welfare: Defense Intellectuals and Urban Problems in Cold War America* (Baltimore: Johns Hopkins University Press, 2005); Alexander, *New Jim Crow*, 76–77.

59. N. Pileggi et al., "Protecting Yourself Against Crime," *New York Magazine*, February 8, 1982, 20–25, 27–41.

60. David M. Alpern, "A Newsweek Poll: 'Deadly Force,'" *Newsweek*, March 11, 1985, 53; Barry Meier, "Reality and Anxiety: Crime and the Fear of It," *New York Times*, February 18, 1993, A14; William C. Cunningham, John J. Strauchs, and Clifford W. Van Meter, *Private Security Trends, 1970–2000: The Hallcrest Report II* (Boston: Butterworth-Heinemann, 1990), 238.

61. Magnuson, "Curse of Violent Crime."

62. See www.livingroomcandidate.org for videos of all TV ads discussed here.

63. Sarah Eschholz, "Racial Composition of Television Offenders and Viewers' Fear of Crime," *Critical Criminology* 11, no. 1 (2001): 41–60.

64. Barry Glassner, *The Culture of Fear: Why Americans Are Afraid of the Wrong Things* (New York: Basic Books, 1999), xv.

65. Poll data from Roper Center for Public Opinion Research, Cornell University, iPoll, https://ropercenter.cornell.edu/ipoll-database.

66. Magnuson, "Curse of Violent Crime"; Meier, "Reality and Anxiety," A14.

67. Meier, "Reality and Anxiety," A14.

68. Rorie Sherman, "Crime's Toll on the U.S.: Fear, Despair and Guns," *National Law Journal*, April 18, 1994, A1, A19–A20, reprinted in John J. Sullivan and Joseph L. Victor, eds., *Annual Editions: Criminal Justice 95/96* (Guilford, CT: Dushkin, 1995), 57–61. For crime statistics, see US Department of Justice, Federal Bureau of Investigation, Uniform Crime Reporting Statistics, https://www.ucrdatatool.gov. For population data, see "Population and Housing Unit Estimates," US Department of Commerce, US Census Bureau, https://www.census.gov/programs-surveys/popest.html; "Table Aa6–8. Population: 1790–2000 [Annual estimates]," in Susan B. Carter et al., eds., *Historical Statistics of the United States*.

69. Roper Center for Public Opinion Research, Cornell University, iPoll, https://ropercenter.cornell.edu/ipoll-database.

70. *Gallup Poll Monthly*, no. 348 (September 1994); Sherman, "Crime's Toll on the U.S.," 57.

71. See William J. Bennett, John J. DiIulio, and John P. Walters, *Body Count: Moral Poverty . . . And How to Win America's War Against Crime and Drugs* (New York: Simon and Schuster, 1996); John DiIulio, "Lock 'Em Up or Else: Huge Wave of Criminally Inclined Coming in Next 10 Years," *Lakeland (FL) Ledger*, March 23, 1996, A11; Joyce Purnick, "Youth Crime: Should Laws Be Tougher?" *New York Times*, May 9, 1996, B1.

72. Quoted in Vincent Schiraldi, "Will the Real John DiIulio Please Stand Up," *Washington Post*, February 5, 2001, A19.

73. Elizabeth Becker, "As Ex-Theorist on Young 'Superpredators,' Bush Aide Has Regrets," *New York Times*, February 9, 2001, www.nytimes.com/2001/02/09/us/as-ex-theorist-on-young-superpredators-bush-aide-has-regrets.html. See also Zimring, *Great American Crime Decline*. Zimring cites John DiIulio, *How to Stop*

the Coming Crime Wave (New York: Manhattan Institute, 1996), 4, and also John DiIulio, "The Coming of the Super-Predators," *Weekly Standard*, November 27, 1995, 23.

74. Zimring, *Great American Crime Decline*, 21–22. Quotation in Zimring from James Q. Wilson, "Crime and Public Policy," and "Concluding Essay in Crime," in James Q. Wilson and Joan Petersilia, eds., *Crime* (San Francisco: Institute for Contemporary Studies Press, 1995), 488–507.

75. James Alan Fox, *Trends in Juvenile Violence: A Report to the United States Attorney General on Current and Future Rates of Juvenile Offending*, US Department of Justice, Bureau of Justice Statistics, March 1996, www.bjs.gov/content/pub/pdf/tjvfox2.pdf; Schiraldi, "Will the Real John DiIulio Please Stand Up"; "'Superpredators' Aren't Mere Kids," *Omaha World Herald*, May 16, 1997, 12.

76. According to government statistics, the juvenile crime rate for both property crimes and violent crimes in 2014 were at their lowest rate in thirty years. See "Law Enforcement and Juvenile Crime: Juvenile Arrest Rate Trends," in Statistical Briefing Book, US Department of Justice, Office of Justice Programs, Office of Juvenile Justice and Delinquency Prevention, www.ojjdp.gov/ojstatbb/crime/JAR_Display.asp?ID=qa05206; James P. Lynch, "Trends in Juvenile Violent Offending: An Analysis of Victim Survey Data," US Department of Justice, Office of Justice Programs, Office of Juvenile Justice and Delinquency Prevention, https://www.ncjrs.gov/pdffiles1/ojjdp/191052.pdf. See also Becker, "As Ex-Theorist on Young 'Superpredators.'"

77. "Clinton State of the Union, January 25, 1994," in Owen Peterson, ed., *Representative American Speeches, 1993–1994*, vol. 66, no. 6 (New York: H. W. Wilson Company, 1994), 9–26.

78. Parenti, *Lockdown America*, esp. chap. 4; Alexander, *New Jim Crow*, 49–50, 53–54, 57, 253; Simon, *Governing Through Crime*, 102–103.

79. Alexander, *New Jim Crow*, 155–156. Davis was sentenced to death, and in 2017 he was still incarcerated on death row.

80. Vincent Shiraldi, Jason Colburn, and Eric Lotke, "Three Strikes and You're Out: An Examination of the Impact of 3-Strikes Laws 10 Years After Their Enactment," *Justice Policy Institute* (2004): 1–23. My thanks to Patrick Wilz for compiling the data.

81. Flamm, *Law and Order*, 183–184. See also Jimmie L. Reeves and Richard Campbell, *Cracked Coverage: Television News, the Anti-Cocaine Crusade, and the Reagan Legacy* (Durham, NC: Duke University Press, 1994).

82. Simon, *Governing Through Crime*, 31, 76. Simon cites Markus Dubbar, *Victims in the War on Crime: The Use and Abuse of Victims' Rights* (New York: New York University Press, 2002).

83. By the end of the twentieth century, one out of every four young black men was in jail, on parole, or on probation. Within the next decade, almost 60 percent of the nation's inmates were black and Latino—twice their combined

percentage of the population. American Indians are also vastly overrepresented in prisons compared to their percentage of the population. Jamaal Bell, "Mass Incarceration: A Destroyer of People of Color and Their Communities," *Huffington Post*, May 17, 2010, www.huffingtonpost.com/jamaal-bell/mass-incarceration-a-dest_b_578854.html.

84. Alexander, *New Jim Crow*, 7.

85. In 1980, there were 41,000 people incarcerated for drug offenses; by 2011, that number had risen to half a million—an increase of 1,100 percent. In 2005, 80 percent of all drug arrests were for possession, and only 20 percent for selling. In 2011, more people were incarcerated for drug offenses than for all offenses combined in 1980. See Alexander, *New Jim Crow*, 60; Gottschalk, *Caught*, 6.

86. Heather Ann Thompson, "Inner-City Violence in the Age of Mass Incarceration," *The Atlantic*, October 30, 2014, www.theatlantic.com/national/archive/2014/10/inner-city-violence-in-the-age-of-mass-incarceration/382154.

87. Germany, for example, incarcerated 93 people for every 100,000 adults and children. The United States incarcerated eight times that many: 750 per 100,000 population, even though their crime rates were similar. See Alexander, *New Jim Crow*, 1–7. See also Walker, *Popular Justice*, 217–218; Gottschalk, *Caught*, 8.

88. "The Threat," Bob Dole presidential campaign television ad, 1996, www.livingroomcandidate.org.

89. David Garland, ed., *Mass Imprisonment: Social Causes and Consequences* (London: Sage, 2001), 2. See also the chapter by Katherine Beckett and Bruce Western, "Governing Social Marginality: Welfare, Incarceration and the Transformation of State Policy," 40, 46.

90. "Private Prisons Are Back," Corrections Project, www.correctionsproject.com/corrections/pris_priv.htm.

91. The rate of increase for prison costs was six times greater than for higher education spending. See "Data Collection: National Prisoner Statistics (NPS) Program," US Department of Justice, Bureau of Justice Statistics, https://www.bjs.gov/index.cfm?ty=dcdetail&iid=269; Ruth Wilson Gilmore, "Globalisation and US Prison Growth: From Military Keynesianism to Post-Keynesian Militarism," *Race & Class* 40 (February/March 1998/1999): 172–174; Gottschalk, *Caught*, 22.

92. Alexander, *New Jim Crow*, 179–180, 208; Peter Wagner and Bernadette Rabuy, "Following the Money of Mass Incarceration," Prison Policy Initiative, January 25, 2017, https://www.prisonpolicy.org/reports/money.html.

93. Alexander, *New Jim Crow*, 1–4; Gottschalk, *Caught*, 2.

94. Thompson, "Inner City Violence."

95. Jeff Manza and Christopher Uggen, *Locked Out: Felon Disenfranchisement and American Democracy* (New York: Oxford University Press, 2006), 49, 76, 77, 78, 94, 112, 162, 179–180, 218.

96. Ibid., 67–68, 78–79, 218; Alexander, *New Jim Crow*, 160.

97. Christopher Uggen, Ryan Larson, and Sarah Shannon, "6 Million Lost Voters: State-Level Estimates of Felony Disfranchisement, 2016," The Sentencing Project, October 6, 2016, www.sentencingproject.org/publications/6-million-lost-voters-state-level-estimates-felony-disenfranchisement-2016; Melissa Franqui, "Felony Disenfranchisement: The Untold Story of the 2016 Election," *Salon*, November 28, 2016, www.salon.com/2016/11/28/felony-disenfranchisement-the-untold-story-of-the-2016-election_partner.

98. Joan Petersilia, *When Prisoners Come Home: Parole and Prisoner Reentry* (New York: Oxford University Press, 2003).

99. Quoted in Alexander, *New Jim Crow*, 8.

100. See Dan Baum, *Smoke and Mirrors: The War on Drugs and the Politics of Failure* (New York: Little, Brown, 1997).

101. Ethan Siegel, "Newt Gingrich Exemplifies Just How Unscientific America Is," *Forbes*, August 5, 2016, https://www.forbes.com/sites/startswithabang/2016/08/05/newt-gingrich-exemplifies-just-how-unscientific-america-is/#56d2e94e5e47.

102. Charles Blow, "Crime and Punishment," *New York Times*, November 30, 2014, www.nytimes.com/2014/12/01/opinion/charles-blow-crime-and-punishment.html. See Carole A. Stabile, *White Victims, Black Villains: Gender, Race, and Crime News in US Culture* (New York: Routledge, 2006).

Chapter 3: Vigilante Virtue: Fantasy, Reality, and the Law

1. Alex Seitz-Wald, "Assault Rifle Company Issues 'Man Cards,'" *Salon*, December 17, 2012, www.salon.com/2012/12/17/bushmasters_horrible_ad_campaign.

2. Leonard J. Moore, *Citizen Klansmen: The Ku Klux Klan in Indiana, 1921–1928* (Chapel Hill: University of North Carolina Press, 1997).

3. "Our History," National Neighborhood Watch—A Division of the National Sheriffs' Association, www.nnw.org/our-history.

4. Research and Forecasts, Inc., with Ardy Friedbert, *America Afraid: How Fear of Crime Changes the Way We Live; Based on the Widely Publicized Figgie Report* (New York: New American Library, 1983), 17.

5. Poll data from "Herald Poll," *Los Angeles Herald*, June 19, 1985, in Lary May, "Redeeming the Lost War: Backlash Films and the Rise of the Punitive State," in Austin Seurat and Charles Ogletree, eds., *Punishment in Popular Culture* (New York: New York University Press, 2015).

6. Pew Research Center, "Public Trust in Government: 1958–2015," November 23, 2015, www.people-press.org/2015/11/23/public-trust-in-government-1958-2015.

7. Elizabeth Mehren, "Cashing In on the Case of the Subway Vigilante: Everything from a Book to 'Thugbuster' T-Shirts Tells Tale of Bernie Goetz," *Los*

Angeles Times, February 13, 1985, http://articles.latimes.com/1985-02-13/news/vw-4748_1_bernie-goetz.

8. David M. Alpern, "A Newsweek Poll: 'Deadly Force,'" *Newsweek*, March 11, 1985, 53; "Behind Tough Public Stance on Criminals," *U.S. News and World Report* 98, no. 2 (January 21, 1985): 60; John J. Goldman, "Goetz Sentenced to Year in Jail, Tells Court Society Needs Protection from Criminals," *Los Angeles Times*, January 14, 1989, http://articles.latimes.com/1989-01-14/news/mn-93_1_one-year-jail-sentence.

9. Steven V. Roberts, "D'Amato and Doonesbury," *New York Times*, February 7, 1985, www.nytimes.com/1985/02/07/us/d-amato-and-doonesbury.html.

10. Goldman, "Goetz Sentenced." Goetz served eight months of his sentence. In 1996, Darrell Cabey won a $43 million judgment against Goetz, who then declared bankruptcy. Goetz ran unsuccessfully for local office twice in the twenty-first century. He continued to maintain that his actions on the subway were justified and had had a positive effect on New York City. In 2014, he had another brush with the law when he was arrested for selling $30 worth of marijuana to an undercover police officer. "Bernhard Goetz, New York City Subway Vigilante, Arrested on Marijuana Charge," CBS News, November 2, 2013, www.cbsnews.com/news/bernhard-goetz-new-york-city-subway-vigilante-arrested-on-marijuana-charge.

11. A classic film in this genre is *The Searchers* (1956) in which John Wayne plays the hero who saves the girl from Comanche captors after the Civil War. Popular television shows and film dramas repeated variations of this plot.

12. Michael Munn, *Clint Eastwood: Hollywood's Loner* (London: Robson Books, 1992), 95.

13. New York epitomized urban danger in much of the media and popular culture. See Brian Lee Tochterman, "Welcome to Fear City: The Cultural Narrative of New York City, 1945–1980" (PhD diss., University of Minnesota, 2011), 11–12, 35; Brian Lee Tochterman, *The Dying City: Postwar New York and the Ideology of Fear* (Chapel Hill: University of North Carolina Press, 2017).

14. Mickey Spillane, *One Lonely Night* (New York: Dutton, 1951), 170–171. For a discussion of Spillane's Cold War themes, see Elaine Tyler May, *Homeward Bound: American Families in the Cold War Era*, 3rd ed. (New York: Basic Books, 2008), 94.

15. Tochterman, "Welcome to Fear City," 50–51, 61–62.

16. Spillane, *The Big Kill* (New York: Dutton, 1951), 186, quoted in Tochterman, "Welcome to Fear City," 72.

17. Vincent Canby, "New York Woes Are Good Box Office," *New York Times*, November 10, 1974. Also quoted in Vincent Cannato, *The Ungovernable City: John Lindsay and His Struggle to Save New York* (New York: Basic Books, 2002), 562. For further discussion, see Tochterman, "Welcome to Fear City," 202–204.

18. Tochterman, "Welcome to Fear City," 222.

19. See Paul Talbot, *Bronson's Loose! The Making of the* Death Wish *Films* (New York: Universe, 2006). The quotation is from the trailer for *Death Wish*, available at https://www.youtube.com/watch?v=_GieK_55uyY.

20. Quotations from May, "Redeeming the Lost War," 1–40.

21. Richard Brandshaft, *Women and Guns* (NRA magazine), January 1992, Letters section. For other audience quotes, see May, "Redeeming the Lost War," 39–40.

22. *Sudden Impact*, Clint Eastwood, dir. (Warner Bros., 1983).

23. May, "Redeeming the Lost War."

24. See Box Office Mojo, "Marvel Cinematic Universe," n.d., http://www.boxofficemojo.com/franchises/chart/?id=avengers.htm. The worldwide total is listed at the bottom. See also Brad Brevet, "'Captain America' #1 Again as the Marvel Cinematic Universe Tops $10 Billion Worldwide," Box Office Mojo, May 15, 2016, www.boxofficemojo.com/news/?id=4187&p=.htm.

25. "Ventura Blasts Star Tribune Outdoors Columnist," transcript of interview with Dennis Anderson, *Star Tribune*, April 5, 2001.

26. Non-gun-owners as well as gun owners favor gun rights. See Jeffrey M. Jones, "Forty-Four Percent Favor Stricter Laws on Firearm Sales," Gallup, October 9, 2009.

27. Tom W. Smith, "Surge in Gun Sales? The Press Misfires," *Public Perspective*, July/August 2002, 5; Roper Center for Public Opinion Research, Cornell University, *Public Perspective*, July/August 2002, https://ropercenter.cornell.edu/public-perspective/ppscan/134/134005.pdf; Pamela Haag, *The Gunning of America: Business and the Making of American Gun Culture* (New York: Basic Books, 2016), for quotations, see xviii, xvi, xix. For the appeal of guns, see also Dan Baum, *Gun Guys: A Road Trip* (New York: Knopf, 2013). See also multi-article feature on guns, "Gun Country," *New York Times*, December 11, 2013, www.nytimes.com/projects/2013/gun-country; Brian Anse Patrick, *Rise of the Anti-Media: In-forming America's Concealed Weapon Carry Movement* (Lanham, MD: Lexington Books, 2010), chap. 6.

28. Emma Gray, "Bushmaster Rifle Ad Reminds Us to Ask More About Masculinity and Gun Violence," *Huffington Post*, December 17, 2012, www.huffingtonpost.com/emma-gray/bushmaster-rifle-ad-masculinity-gun-violence-newtown-adam-lanza_b_2317924.html. Alternet's Chauncey DeVega was asked why we are so reluctant to "delve deeper into the relationship(s) between whiteness, masculinity, and gun violence." See Chauncey DeVega, "Is a Crisis in White Masculinity Leading to Horrific Gun Crimes Like the Sandy Hook Shootings?" *Alternet*, December 14, 2012, www.alternet.org/visions/crisis-white-masculinity-leading-horrific-gun-crimes-sandy-hook-shootings. In a press release for his 2008 book on the subject of hypermasculinity and violence, UCLA professor of education Douglas Kellner said, "The school shooters and domestic terrorists

examined in this book all exhibit male rage, attempt to resolve a crisis of masculinity through violent behavior, demonstrate a fetish for guns or weapons, and represent, in general, a situation of guys and guns amok." See "School Shootings the Result of Crisis of Masculinity, Gun Culture, Professor Argues," *Science Daily*, February 18, 2008, www.sciencedaily.com/releases/2008/02/080217133643.htm; Seitz-Wald, "Assault Rifle Company Issues 'Man Cards.'" After the Sandy Hook shooting, Bushmaster, the gun company that produced the weapon used by Adam Lanza, removed its 'Man Card' advertisement. See Charles Johnson, "Bushmaster Gun Company Shamed into Removing 'Man Card' Advertisement," *Little Green Footballs*, December 19, 2012, http://littlegreenfootballs.com/article/41361_Bushmaster_Gun_Company_Shamed_Into_Removing_Man_Card_Advertisement.

29. John Burnett, "Does Carrying a Pistol Make You Safer?" National Public Radio, *Morning Edition*, April 12, 2016, www.npr.org/2016/04/12/473391286/does-carrying-a-pistol-make-you-safer.

30. See Jennifer Carlson, *Citizen-Protectors: The Everyday Politics of Guns in an Age of Decline* (New York: Oxford University Press, 2015).

31. In 1927, Congress banned the mailing of concealable weapons, but it did not ban the weapons themselves.

32. Fox Butterfield, "Ideas & Trends: Southern Curse; Why America's Murder Rate Is So High," *New York Times*, July 26, 1998, www.nytimes.com/1998/07/26/weekinreview/ideas-trends-southern-curse-why-america-s-murder-rate-is-so-high.html.

33. Michael Flamm, *Law and Order: Street Crime, Civil Unrest, and the Crisis of Liberalism in the 1960s* (New York: Columbia University Press, 2007), 126–127. For the Hoover quote, see p. 127. Hoover's enthusiasm for gun control was motivated, in part, by the brazen public display of firearms by the Black Panthers in the late 1960s. See *The Black Panthers: Vanguard of the Revolution*, Stanley Nelson, director (Public Broadcasting System, 2015).

34. Gallup poll (American Institute of Public Opinion), July 1959; Fox News Poll, December 2015. See also Roper Center for Public Opinion Research, Cornell University, iPoll, https://ropercenter.cornell.edu/ipoll-database.

35. In 1986, although laws that year increased some penalties for violations of gun control laws and banned so-called cop killer bullets, the Firearm Owners Protection Act of that year limited the Bureau of Alcohol, Tobacco, and Firearms to one inspection of federally licensed dealerships per year and forbade the government from creating a national registry of gun ownership.

36. "A Brief History of the NRA," National Rifle Association, n.d., https://home.nra.org/about-the-nra.

37. Joel Achenbach, Scott Higham, and Sari Horwitz, "How NRA's True Believers Converted a Marksmanship Group into a Mighty Gun Lobby," *Washington*

Post, January 12, 2013, https://www.washingtonpost.com/politics/how-nras-true-believers-converted-a-marksmanship-group-into-a-mighty-gun-lobby/2013/01/12/51c62288-59b9-11e2-88d0-c4cf65c3ad15_story.html.

38. John Sides, "Gun Owners vs. the NRA: What the Polling Shows," *Washington Post*, December 23, 2012, https://www.washingtonpost.com/news/wonk/wp/2012/12/23/gun-owners-vs-the-nra-what-the-polling-shows.

39. Public opinion on this matter has changed dramatically over the past half-century. See "Guns," Polling Report, www.pollingreport.com/guns.htm.

40. "History of Gun-Control Legislation," *Washington Post*, December 22, 2012, www.washingtonpost.com/national/history-of-gun-control-legislation/2012/12/22/80c8d624-4ad3-11e2-9a42-d1ce6d0ed278_story.html; Robert Longley, "US Gun Control Timeline," ThoughtCo, updated March 9, 2017, https://www.thoughtco.com/us-gun-control-timeline-3963620.

41. Patrick, *Rise of the Anti-Media*, ix, xi, xii, xvi, 40, 90, 155.

42. Ian Urbina, "Locked, Loaded, and Ready to Caffeinate," *New York Times*, March 8, 2010, A11.

43. John Burnett, "Does Carrying a Pistol Make You Safer?" National Public Radio, *Morning Edition*, April 12, 2016, www.npr.org/2016/04/12/473391286/does-carrying-a-pistol-make-you-safer; Sociologist Jennifer Carlson noted, "It's not just the idea of if I conceal carry then I'm safer. It's the idea that if I just imagine there's people out there who are conceal carrying then the world is safer." See Jennifer Carlson, *Citizen-Protectors: The Everyday Politics of Guns in an Age of Decline* (New York: Oxford University Press, 2015).

44. Kim Severson, "Want Guns with That? Chefs Find Politics Hotter Than Kitchen," *New York Times*, April 1, 2014, 1.

45. "Concealed Carry's Body Count," editorial, *New York Times*, February 11, 2015, A26. See also "Unintended Consequences: Pro-Handgun Experts Prove That Handguns Are a Dangerous Choice for Self-Defense," Violence Policy Center, 2001, www.vpc.org/studies/uninsum.htm; "The Concealed-Carry Fantasy," editorial, *New York Times*, October 26, 2015, www.nytimes.com/2015/10/26/opinion/the-concealed-carry-fantasy.html.

46. Abby Goodnough, "Florida Expands Right to Use Deadly Force in Self-Defense," *New York Times*, April 27, 2005, www.nytimes.com/2005/04/27/us/florida-expands-right-to-use-deadly-force-in-selfdefense.html.

47. Goodnough, "Florida Expands Right."

48. "Remarks by the President on Trayvon Martin," White House, Office of the Press Secretary, July 19, 2013, https://www.whitehouse.gov/the-press-office/2013/07/19/remarks-president-trayvon-martin.

49. Alana Levinson, "Polls Show Wide Racial Gap on Trayvon Martin Case," National Public Radio, July 22, 2013 (updated July 23, 2013), www.npr.org/sections/itsallpolitics/2013/07/22/204595068/polls-show-wide-racial-gap-on-trayvon-martin-case. See also ABC News/*Washington Post* poll, in Gary

Langer, "Vast Racial Gap on Trayvon Martin Case Marks a Challenging Conversation," ABC News, July 22, 2013, http://abcnews.go.com/blogs/politics/2013/07/vast-racial-gap-on-trayvon-martin-case-marks-a-challenging-conversation.

50. Data from states with stand-your-ground laws raise questions about how notions of self-defense are evolving and whether, under such laws, race-based fears are more likely to influence juries. According to Darren Hutchinson, a law professor and civil rights law expert at the University of Florida in Gainesville, studies show "that it's just harder for black defendants to assert stand-your-ground defense if the victim is white, and easier for whites to raise a stand-your-ground defense if the victims are black. The bottom line is that it's really easy for juries to accept that whites had to defend themselves against persons of color." See Patrik Jonsson, "Racial Bias and 'Stand Your Ground' Laws: What the Data Show," *Christian Science Monitor*, August 6, 2013, www.csmonitor.com/USA/Justice/2013/0806/Racial-bias-and-stand-your-ground-laws-what-the-data-show. This article notes that the Trayvon Martin case was not technically brought under Florida's stand-your-ground law, but the law had an impact on the jury's decision.

51. Adrienne Cutway, "George Zimmerman Discusses Gun Auction in TV Interview," *Orlando Sentinel*, May 24, 2016, www.orlandosentinel.com/features/gone-viral/os-george-zimmerman-gun-auction-video-20160524-story.html.

52. *State of Florida vs. Curtis Reeves*, www.curtisreevestrial.com.

53. "More Stand Your Ground Mischief in Florida," editorial, *New York Times*, November 2, 2015, www.nytimes.com/2015/11/02/opinion/more-stand-your-ground-mischief-in-florida.html. For the passage of the statute, see Ramsey Touchberry, "Florida Legislature Passes Bill to Strengthen Stand Your Ground Law," Florida's WUFT-FM, May 8, 2017, https://www.wuft.org/news/2017/05/08/florida-legislature-passes-bill-to-strengthen-stand-your-ground-law.

54. David A. Love, "These Are the States That Have 'Stand Your Ground' Laws," *Takepart*, December 16, 2015, www.takepart.com/article/2015/05/27/these-are-states-have-stand-your-ground-laws. See also Victor Li, "States with Stand-Your-Ground Laws Have Seen an Increase in Homicides, Reports Task Force," *ABA Journal*, August 8, 2014, www.abajournal.com/news/article/states_with_stand_your_ground_laws_have_more_homicides.

55. Graduate Institute of International Studies (Geneva), *Small Arms Survey 2007: Guns and the City* (New York: Cambridge University Press, 2007), 47; Graduate Institute of International Studies (Geneva), *Small Arms Survey 2003: Development Denied* (Oxford: Oxford University Press, 2003), 4; Robert Hahn et al., "First Reports Evaluating the Effectiveness of Strategies for Preventing Violence: Firearms Laws: Findings from the Task Force on Community Preventive Services," Centers for Disease Control and Prevention, Morbidity and Mortality Weekly Report, October 3, 2003, www.cdc.gov/mmwr/preview/mmwrhtml/rr5214a2.htm; "Population and Housing Unit Estimates," US Department of

Commerce, US Census Bureau, https://www.census.gov/programs-surveys/popest.html; "Table Aa6–8. Population: 1790–2000 [Annual estimates]," in Susan B. Carter et al., eds., *Historical Statistics of the United States: Millennial Edition Online* (New York: Cambridge University Press, 2006), http://hsus.cambridge.org/HSUSWeb/HSUSEntryServlet.

56. For data on gun ownership, see Tom W. Smith and Jaesok Son, "General Social Survey Final Report: Trends in Gun Ownership in the United States, 1972–2014," March 2015, NORC at the University of Chicago, www.norc.org/PDFs/GSS%20Reports/GSS_Trends%20in%20Gun%20Ownership_US_1972–2014.pdf; David Frum, "America's Gun Problem Is Not a Race Problem," CNN, January 16, 2013, www.cnn.com/2013/01/15/opinion/frum-guns-race.

57. D'Vera Cohn, Paul Taylor, Mark Hugo Lopez, Catharine A. Gallagher, Kim Parker, and Kevin T. Maass, "Gun Homicide Rate Down 49% Since 1993 Peak; Public Unaware," Pew Research Center Social and Demographic Trends, May 7, 2013, www.pewsocialtrends.org/2013/05/07/gun-homicide-rate-down-49-since-1993-peak-public-unaware.

58. "Gallup Historical Trends: Crime, Guns," Gallup, www.gallup.com/poll/1645/guns.aspx. The data showed 60 percent in favor of the ban on assault weapons in January 2013, and 56 percent in April 2013. See also "Guns," Polling Report, www.pollingreport.com/guns.htm; "The Concealed-Carry Fantasy," editorial, *New York Times*, October 26, 2015, www.nytimes.com/2015/10/26/opinion/the-concealed-carry-fantasy.html; "Growing Public Support for Gun Rights," Pew Research Center, December 10, 2014, www.people-press.org/2014/12/10/growing-public-support-for-gun-rights.

59. Frank Zimring and Gordon Hawkins, *Crime Is Not the Problem: Lethal Violence in America* (New York: Oxford University Press, 1999). According to research by the Harvard School of Public Health's Injury Control Center in 2013, there were 29.7 gun homicides per million in the United States, compared to the next highest country, Switzerland, with 7.7 gun homicides per million. See www.hsph.harvard.edu/hicrc.

60. Jason Millman, "Many More People Are Dying from Gun Suicides Than Gun-Related Homicides," *Washington Post*, January 14, 2015, https://www.washingtonpost.com/news/wonk/wp/2015/01/14/many-more-people-are-dying-from-gun-suicides-than-homicides.

61. Abbey Oldham, "2015: The Year of Mass Shootings," PBS Newshour, January 4, 2016, www.pbs.org/newshour/rundown/2015-the-year-of-mass-shootings.

62. David Cunningham, "Five Myths About the Ku Klux Klan," *Washington Post*, March 11, 2016, https://www.washingtonpost.com/opinions/five-myths-about-the-ku-klux-klan/2016/03/11/cddfa6f6-e55b-11e5-a6f3-21ccdbc5f74e_story.html; Carimah Townes, "KKK Forms Neighborhood Watch to Complement Police in Pennsylvania Town," Think Progress, April 22, 2014, http://thinkprogress.org/justice/2014/04/22/3429509/pennsylvania-town-may-experience

-zimmerman-like-murders. For the Urban Institute study cited, see Sarah Childress, "Is There Racial Bias in 'Stand Your Ground' Laws?" *Frontline*, July 31, 2012, www.pbs.org/wgbh/frontline/article/is-there-racial-bias-in-stand-your-ground-laws.

Chapter 4: Women: Victims or Villains?

1. Representative Steve Stockman's (R-TX) campaign bumper sticker in 2013 read: "If babies had guns, they wouldn't be aborted. Vote Pro-Life!" This story received quite a bit of press coverage. See, for example, Mark Sappenfield, "'If Babies Had Guns They Wouldn't Be Aborted.' Is Rep. Steve Stockman Serious?" *Christian Science Monitor*, April 14, 2013, www.csmonitor.com/USA/Politics/Decoder/2013/0414/If-babies-had-guns-they-wouldn-t-be-aborted.-Is-Rep.-Steve-Stockman-serious.

2. Sara Dubow, *Ourselves Unborn: A History of the Fetus in Modern America* (New York: Oxford University Press, 2011).

3. Kimberly Hutcherson, "A Brief History of Anti-Abortion Violence," CNN, December 1, 2015, www.cnn.com/2015/11/30/us/anti-abortion-violence; Liam Stack, "A Brief History of Deadly Attacks on Abortion Providers," *New York Times,* November 29, 2015, www.nytimes.com/interactive/2015/11/29/us/30 abortion-clinic-violence.html.

4. Carol Mason, *Killing for Life: The Apocalyptic Narrative of Pro-Life Politics* (Ithaca, NY: Cornell University Press, 2002).

5. See Leslie J. Reagan, *When Abortion Was a Crime: Women, Medicine, and Law in the United States, 1867–1973* (Berkeley: University of California Press, 1997).

6. Dubow, *Ourselves Unborn*, 112.

7. Guttmacher Institute, "Last Five Years Account for More Than One-Quarter of All Abortion Restrictions Enacted Since Roe, Guttmacher Institute," News in Context, https://www.guttmacher.org/article/2016/01/last-five-years-account-more-one-quarter-all-abortion-restrictions-enacted-roe.

8. The study can be found in Veronica Kolder, Janet Gallagher, and Michael Parsons, "Court Ordered Obstetrical Interventions," *New England Journal of Medicine* 316 (May 7, 1987): 1192, cited in Dubow, *Ourselves Unborn*, 118.

9. Susan Okiejan, "The Epidemic That Wasn't," *New York Times*, January 26, 2009, www.nytimes.com/2009/01/27/health/27coca.html; Michael Winerip, "Revisiting the 'Crack Babies' Epidemic That Was Not," *New York Times*, Retro Report, May 20, 2013, www.nytimes.com/2013/05/20/booming/revisiting-the-crack-babies-epidemic-that-was-not.html.

10. Dubow, *Ourselves Unborn*, 135–152; Dorothy Roberts, *Killing the Black Body: Race, Reproduction, and the Meaning of Liberty* (New York: Vintage, 1998), 194. See also Jimmie L. Reeves and Richard Campbell, *Cracked Coverage:*

Television News, The Anti-Cocaine Crusade, and the Reagan Legacy (Durham, NC: Duke University Press, 1994).

11. Amanda Sakuma, "Tennessee Passes Law Criminalizing Moms Who Used Drugs While Pregnant," MSNBC, April 30, 2014, www.msnbc.com/msnbc/tennessee-passes-law-criminalize-moms-drugs; "Criminalizing Expectant Mothers," editorial, *New York Times*, April 16, 2014, www.nytimes.com/2014/04/17/opinion/criminalizing-expectant-mothers.html.

12. Molly Ladd Taylor and Lauri Umanski, *Bad Mothers: The Politics of Blame in Twentieth-Century America* (New York: New York University Press, 1998).

13. On changing expectations for fathers, see Robert L. Griswold, *Fatherhood in America: A History* (New York: Basic Books, 1993).

14. Donald M. Fisk, US Department of Labor, Bureau of Labor Statistics, "American Labor in the 20th Century," *Compensation and Working Conditions*, Fall 2001, www.bls.gov/opub/mlr/cwc/american-labor-in-the-20th-century.pdf; Jeanne Boydston, "Women in the Labor Force," in Paul S. Boyer, ed., *The Oxford Companion to United States History* (New York: Oxford University Press, 2001), www.anb.org/cushwsuffrage.html.

15. Laura Flynn McCarthy, "The Discipline Solution," *Working Mother*, September 13, 2007, www.workingmother.com/content/discipline-solution; Lisa Belkin, "Dr. Spock Changes His Mind," *Huffington Post*, January 27, 2012 (updated March 20, 2012), www.huffingtonpost.com/lisa-belkin/dr-spock-changes_b_1215745.html.

16. Edward George (California corrections officer), with Dary Matera, *Taming the Beast: Charles Manson's Life Behind Bars* (New York: St. Martin's Press, 1998), xi.

17. Ed Magnuson, "The Curse of Violent Crime," *Time*, March 23, 1981, http://content.time.com/time/magazine/article/0,9171,952929,00.html.

18. Ibid.

19. Thomas Dale Cowan, *Popular Mechanics Home Security Handbook* (New York: Cloverdale Press, 1982), chap. 5; Donald R. Brann, *How to Install Protective Alarm Devices* (Briarcliff Manor, NY: Directions Simplified, 1972).

20. Janet L. Lauritsen and Karen Heimer, *Gender and Violent Victimization*, US Department of Justice, December 2009, https://www.ncjrs.gov/pdffiles1/nij/grants/229133.pdf. Data on domestic violence is inconclusive before the 1980s because assaults by intimate partners were often not reported.

21. Susan Douglas, *Where the Girls Are: Growing Up Female with the Mass Media* (New York: Times Books, 1995), 209–211. Poll data examined from online opinion polls, "Self Defense, Personal Safety—Public Opinion Polls," Roper Center for Public Opinion Research, Cornell University, https://ropercenter.cornell.edu. For example, polls taken in 1981, 1990, 1995, and 1998 indicate that women are more fearful than men. On crime statistics, see Eric H. Monkkonen, *Murder in New York City* (Berkeley: University of California Press, 2000), esp. chap. 3, which discusses the fact that most violent offenders—as well as

victims—are men, and chap. 6, which discusses the fact that black men are disproportionately victims of violent crime.

22. David S. Machlowitz (New York City attorney), "Lawyer on the Aisle," *American Bar Association Journal* 71 (June 1985): 120.

23. By 1992, non-stranger violence against women came to exceed non-stranger violence against men. See Karen Heimer and Janet L. Lauritsen, "Gender and Violence in the United States: Trends in Offending and Victimization," in *Understanding Crime Trends: Workshop Report* (Washington, DC: National Research Council, 2008), 78. See also Irene Hanson Frieze and Nam Yu Li, "Gender, Aggression, and Prosocial Behavior," in Joan C. Chrisler and Donald R. McCreary, eds., *Handbook of Gender Research in Psychology*, vol. 2, *Gender Research in Social and Applied Psychology* (New York: Springer, 2010), 311–336. Frieze and Nam Yu Li find that except in cases of sexual assault and rape, men were more likely than women to be victims of violent crime. See also Candice Batton, "Gender Differences in Lethal Violence: Historical Trends in the Relationship Between Homicide and Suicide Rates, 1960–2000," *Justice Quarterly* 21, no. 3 (September 2004): 423–461.

24. Bruce Tegner, *Self Defense for Women: A Simple Method*, pamphlet (Ventura, CA: Thor Publishing, 1961), 14. There were revised editions of the pamphlet in 1966 and 1969. Available at Schlesinger Library, Radcliffe Institute for Advanced Study, Harvard University.

25. Tegner, *Self Defense for Women*, 19–25.

26. "Street-Safety Precautions Every Woman Should Follow," *Good Housekeeping*, October 1972, 193.

27. Richard D. Lyons, "Safety of Chemical Mace Is Questioned by Many," *New York Times*, May 11, 1968, 43.

28. William D. Marbach, with Marc Frons and Jeff B. Copeland, "Capitalizing on Crime," *Newsweek*, March 9, 1981, 66.

29. Lyons, "Safety of Chemical Mace," 43.

30. The Take Back the Night movement dates back to the 1970s. See, for example, http://takebackthenight.org. For the Roxanne Dunbar-Ortiz quotation, see Roxanne Dunbar-Ortiz, interview for documentary film *She's Beautiful When She's Angry*, Mary Dore, director, November 13, 2014, www.shesbeautifulwhenshesangry.com/roxanne-dunbar-ortiz.

31. Self-Defense for Women, a Boston-area feminist group concerned about violence against women, distributed the flyer, "Information Sheet for Members of the Press," February 24, 1973, Schlesinger Library.

32. Susan G. Peterson, *Self-Defense for Women: The West Point Way* (New York: Simon and Schuster, 1979), 9, 11, 13, 15, 226, Schlesinger Library. The book advertises: "The first woman physical education instructor in the history of the US Military Academy shows civilian women of all ages how to protect everything from their possessions to their very lives."

33. Eileen Keerdoja, with William Slate, "The Hillside Strangler," *Newsweek*, January 1, 1979, 8.

34. See, for example, Martha Fineman and Roxanne Mykitiuk, eds., *The Public Nature of Private Violence: The Discovery of Domestic Abuse* (New York: Routledge, 1994); Patricia Searles and Ronald J. Berger, "The Feminist Self-Defense Movement: A Case Study," *Gender and Society* 1 no. 1 (March 1987): 61–84. See also Patricia Searles and Ronald Berger, eds., *Rape and Society: Readings on the Problem of Sexual Assault, Crime and Society* (Boulder: Westview Press, 1995); Research and Forecasts, Inc., with Ardy Friedbert, *America Afraid: How Fear of Crime Changes the Way We Live. Based on the Widely Publicized Figgie Report* (New York: New American Library, 1983), 76; poll data from Roper Center for Public Opinion Research, Cornell University, iPoll, https://ropercenter.cornell.edu/ipoll-database.

35. "Women's Outdoor Safety," *U.S. News and World Report*, April 21, 1980, 90.

36. See the Ken Burns documentary *The Central Park Five*, 2013; Sarah Burns, "Why Trump Doubled Down on the Central Park Five," *New York Times*, October 17, 2016, https://www.nytimes.com/2016/10/18/opinion/why-trump-doubled-down-on-the-central-park-five.html.

37. Kristin Eddy, "Taking a Beating," *Washington Post Magazine*, November 11, 1990, W14.

38. For an analysis of the positive psychological and physical benefits of women's self-defense training, see Martha McCaughey, "The Fighting Spirit: Women's Self-Defense Training and the Discourse of Sexed Embodiment," *Gender and Society* 12, no. 3 (1998): 277–300.

39. Al Marrewa, *Feminine Warrior: A Woman's Guide to Verbal, Psychological and Physical Empowerment* (Collingdale, PA: Diane Publishing, 1998), 18–20, 211–216, 220–241, 245–247. See also Elizabeth Pennell, *Self-Defense for Women: Techniques to Get You Home Safely* (Holbrook, MA: Adams Media, 2000).

40. Self-defense and personal safety public opinion polls taken from Roper Center for Public Opinion Research, Cornell University, https://ropercenter.cornell.edu. In November 1997 and again in October 2000, 18 percent obtained self-defense training or education to protect from crime. By March 2001, this figure had risen to 25 percent, and by May 2001, 17 percent.

41. There were some exceptions: some films in the World War I era featured women who rescued men. See Lynn Dumenil, *The Second Line of Defense: American Women and World War I* (Chapel Hill: University of North Carolina Press, forthcoming); *His Girl Friday*, Howard Hawks, director (Columbia Pictures, 1940); *Best Years of Our Lives*, William Wyler, director (Samuel Goldwyn, 1946).

42. See, for example, *The Brave One*, Neil Jordan, director (Warner Bros., 2007).

43. An exception is *Gran Torino*, Clint Eastwood, director (Matten Productions, 2008), in which Clint Eastwood as the hero sacrifices himself in the end.

44. Gretel Kauffman, "Why the Gender Gap in Gun Ownership Is Shrinking," *Christian Science Monitor*, September 22, 2016, www.csmonitor.com/USA/Society/2016/0922/Why-the-gender-gap-in-gun-ownership-is-shrinking.

45. Brian Anse Patrick, *Rise of the Anti-Media: In-forming America's Concealed Weapon Carry Movement* (Lanham, MD: Lexington Books, 2010); see also Deborah Homsher, *Women and Guns: Politics and the Culture of Firearms in America*, expanded ed. (New York: Routledge, 2001).

46. See the website for A Girl and a Gun Women's Shooting League, www.agirlandagun.org; the website for The Well Armed Woman, Where The Feminine and Firearms Meet, www.thewellarmedwoman.com/media/chapters-press; and the website for the National Rifle Association's Women's Programs, http://women.nra.org.

47. See *Women and Guns*, January 1992, 14, 17.

48. Peggy Tartaro, "Who's Afraid," *Women and Guns*, January 1992, 16, 19–22, 43.

49. The magazine also promoted a 1989 book by Paxton Quigley, *Armed and Female: Twelve Million American Women Own Guns. Should You?* (New York: St. Martin's Press, 1990). *Publisher's Weekly* reviewed the book on April 30, 1989, calling it a "disturbing, controversial book." See the review at "Armed and Female: Paxton Quigley, Author," *Publishers Weekly*, n.d., https://www.publishersweekly.com/978-0-525-24742-5. Advertisements for products and the book appear in *Women and Guns*, January 1992, 29, 48–49.

50. Tartaro, "Who's Afraid," 50.

51. Ibid., 33.

52. Erica Goode, "Rising Voice of Gun Ownership Is Female," *New York Times*, February 10, 2013, www.nytimes.com/2013/02/11/us/rising-voice-of-gun-ownership-is-female.html. A version of this article appeared in print on February 11, 2013, on p. A9 of the New York edition, with the headline "Rising Voice of Gun Ownership Is Female."

53. Celia Bigelow, "Why Female Gun Ownership Is Up 77% Since 2005," *Town Hall*, February 27, 2013, http://townhall.com/columnists/celiabigelow/2013/02/27/why-female-gun-ownership-is-up-77-since-2005-n1521739/page/full.

54. W. J. Cassidy, "Her Right to Bear Arms: The Rise of Women's Gun Culture," *Rolling Stone*, July 14, 2014, www.rollingstone.com/politics/news/her-right-to-bear-arms-the-rise-of-womens-gun-culture-20140714; Nicholas D. Kristof, "Chicks with Guns," *New York Times*, March 8, 2002, www.nytimes.com/2002/03/08/opinion/chicks-with-guns.html.

55. Lindsay McCrum, *Chicks with Guns* (New York: Vendome Press, 2011), 58–59, 88–89, 130–131.

56. John Burnett, "Does Carrying a Pistol Make You Safer?" National Public Radio, *Morning Edition*, April 12, 2016, www.npr.org/2016/04/12/473391286/does-carrying-a-pistol-make-you-safer. Crime statistics are from the FBI. For

violent crime data, see "Crime in the U.S. 2013, Violent Crime," US Department of Justice, Federal Bureau of Investigation, Criminal Justice Information Services Division, https://www.fbi.gov/about-us/cjis/ucr/crime-in-the-u.s/2013/crime-in-the-u.s.-2013/violent-crime/violent-crime-topic-page/violentcrimemain_final. For property crime data, see "Crime in the United States 2011, Property Crime," US Department of Justice, Federal Bureau of Investigation, Criminal Justice Information Services Division, https://www.fbi.gov/about-us/cjis/ucr/crime-in-the-u.s/2011/crime-in-the-u.s.-2011/property-crime/property-crime. For firearms fashions, see Lauren Silverman, "Gun-Toting Women Give Rise to Firearms Fashion Accessories," National Public Radio, *All Things Considered*, January 27, 2016, www.npr.org/2016/01/27/464571529/gun-toting-women-give-rise-to-firearms-fashion-accessories.

57. Estelle B. Freedman, "'Uncontrolled Desires': The Response to the Sexual Psychopath, 1920–1960," *Journal of American History* 74, no. 1 (1987): 83–106.

58. Alexandra Heller-Nicholas, "Strangers with Candy: The Highway Safety Foundation and *The Child Molester* (1964)," *Bright Lights Film Journal*, April 30, 2011, http://brightlightsfilm.com/strangers-with-candy-the-highway-safety-foundation-and-the-child-molester-1964/#.WSZVAKK1u70.

59. *The Child Molester* (Highway Safety Foundation, 1964), https://archive.org/details/CHILD. See comments on the same web page.

60. George Hunter, *How to Defend Yourself, Your Family, and Your Home* (New York: David McKay, 1967), chap. 9.

61. Paul Mokrzycki Renfro, "Stranger Danger: The Politics of Child Safety in the Age of Reagan" (PhD diss., University of Iowa, 2016), viii. See also Gillian Frank, "Save Our Children: The Sexual Politics of Child Protection, 1965–1990" (PhD diss., Brown University, 2009); Gillian Frank, "Anti-Abortion and Anti-Busing Politics in Michigan, 1967–1972," paper presented at the Organization of American Historians, 2012. See also Frank's book in progress, *Save Our Children: Sexual Politics and Cultural Conservatism in the United States, 1965–1990*.

62. Timothy Griffin and Monica K. Miller, "Child Abduction, AMBER Alert, and Crime Control Theater," *Criminal Justice Review* 33, no. 2 (June 2008): 159–176.

63. Mokrzycki Renfro, "Stranger Danger," 145–150; see also "Missing Children Milk Carton Program," Natonal Child Safety Council, www.nationalchildsafetycouncil.org/about/missing-children-efforts.

64. Mokrzycki Renfro, "Stranger Danger," 3.

65. Ibid., 1–2; Benjamin Radford, "Child Abductions by Strangers Very Rare," *Discovery*, May 4, 2013, http://news.discovery.com/human/psychology/stranger-child-abductions-actually-very-rare-130514.htm; Clemens Wergin, "The Case for Free-Range Parenting," *New York Times*, March 20, 2015, A29. Clemens Wergin is the Washington bureau chief for the newspaper *Die Welt*; see Freedman, "'Uncontrolled Desires.'"

66. David Finkelhor, "Five Myths About Missing Children," *Washington Post*, May 10, 2013, www.washingtonpost.com/opinions/five-myths-about-missing-children/2013/05/10/efee398c-b8b4-11e2-aa9e-a02b765ff0ea_story.html. David Finkelhor is the director of the Crimes Against Children Research Center at the University of New Hampshire and a researcher for the National Incidence Studies of Missing, Abducted, Runaway, and Thrownaway Children.

67. Mokrzycki Renfro, "Stranger Danger," 9, 229–230.

68. In 1967, 49 percent of mothers were stay-at-home mothers. That proportion steadily dropped through the decades until 1999, when only 23 percent of moms stayed at home. In 1999, the percentage of mothers who stayed at home began to increase again, rising by 6 points, to 29 percent, in 2012. See Jacob Galley, "Stay-at-Home Mothers Through the Years," US Department of Labor, Bureau of Labor Statistics, September 2014, www.bls.gov/opub/mlr/2014/beyond-bls/stay-at-home-mothers-through-the-years.pdf.

69. Sandra L. Hofferth, "Child Care in the United States Today," *The Future of Children: Financing Child Care* 6, no. 2 (Summer/Fall 1996), https://www.princeton.edu/futureofchildren/publications/docs/06_02_02.pdf.

70. See, for example, Ellen Ruppel Shell, "Babes in Day Care: The Controversy over Whether Nonmaternal Care Harms Infants," *Atlantic Monthly*, August 1988, www.theatlantic.com/past/docs/issues/88aug/babe.htm; Beth Azar, "The Debate over Child Care Isn't Over Yet . . .," *Monitor on Psychology* 31, no. 3 (March 2000): 32.

71. Sarah Hughes, "American Monsters: The Media and the Creation of the Child Safety Panic, 1975–2000," paper presented to the Organization of American Historians, April 2013. See also Sarah Hughes, "American Monsters: Tabloid Media and the Satanic Panic, 1970–2010" (PhD diss., Temple University, 2015); Debbie Nathan and Michael Snedecker, *Satan's Silence: Ritual Abuse and the Making of a Modern American Witch Hunt* (San Jose, CA: Authors Choice Press, 1995); Barbara J. Nelson, *Making an Issue of Child Abuse: Political Agenda Setting for Social Problems* (Chicago: University of Chicago Press, 1986). Nelson notes that child abuse is primarily a domestic issue.

72. Eric S. Janus, *Failure to Protect: America's Sexual Predator Laws and the Rise of the Preventive State* (Ithaca, NY: Cornell University Press, 2006), esp. chap. 3. See also "Child Sexual Abuse: What Parents Should Inow," American Psychological Association, www.apa.org/pi/families/resources/child-sexual-abuse.aspx. The report points out that it is difficult to know the extent of child sexual abuse—it is generally underreported and definitions are not always consistent.

73. Sandra L. Hofferth, "Changes in American Children's Time—1997 to 2003," *Electronic International Journal of Time Use Research* 6, no. 1 (2009): 26–47; S. A. Ham, S. Martin, and H. W. Kohl III, "Changes in the Percentage of Students Who Walk or Bike to School—United States, 1969 and 2001," *Journal of Physical Activity and Health* 5, no. 2 (2008): 205–215. According to the abstract

for Ham et al., "This report describes changes in the percentage of US students (age 5 to 18 years) who walked or bicycled to school and in the distance that they lived from or traveled to their school in 1969 and 2001 and travel patterns in 2001."

74. Solveig Moen Brown, "Minnesota Mothering: An Anthropological Exploration of How Mothers Negotiate Motherhood in American Culture" (PhD diss., University of Minnesota, 2012), chap. 6, "The Work of Mothering: Mothers' Thoughts on Safety, Consumerism, Individualism and Religion." Quotations are from 318, 319, 324, 325. See also Caryl Rivers, *Selling Anxiety: How the News Media Scare Women* (Hanover, NH: University Press of New England, 2008).

75. Wergin, "Case for Free-Range Parenting."

76. Brown, "Minnesota Mothering."

77. There are many such products advertised and sold. For this advertisement, see "Nanny Cams to Protect What Matters Most," Brick House Security, www.brickhousesecurity.com/category/hidden+cameras/nanny+cams.do.

78. Brown, "Minnesota Mothering."

79. Ibid.; Andrea McCarren, "Parents in Trouble Again for Letting Kids Walk Alone," *USA Today*, April 13, 2015, https://www.usatoday.com/story/news/nation/2015/04/13/parents-investigated-letting-children-walk-alone/25700823.

80. Catherine Ellsworth, "Mother Arrested for Briefly Leaving Child in Car," *Telegraph*, March 13, 2008, www.telegraph.co.uk/news/worldnews/1581596/Mother-arrested-for-briefly-leaving-child-in-car.html; Lenore Skenazy, "The Day She Let Her Son Wait in the Car," *Huffington Post*, August 9, 2014, www.huffingtonpost.com/lenore-skenazy/the-day-she-let-her-son-wait-in-the-car_b_5455439.html.

81. Wergin, "Case for Free-Range Parenting."

82. David Villano, "The Kids Really Are All Right," *Pacific Standard*, May 28, 2013, www.psmag.com/books-and-culture/the-kids-really-are-all-right-58651.

83. "Statistics," National Coalition Against Domestic Violence, http://ncadv.org/learn-more/statistics; "Child Hunger Facts," *Feeding America*, www.feedingamerica.org/hunger-in-america/impact-of-hunger/child-hunger/child-hunger-fact-sheet.html; Christopher Ingraham, "Our Infant Mortality Rate Is a National Embarrassment," *Washington Post*, September 29, 2014, https://www.washingtonpost.com/news/wonk/wp/2014/09/29/our-infant-mortality-rate-is-a-national-embarrassment/?utm_term=.a555697bfda7.

Chapter 5: Locked-Up America: Self-Incarceration and the Illusion of Security

1. Timothy Egan, "The Serene Fortress: A Special Report. Many Seek Security in Private Communities," *New York Times*, September 3, 1995, 1.

2. Full-page illustration, *House Beautiful* 106, no. 7 (July 1964): 100.

3. "Making Your Home Safe Against Intruders," *Ladies' Home Journal* 85, no. 7 (1968): 66.

4. David Monteyne, *Fallout Shelter: Designing for Civil Defense in the Cold War* (Minneapolis: University of Minnesota Press, 2011), xiii–xxi, and chap. 7 on the Boston City Hall.

5. The Uniform Crime Reporting (UCR) Program is the starting place for those seeking information on crime in the nation. The UCR compiles statistics from over 18,000 law enforcement agencies voluntarily participating in the program. According to these data, the population increased by approximately 9 percent, and the crime rate (total crime as well as violent crime) increased by approximately 6 percent. See "United States Crime Rates 1960–2015," Disaster Center, National Terrorism Advisory System, www.disastercenter.com/crime/uscrime.htm.

6. Advertisement, General Telephone and Electronics, *Time* 96, no. 2 (July 13, 1970): 60–61. The Boston Strangler referred to the murderer of thirteen women in the Boston area in the early 1960s.

7. Research and Forecasts, Inc., with Ardy Friedbert, *America Afraid: How Fear of Crime Changes the Way We Live. Based on the Widely Publicized Figgie Report* (New York: New American Library, 1983), 17; Donald Brann, *How to Install Protective Alarm Devices* (Briarcliff Manor, NY: Directions Simplified, 1972); Thomas Dale Cowan, *Popular Mechanics Home Security Handbook* (New York: Cloverdale Press, 1982).

8. William D. Marbach, with Marc Frons and Jeff B. Copeland, "Capitalizing on Crime," *Newsweek*, March 9, 1981, 66; William C. Cunningham, John J. Strauchs, and Clifford W. Van Meter, *Private Security Trends, 1970–2000: The Hallcrest Report II* (Boston: Butterworth-Heinemann, 1990), 238.

9. See Cowan, *Popular Mechanics Home Security Handbook.*

10. Marbach et al., "Capitalizing on Crime," 66. For an ad for the Quantum Sleeper, see https://www.geeksaresexy.net/2008/06/27/quantum-sleeper-the-anti-apocalypse-bed.

11. Jonathan Simon, *Governing Through Crime: How the War on Crime Transformed American Democracy and Created a Culture of Fear* (New York: Oxford University Press, 2007), 6–7, 10, 15–16.

12. Edward J. Blakely and Mary Gail Snyder, *Fortress America: Gated Communities in the United States* (Washington, DC: Brookings Institution Press, 1999), 3; Lester Thurow, "The Rich: Why Their World Might Crumble," *New York Times*, November 19, 1995, 78; Setha Low, "Imprisoned by the Walls Built to Keep 'the Others' Out," *Los Angeles Times*, December 19, 2003, http://articles.latimes.com/2003/dec/19/opinion/oe-low19. See also Setha Low, *Behind the Gates: Life, Security and the Pursuit of Happiness in Fortress America* (New York: Routledge, 2003).

13. Blakely and Snyder, *Fortress America*, 8, 20.

14. Ibid., 10–11.

15. Ibid., 100, 127.

16. Ibid., 153, 18–19.

17. Ibid., 61.

18. Ibid., 65, 95.

19. Egan, "Serene Fortress."

20. Taylor Ward, "Neighborhoods Are Shutting Gates on Crime," *St. Petersburg (FL) Times*, August 27, 1995, 1A.

21. Low, "Imprisoned by the Walls."

22. Blakely and Snyder, *Fortress America*, 21.

23. Ibid., 33.

24. Ibid., 34, 71, 94.

25. Andres Duany, Elizabeth Plater-Zyberk, and Jeff Speck, *Suburban Nation: The Rise of Sprawl and the Decline of the American Dream* (New York: North Point Press, 2000), 43–45; Georjeanna Wilson-Doenges, "An Exploration of Sense of Community and Fear of Crime in Gated Communities," *Environment and Behavior* 32, no. 5 (September 2000): 597–611; Blakely and Snyder, *Fortress America*, 60, 59, 130–132, 135.

26. Sharon Waxman, "Paradise Bought in Los Angeles," *New York Times*, July 2, 2006, www.nytimes.com/2006/07/02/fashion/02mansion.html.

27. Matt A.V. Chaban, "Still Secret and Secure, Safe Rooms Now Hide in Plain Sight," *New York Times*, May 25, 2015, https://www.nytimes.com/2015/05/26/nyregion/still-secret-and-secure-safe-rooms-now-hide-in-plain-sight.html.

28. Ibid.

29. Randel Hanson, "A Gated Community on Wheels," in Elaine Cardenas and Ellen Gorman, eds., *The Hummer: Myths and Consumer Culture* (Lanham, MD: Lexington Books, 2007), 3–13.

30. David Campbell, "The Biopolitics of Security: Oil, Empire, and the Sports Utility Vehicle," *American Quarterly* 57, no. 3 (September 2005): 943–972.

31. Keith Bradsher, *High and Mighty: SUVs—The World's Most Dangerous Vehicles and How They Got That Way* (New York: PublicAffairs, 2002); Campbell, "Biopolitics," data on 963–964. See also Malcolm Gladwell, "Big and Bad: How the S.U.V. Ran Over Automotive Safety," *New Yorker*, January 12, 2004, 28–33.

32. Keith Bradsher, "Was Freud a Minivan or S.U.V. Kind of Guy?" *New York Times*, July 17, 2000, www.nytimes.com/2000/07/17/business/was-freud-a-minivan-or-suv-kind-of-guy.html.

33. Campbell, "Biopolitics," 957–963; Hanson, "Gated Community on Wheels," 8–9.

34. Bradsher, "Was Freud a Minivan or S.U.V. Kind of Guy?"

35. Hanson, "Gated Community on Wheels," 6, 9; Campbell, "Biopolitics," 962.

36. Campbell, "Biopolitics," 958–959.

37. Bradsher, "Was Freud a Minivan or S.U.V. Kind of Guy?"

38. Campbell, "Biopolitics," 961; Mike Kaszuba, "THEY'RE COMIN' AT YOU: Both Mystique and Miff Surround the Beloved or Reviled Hummer," *Minneapolis Star Tribune*, November 16, 2003, 1A; Joe Mathews, "The Hummer and Schwarzenegger: They Probably Won't Be Back," *Washington Post*, February 28, 2010, www.washingtonpost.com/wp-dyn/content/article/2010/02/26/AR2010022603248.html.

39. Campbell, "Biopolitics," 961; Kaszuba, "THEY'RE COMIN' AT YOU."

40. Andrew A. Nelles (Associated Press), "Booming SUV Market Gets New Entries," *The Ledger*, February 12, 2015, www.theledger.com/article/20150212/NEWS/150219743.

41. Evan Osnos, "Doomsday Prep for the Super Rich," *New Yorker*, January 30, 2017.

42. Ibid.

43. Ibid.

44. *Doomsday Preppers*, National Geographic, http://channel.nationalgeographic.com/doomsday-preppers.

Epilogue: Back to the Future: The Twenty-First Century

1. Quotation by Joe Modzeleweski, *Miami Herald*, November 10, 2002, quoted in Jonathan Simon, *Governing Through Crime: How the War on Crime Transformed American Democracy and Created a Culture of Fear* (New York: Oxford University Press, 2009), 75.

2. Much of the material in this epilogue is drawn from Elaine Tyler May, "Echoes of the Cold War: The Aftermath of September 11 at Home," in Mary Dudziak, ed., *September 11 in History: A Watershed Moment?* (Durham, NC: Duke University Press, 2003), 35–54.

3. Jonathan Kaminsky, "Everything We Know About Security Is Wrong," *City Pages*, August 22, 2007, www.citypages.com/news/everything-we-know-about-security-is-wrong-6686282.

4. See, for example, Steve Samuel, "A Weak Spot: The Luggage Hold," *New York Times*, October 11, 2001, A25.

5. Anthropologist Joseph Masco observed, "The 'new' counterterror state in 2001 was actually a repetition, modeled in language and tone on the launch of the national security state in 1947. Both projects involved the designation of new insecurities, new institutions to fight them, a public mobilization campaign grounded in fear, and above all, official claims that a new kind of war (a cold war or a war on terror) was a multigenerational commitment, constituting a new mode of everyday life rather than a brief intensity of conflict." Joseph Masco, *Theater of Operations: National Security Affect from the Cold War to the War on Terror* (Durham: University of North Carolina Press, 2014), 5. See also Kenneth

Burke, *Attitudes Toward History*, 3rd ed. (Berkeley: University of California Press, 1984), 132–133. According to legal scholar Jonathan Simon, the September 11 attacks "created a kind of amnesia wherein a quarter century of fearing crime and securing social spaces [were] suddenly recognized, but misidentified as a response to an astounding act of terrorism, rather than a generation-long pattern of political and social change." Simon, *Governing Through Crime*, 11.

6. Roper Center for Public Opinion Research, Cornell University, iPoll, https://ropercenter.cornell.edu/ipoll-database.

7. See Garrett M. Graff, *The Story of the U.S. Government's Secret Plan to Save Itself—While The Rest of Us Die* (New York: Simon and Schuster, 2017).

8. Scott Shane, "Non-Jihadists Tied to Deadlier Toll in U.S. Since 9/11," *New York Times*, June 25, 2015, 1A. The story follows the killings in the Charleston church and documents research showing forty-eight killings by non-Muslim extremists compared to twenty-six by self-proclaimed jihadists. See also Gardiner Harris and Michael D. Shear, "President Says of Terrorism Threat: 'We Will Overcome It,'" *New York Times*, December 7, 2015, A1, A15. According to Harris and Shear, "Jihadi-inspired attacks include the 2015 attacks in San Bernardino that killed 14 people; attacks by American terrorists include the 2015 murder of 9 African Americans in a Charleston church in 2015 by white supremacist Dylann Roof, and the attacks on abortion providers by anti-abortion terrorists over many years" (p. A15).

9. Michael S. Sherry, *In the Shadow of War: The United States Since the 1930s* (New Haven, CT: Yale University Press, 1995), x.

10. Frank Rich, "The Wimps of War," *New York Times*, March 30, 2002, A15; Michael R. Gordon, "U.S. Nuclear Plan Sees New Weapons and New Targets," *New York Times*, March 10, 2002, A1.

11. Aristide Zolberg, "Guarding the Gates in a World on the Move," Social Science Research Council, After September 11 Archive, www.ssrc.org/sept11/essays.

12. Ann McFeatters, "Bush Signs Anti-Terror Bill; Says Tough Law Will Preserve Constitutional Rights," *Pittsburgh Post-Gazette*, October 27, 2001, A6; Jacques Steinberg, "A Nation Challenged: The Students; U.S. Has Covered 200 Campuses to Check Up on Mideast Students," *New York Times*, November 12, 2001, A1.

13. "Closing the Safety Gap," editorial, *Christian Science Monitor*, October 11, 2001, 8.

14. James Traub, "The Dark History of Defending the 'Homeland,'" *New York Times Magazine*, April 5, 2016, www.nytimes.com/2016/04/10/magazine/the-dark-history-of-defending-the-homeland.html. See also Amy Kaplan, "Homeland Insecurities: Transformations in Language and Space," in Dudziak, ed., *September 11 in History*, 55–69.

15. See Susan Faludi, *Backlash: The Undeclared War Against American Women* (New York: Crown/Archetype, 2009 [1991]).

16. Susan Faludi, *Terror Dream: Fear and Fantasy in Post-9/11 America* (New York: Metropolitan Books, 2007), 20–21, 35–39, 137, 139, 149.

17. See ibid., chap. 7.

18. Ibid., 157, 161–162. Nevertheless, the term caught on. See Juliette Kayyem, *Security Mom: An Unclassified Guide to Protecting Our Homeland and Your Home* (New York: Simon and Schuster, 2016).

19. Michelle Ye Hee Lee, "Donald Trump's False Comments Connecting Mexican Immigrants and Crime," *Washington Post*, July 8, 2015, https://www.washingtonpost.com/news/fact-checker/wp/2015/07/08/donald-trumps-false-comments-connecting-mexican-immigrants-and-crime/?utm_term=.9b0e5e962c7e.

20. Jeremy Diamond, "Trump Falsely Claims US Murder Rate Is 'Highest' in 47 Years," CNN, February 7, 2017, www.cnn.com/2017/02/07/politics/donald-trump-murder-rate-fact-check.

21. Nicolaus Mills, *The Triumph of Meanness: America's War Against Its Better Self* (New York: Houghton Mifflin, 1997), 7.

22. Aaron Blake, "It's Almost Like Donald Trump's Secret Plan to Defeat ISIS Never Actually Existed," *Washington Post*, September 7, 2016, https://www.washingtonpost.com/news/the-fix/wp/2016/09/07/donald-trump-said-he-had-a-secret-plan-to-defeat-isis-as-of-now-hes-not-planning-to-use-it/?utm_term=.40047573e978.

23. Melissa Fares, "Trump 'Arms Race' Comment Sows More Doubt on Nuclear Policy," Reuters, December 23, 2016, www.reuters.com/article/us-usa-trump-nuclear-idUSKBN14B1ZZ.

24. "Donald Trump's Economic Promises," BBC News, November 9, 2016, www.bbc.com/news/business-37921635.

25. Aaron Blake, "Donald Trump's Defenses of Not Paying Taxes Pretty Much Say It All," *Washington Post*, October 2, 2016, https://www.washingtonpost.com/news/the-fix/wp/2016/09/28/donald-trumps-defense-of-not-paying-taxes-is-remarkable/?utm_term=.5b475fffbc0e; "Pages from Donald Trump's 1995 Income Tax Records," *New York Times*, October 1, 2016, https://www.nytimes.com/interactive/2016/10/01/us/politics/donald-trump-taxes.html; David Barstow, Susanne Craig, Russ Buettner, and Megan Twohey, "Donald Trump Tax Records Show He Could Have Avoided Taxes for Nearly Two Decades, The Times Found," *New York Times*, October 1, 2016, https://www.nytimes.com/2016/10/02/us/politics/donald-trump-taxes.html.

26. Daniel Victor and Liam Stack, "Stephen Bannon and Breitbart News, in Their Words," *New York Times*, November 14, 2016, https://www.nytimes.com/2016/11/15/us/politics/stephen-bannon-breitbart-words.html.

27. Christopher Uggen, Ryan Larson, and Sarah Shannon, "6 Million Lost Voters: State-Level Estimates of Felony Disenfranchisement, 2016," The Sentencing

Project, October 6, 2016, www.sentencingproject.org/publications/6-million-lost-voters-state-level-estimates-felony-disenfranchisement-2016.

28. The researchers Josh Pasek, Jon A. Krosnick, and Trevor Tompson found that in 2012, 32 percent of Democrats held antiblack views, while 79 percent of Republicans did. For the impact of race on Obama's presidency and the 2016 election, including the survey noted above, see Ta-Nehisi Coates, "My President Was Black: A History of the First African American White House—and of What Came Next," *The Atlantic*, January/February 2017, https://www.theatlantic.com/magazine/archive/2017/01/my-president-was-black/508793.

29. Grainne Dunne, "Four Ways the Obama Administration Has Advanced Criminal Justice Reform," Brennan Center for Justice, New York University School of Law, May 19, 2016, https://www.brennancenter.org/blog/four-ways-obama-administration-has-advanced-criminal-justice-reform; Matt Ferner, "Americans Are Sick of the 'Tough on Crime' Era: An Overwhelming Number of Voters Want to Reform the Federal Justice System, a New Poll Finds," *Huffington Post*, February 13, 2016, www.huffingtonpost.com/entry/federal-justice-reform-poll_us_56be1a95e4b08ffac124f71e; Max Ehrenfreund, "Obama's Advisers Just Revealed an Unconventional Solution to Mass Incarceration," *Washington Post*, April 25, 2016, https://www.washingtonpost.com/news/wonk/wp/2016/04/25/how-to-reduce-crime-without-courts-or-prisons.

30. Laurel Wamsley, "Big Newspapers Are Booming: 'Washington Post' to Add 60 Newsroom Jobs," National Public Radio, December 27, 2016, www.npr.org/sections/thetwo-way/2016/12/27/507140760/big-newspapers-are-booming-washington-post-to-add-sixty-newsroom-jobs.

31. Quoted in Daniel May, "How to Revive the Peace Movement: We Need to Merge Social-Justice and Antiwar Activism," *The Nation*, April 3, 2017, 12–18, https://www.thenation.com/article/how-to-revive-the-peace-movement-in-the-trump-era.

32. Jonah Engel Bromwich, "Doomsday Clock Registers Cold-War-Type Pessimism," *New York Times*, January 27, 2017, A17; Jill Lepore, "Autumn of the Atom," *New Yorker*, January 30, 2017, 22–28.

INDEX

Elaine Tyler May is Regents Professor of American Studies and History at the University of Minnesota. The award-winning author of six books, including *Homeward Bound: American Families in the Cold War Era*, May is the former president of the Organization of American Historians and the American Studies Association. She lives in Minneapolis, Minnesota.

Photograph by Lisa Miller